P9-CST-684

Culinary BIRDS

Culinary BIRDS

THE ULTIMATE POULTRY COOKBOOK

James Beard-Award Winning Chef John Ash and James O. Fraioli

Foreword by Mike Leventini, President of Petaluma Poultry
Photography by Jessica Nicosia-Nadler

RUNNING PRESS
PHILADELPHIA · LONDON

Books published by Running Press are available at special discounts for bulk purchases in the United States by corporations, institutions, and other organizations. For more information, please contact the Special Markets Department at the Perseus Books Group, 2300 Chestnut Street, Suite 200, Philadelphia, PA 19103, or call (800) 810-4145, ext. 5000, or e-mail special.markets@perseusbooks.com.

ISBN 978-0-7624-4484-7
Library of Congress Control Number: 2013938633

E-book ISBN 978-0-7624-5065-7

9 8 7 6 5 4 3 2 1
Digit on the right indicates the number of this printing

Interior design by Debra McQuiston
Edited by Geoff Stone
Typography: DIN, Helvetica and Boton

Running Press Book Publishers
2300 Chestnut Street
Philadelphia, PA 19103-4371

Visit us on the web!
www.runningpresscooks.com

The Authors would like to personally thank: Chef John Hall and the extraordinary culinary team at Le Cordon Bleu College of Culinary Arts - Sacramento, California; Chef Richard Jensen II, Torrey Crable, Patricia Nicosia, Jenn Allen, Enjoli D. Crayton, Rita Evans, Ashanique Gaines, Joseph Gray, Gabriela Gutierrez, Shamara Jones, Danushka Jung-Maisel, Sonnie Keokesa, Elizabeth Miranda, Erin J. Shepherd, and Kempton Stafford. The terrific recipe testers Kainoa Raymond, Lorri Allen and Biff Owen. Photographer extraordinaire Jessica Nicosia-Nadler. Mike Leventini and Petaluma-Poultry. Andrea Hurst & Associates. Geoffrey Stone at Running Press/Perseus Books.

contents

poultry

poul•try (noun) \pol-tre\

Domesticated
birds kept for eggs
or meat.

FOREWORD

BY MIKE LEVENTINI, PRESIDENT OF PETALUMA POULTRY

Poultry. It's a mainstay of the American diet. It's the low fat, nutritious, versatile and familiar protein that we all know and love. It's rich in protein, niacin, vitamin B6 and selenium, helps fight against bone loss, contribute to healthy circulation, support immunity, and even offer protection against cancer and heart disease. Although the mass production of poultry was developed in America, it was only less than a century ago that chickens were bred more for exhibition than consumption. The bird, today well known as a dinner table centerpiece, was once little more than a prized showpiece. It wasn't until around 1910 that raising chicken for eggs and meat began to trump raising them for show.

In 1928 when Herbert Hoover claimed that if he won the presidential campaign there would be "a chicken in every pot," Americans were eating an average of only a half-pound of chicken a year. It wasn't until after World War II that the tides began to change. Food production became more industrialized, and the growing demand and need for affordability led to the implementation of large scale production methods. The farms and processing facilities became bigger and more efficient and the product more affordable to the consumer—keeping the cost of chicken down even in today's high-priced economy. Houses and cars cost fourteen times what they did fifty years prior, but the price of chicken hasn't even doubled. As Joel Stein with *Time* magazine wrote, that helps explain why we eat 150 times as many chickens a year as we did eighty years ago. In fact, according to the National Chicken Council, current chicken consumption per capita is around ninety pounds a year, over half a bird a week. And while chicken was more expensive than steak or lobster one hundred years ago in the United States, it may now be cheaper than the potatoes it's served with.

I came to learn the impact of free range, vegetarian feed, and antibiotic-free husbandry practices on the quality and taste of poultry...'you are what you eat,' began to make a whole lot of sense, as you can taste that adage in every bite.

The low-cost production system came with benefits, such as making poultry more accessible to the average consumer, but it also led to significant issues. Animals were raised in crowded environments, farms became reliant on growth promotants, antibiotics were used as a preventative means to keep livestock healthy, and low-cost feed formulations including animal by-products became the standard. Unfortunately, animal welfare considerations took a back seat to saving money at what were seen as "factory farms" in the eyes of some consumers, and waterway pollution and employee welfare became issues needing to be addressed.

Not only did the farming methods change, but the form of poultry changed as well. As little as thirty years ago, the majority of poultry was sold as bulk, either whole or cut up. Now, you can buy your poultry in a tray or box, raw or cooked, chopped, formed, sliced or diced. While there have always been birds raised on small farms or in backyards by farmers who have shunned these large-scale methods and kept old fashioned breeds and flavor profiles, it was certainly hard to find them other than at your local farmer's market.

Numerous food safety issues and a mad cow outbreak later, consumers were forced to care more about how their animals are raised, what happens from the farm to the fork, and what's behind terms such as free range, organic, antibiotic free, and vegetarian fed.

Similar to John Ash, I grew up around livestock and was involved in 4H and the FFA (Future Farmers of America). My dad is a retired high school agriculture teacher and his small farm is a place of fond memories for me and my children. I've been raising poultry for twenty-three years, but it wasn't until about eight years ago, when I joined the team at Petaluma Poultry, that I learned the saying "a chicken is chicken" is by no means valid.

My career in poultry began with a conventional poultry company that I joined out of college, and I worked there for fifteen years. In the fall of 2003, I received an invitation to move over to Petaluma Poultry. I was married with three young children and I wanted to make sure that the change and tough transition would be worth it. Before I accepted the offer, I came home with a Rocky Free-Range Chicken and a conventional bird. We baked both birds side by side and served them to the family. My reaction to the Rocky bird: Wow! It made me immediately curious to understand the reasons why the flavor and texture were so different.

I'll give my kids credit. They picked the conventional bird. Of course, they knew that if they picked the Rocky, they would have to move. The winning candidate was more than obvious. I quickly came to learn the impact of free range, vegetarian feed, and antibiotic-free husbandry practices on the quality and taste of poultry. My mom's motto, "you are what you eat," began to make a whole lot of sense, as you can taste that adage in every bite.

Our chicken taste test made the decision easy, and the family and I moved to Sonoma County in Northern California. I joined Petaluma Poultry shortly after its founder, Allen Shainsky, had passed away. Chicken husbandry and working the land had been part of Shainsky's daily life for sixty-nine years until his passing in 2000. His legacy and guiding principles continue to be the foundation for Petaluma Poultry, which still operates much like when it began as a small farm and processing company. I quickly grew an understanding and passion for the way we raise our animals.

In John's chapter, In Honor of Chickens, he mentions that the best chicken he ever ate was in France and that it had a distinctive flavor. Coincidentally, in the 1980s, Shainsky actually began his quest for developing a bird that had what Bay Area chefs described as the French-style flavor they experienced in their schooling in Europe. Shainsky spent months in Loire Valley in France to learn how to raise poultry the artisanal way.

Upon returning to Petaluma, he and his partner Dick Krengel developed a balanced vegetarian feed without animal by-products and stopped using antibiotics. Instead, they relied on raising birds in roomy, well-ventilated houses with access to free range and applying sound animal husbandry to build immune systems naturally.

In 1999, Rocky the Range Chicken was introduced in the local, Northern California marketplace as the first USDA approved free-range chicken. Shainsky then followed up with Rosie, the first USDA approved organic chicken. Today these birds are sold in all western states, although they still have the strongest following in the local, Northern California market. Produced under the watchful eye of third-party animal welfare certifiers, not only are these chickens raised without antibiotics and animal byproducts and allowed to roam freely outside, they are also provided an "enriched" environment where they can express natural behaviors. It is the attention to detail, ranging from balanced feed rations, bird-focused animal husbandry practices, and welfare prioritized over low-cost that produces a healthy, happy, tasty chicken.

Until recently, your local natural food store, butcher shop, or farmers market was the only place to find animals raised to these standards. However, with the recent consumer awareness of what we are eating and how it was reared, more and more retail chains and club stores are not only carrying these products but enjoying rapid growth.

In addition, there are numerous companies working to adhere to these production methods—not only across the nation, but also across other species of poultry. You can find organic turkeys, ducks, squab, and other game birds at your local market.

There is a Sonoma County/Northern California perspective on agriculture and an appreciation for food that I share closely with John Ash. John represents the mindset of Sonoma County. He appreciates good food, good flavor, organic poultry, and sustainable farming methods.

When I moved to Sonoma County, I too became a foodie. My wife makes her own beer and cheese; we have a garden in the back, and on my cell phone I not only have pictures of my kids, but also of my killer Brandywine tomatoes. What I've learned is that once you start eating fresh, good-quality food, you can't go back. Once you've eaten fresh fish, enjoyed fine wine, picked a fresh mushroom under an oak tree, once you've eaten organic chicken . . . you've crossed over. You can't eat fast food anymore; you can't go back to bulk wine in a box.

I'm heartened and happy that John is helping to educate consumers about sustainable farming, and what safety, quality, and good taste mean in regard to poultry—a protein that has become a standard and expected part of the American diet. With the efforts of companies like Petaluma Poultry and the support of chefs like John Ash, I hope there will be an organic chicken in every pot—on every plate—in every kitchen. Life's simply too short to drink bad wine and eat ordinary chicken.

INTRODUCTION

Poultry History

More than three thousand years ago in China, farmers were breeding for food various types of poultry such as ducks, geese, and pigeons. Around the same time, chickens, descendents of the wild red junglefowl in southeast Asia, were being domesticated after people discovered they were quite delicious. Other species such as guinea fowl, partridge, pheasant and quail have similar histories. Guinea hens (or fowl), which originated in Africa, were successfully domesticated and introduced elsewhere as game birds, enjoyed by hunters for both sport and dining pleasure. The same with partridge and quail, which are native to Europe, Asia, and Africa. And the same with the popular ring-necked pheasant, which is native to Asia and Europe, and which was once hunted by cavemen in prehistoric times like other birds that prefer to forage on the ground, such as grouse, partridges, and junglefowl.

In medieval times geese, pheasant, and quail were popular game birds. And the chicken was being raised primarily for cockfighting, particularly in Greece. Cockfighting excited warriors and got them ready for battle. It wasn't until the arrival of early explorers to the New World that chickens finally made their way to North America.

In the early 1600s, the Native American Wampanoag tribe introduced the turkey to newly arrived Pilgrims. Because many of the Pilgrims were malnourished from their harrowing trip to America, the Indians encouraged the hungry settlers to sample America's native foods, which included turkey. The first Thanksgiving meal was celebrated in 1621. However, it wasn't until October 3, 1863, that President Abraham Lincoln declared Thanksgiving an official holiday in the United States, thanks to the beckoning of American writer and editor Sarah Josephea Hale.

Prior to the 1800s, American farms didn't raise many domesticated birds due to the large amount of wild game available. Farmers didn't need to spend the money and put in the time raising birds when there were plenty of wild animals to feed upon. But as the United States grew and become more populated, the consumption of some wild birds began to decline as domesticated birds increased in popularity.

During the nineteenth century, around the time cockfighting was outlawed across the United States, more families found themselves raising birds such as chickens, ducks, geese, turkey, and pheasant. Chickens were the dominate domesticated birds because of their consistent egg production. The Dominique variety—a medium-size chicken with black-and-white feathers and yellow legs—was the most popular chicken at the time. The Dominique, also known as Pilgrim Fowl, was a descendant of early colonial chickens. At the turn of the century, though, many farmers were losing interest in the Dominique variety. New Asiatic breeds and strains were being developed by scientists. Naturally, these experiments and discoveries by early scientists drove the expansion of the breeding industry, and bird consumption continued to rise as a result. Meanwhile, around the 1870s, game birds such as the Pekin duck found their way to America from China. It's believed the Pekin was first introduced in San Francisco before making its way to the East coast.

Scientists were also discovering around this time that red meat was high in LDL cholesterol, which increases the risk of heart disease, due to large amounts of

saturated fats and the use of preservatives in processed meat. Naturally, poultry was soon evaluated as a healthy and safe alternative to red meat, which remains true to this day. This is because poultry is loaded with essential vitamins and minerals, including the cancer-preventative B vitamin, niacin. A four-ounce serving of chicken, for example, provides more than 70 percent of the daily value for niacin. A five-ounce serving of turkey provides about half the recommended daily allowance of folic acid and is a good source of potassium, vitamin B, B1, B6, and zinc, which helps keep the bad cholesterol down, strengthens the immune system, and aids in fighting off disease. Studies show that niacin-rich foods, like poultry, also help to protect against Alzheimer's. Other essential vitamins and minerals found in poultry include vitamin A, vitamin D, calcium, iron, potassium, and phosphorous.

Meat from duck and geese were also studied and the results were positive. Such birds are healthy for the human body and loaded with essential vitamins and minerals, but they do need more prep work in the kitchen. For example, most duck meat, which is low in sodium and high in protein, comes from the breast and legs, which tend to be fattier than chicken. This is because ducks are waterfowl, and to keep warm, their bodies have developed an insulating layer of thick fat between the skin and the meat. For healthy dishes, and to reduce the amount of saturated fat in your diet, both the skin and fat from a duck should be removed prior to eating. The same principle applies to goose meat, which is also low in sodium and high in protein. The skin is high in saturated fats and should be removed prior to consumption.

Early studies also proved birds like pheasant to be low in sodium and a good source of protein and vitamins and minerals including niacin, phosphorous, selenium, vitamin B6, and B12. However, unlike other poultry, pheasant is high in LDL cholesterol. The same holds true for guinea fowl and quail meat, which are also packed with essential vitamins and minerals but are high in the bad cholesterol. Of course, wild game meat is better for you than processed meats, as wild birds

The ring-necked pheasant is a colorful and delicious game bird.

have not been injected with any hormones, steroids, or artificial preservatives. But just because it's wild doesn't mean you have to stop paying close attention to what you're eating.

With "white meat" being touted as a better alternative to red meat, poultry marketing campaigns began encouraging Americans, who were becoming more health conscious, to make the switch. Better home appliances also made preparing a variety of poultry at home relatively easy. This new "white meat" movement led to a rapid rise in poultry production. In 1954, the National Broiler Council (now the National Chicken Council) formed to increase consumer demand for chicken poultry. Five years later, the federal inspection of poultry meat became mandatory. As Americans were now consuming chicken at such a high rate, new safety standards and production guidelines had to be implemented to ensure that what was being fed to Americans was safe and was being inspected before it reached the consumer. When environmental pioneers during the '60s questioned the negative aspects of factory-farmed poultry, federal inspections were even more important, especially when it involved the public's—and the birds'—well being. While the government was doing its part, poultry continued to be produced in mass numbers.

According to *D'Artagnan,*
a specialty company raising all-natural
and organic game birds, the
Muscovy duck has less fat and less calories
per pound than turkey.

With the invention of the popular "buffalo wings" in the mid-1960s and more fast food chains adding chicken to their menus, poultry rapidly grew into a billion-dollar industry. Throughout the 1970s, fast food chains like Kentucky Fried Chicken and Popeye's encouraged Americans to keep eating poultry, primarily chicken. In the '80s, animal activists knew little about poultry and how the birds were raised and processed, so consumption trumped what was going on behind the scenes. Today, the poultry industry continues to increase as the United States'—and the world's—population continues to expand and consume more poultry at the table.

Presently, only a few strains of birds dominate today's market, and only a handful of companies are responsible for the majority of the broiler chickens, laying hens, and turkey production in the world. Flocks are now as large as 350,000 hens or more, and, according to the American Meat Institute, the average American consumes almost ninety pounds of poultry per year. Popular duck species include the Pekin (the most consumed in the United States), the Muscovy (originating from South America and considered the leanest duck breed), and the Moulard (a cross between a Pekin and Muscovy, not to be confused with the Mallard). According to the USDA, nearly thirty million ducks were eaten in the United States in 2010. The rich foie gras, or "fattened liver," typically comes from the Moulard duck.

The leading producers of poultry are China, the Russian Federation, the United States, Brazil, Japan, and Mexico.

Did you Know?

Humans and animals need protein to maintain adequate health and strength. Our cell structure is built on protein. We derive our amino acids from protein. Poultry meat, primarily the breast, that has been properly skinned is very lean, low in fat, and contains high-quality protein. Just four ounces of chicken, for instance, provides almost 70 percent of the daily value for protein for the average person.

Studies have found that skinless poultry plays a vital role in human growth and development, can help overweight and obese people lose weight fast, and can even help slow the aging process. Scientists have found in poultry the anti-aging mineral selenium, which works as an antioxidant to help strengthen the immune system. In older people, protein from poultry can help prevent bone loss, particularly in the hip and spine.

Poultry has long been a staple in people's diets and today we continue to discover and learn how healthy it is for us. Because we live in a country that cares about the environment and the well-being of the animals we produce, there is no shortage of organic, free-range, and chemical-free poultry on the market. The next time you are craving a steak, give your heart a break and consider a nice piece of juicy poultry. You'll feel better knowing you're fueling your body with essential proteins while reducing your saturated fat and cholesterol intake.

The Sustainable Poultry Movement

Free range, pasture raised, cage free, vegetarian fed, antibiotic free, non-factory farmed, organic, air chilled—a trip through today's meat section at the supermarket seems to require a degree in agriculture and maybe experience working on a poultry farm. What are these terms? Are they important? Do I need to alter my cooking methods? Most importantly, which poultry should I really be eating?

With enthusiasm for poultry dishes at an all-time high and overnight airfreight shrinking the globe, professionals and home cooks are faced with an array of choices like never before. It is no longer a world of generic chicken and eggs and generic poultry recipes. In today's environmental and health conscious world, chefs and consumers would like to know more about what they are eating, while making it look and taste delicious on the plate.

What is the "best" poultry one can buy?

In order to explore this all-important question, we must first understand the terms that help define the word "best."

Organic Poultry

Organic foods are not limited to just fruits and vegetables. You can also buy organic poultry.

Organic-certified poultry are birds that are not treated with growth hormones or other non-veterinary medicine on a regular and consistent basis, which is often the case with non-organic poultry. Organic poultry are fed an organic diet, consisting of cereals, vegetable proteins, vitamins and minerals, and a small amount of fish meal. To be completely organic, birds must be fed a diet containing ingredients that have been grown or produced organically, without any artificial fertilizers or pesticides. Vegetarian feed often falls into this category.

Organic poultry, like free-range or pasture-raised poultry, must have access to the outdoors so the birds are able to freely roam outside, and not be contained or restrained indoors.

National Organic Standards Board

Poultry producers who meet the standards set by the USDA (United States Department of Agriculture) National Organic Program are entitled to label their products as "USDA Certified Organic."

Sustainability

According to *Sustainable Table* (www.sustainabletable.org), a product can be considered sustainable if its production enables the resources from which it was made to continue to be available for future generations. A sustainable product can thus be created repeatedly without generating negative environmental effects, without causing waste products to accumulate as pollution, and without compromising the well-being of workers or communities. Many different agricultural techniques can be utilized to help make food production more sustainable. The drawback of the term *sustainable* is that the term lacks a clear-cut, universally-accepted, enforceable definition—thus it can be interpreted in different ways. It is more of a philosophy or way of life than a label.

backyard poultry:

Traditional, Sustainable and
Environmentally-Friendly.

According to the
World's Healthiest Foods, skinned chicken
breast has less than half the fat of
a trimmed T-bone steak. The fat in chicken
is also less saturated than beef fat.

According to the USDA, "Organic food is produced by farmers who emphasize the use of renewable resources and the conservation of soil and water to enhance environmental quality for future generations. Organic poultry and egg products come from birds that are given no antibiotics or growth hormones. Organic food is produced without using most conventional pesticides; fertilizers made with synthetic ingredients or sewage sludge; bioengineering; or ionizing radiation. Before a product can be labeled 'organic,' a Government-approved certifier inspects the farm where the food is grown to make sure the farmer is following all the rules necessary to meet USDA organic standards. Companies that handle or process organic food before it gets to your local supermarket or restaurant must be certified, too."

Free Range and Pasture Raised

According to the USDA, free-range and pasture-raised poultry, including cage-free hens raised for egg production, must have access to the outside to receive a "Free Range" certification.

"Free Range" means the birds are able to roam freely outdoors and are not contained or restrained without the ability to nest, roost, and share space according to their natural behavior. The definition of the free roaming space is somewhat limited because of commonly used perimeter fencing that is necessary to keep birds from wandering off the property. In addition, the USDA does not define the size of the freely roaming space, nor does it specify a particular amount of time the birds are allowed outside. There's also no definition for "outside," which means a free-range environment could include thousands of birds crowded inside a shed with a single exit leading to an outdoor strip of dirt or gravel, and not the grassy range we all picture on our grandfather's farm or ranch.

"Pasture Raised" is similar to Free Range, but the birds are free to roam outside on an ongoing basis throughout their lives—similar to what you would find on a rural farm. Notable author Joel Salatin created the term "Pastured Poultry," which simply means the poultry (in his case broiler chickens) are raised outside on grass pastures all of their lives, helping to reduce the carbon footprint.

Factory-Farmed Poultry

"Factory-farmed" poultry is what most Americans are eating today. Because the United States—and the world—purchases and consumes so much poultry, primarily chicken and turkey, supply must be able to keep up with the high demand. Introduce the factory farm. These modern-day, large-scale farming facilities produce the highest output of poultry at the lowest cost because they rely on a system that includes raising the most animals as quick as possible in the smallest area to maximize space and profit. The problem is, as many might agree, such birds are devoid of a healthy way of life.

Factory-farmed poultry, like much of the mass-produced chicken and turkey available on the market today, are kept indoors in a densely populated shed under artificial lights to encourage them to eat more

The average weight for turkeys purchased for Thanksgiving is sixteen pounds.

and sleep less. They are placed in cramped conditions with less than half a square foot of space for each bird (three square feet for turkey). After hatching, the birds often have part of their beaks removed (turkeys also have their toes clipped) without anesthesia to minimize injury due to aggression with other birds. The birds are never allowed outdoors and are unable to roam, scratch, or coexist with other birds like the organic and free-range birds.

Today's mass produced birds like "broiler" chickens (chickens raised for their flesh) are bred to gain weight as fast as possible. They are fed inexpensive food along with supplements to prevent illness and encourage rapid growth. In fact, such birds have been genetically altered to grow twice as fast as they would

in their natural environment. Because these birds grow so rapidly, their internal organs are under a lot of strain, resulting in congestive heart failure and a high mortality rate. Many of these birds have leg disorders, as their limbs are unable to support their abnormally heavy bodies. The same holds true for turkeys, which have been genetically manipulated to produce extraordinarily large breasts to meet today's demand. Many birds raised in these unfortunate conditions also die from dehydration, heat stroke, and infectious disease. Because of the high volume of accumulated waste, ammonia levels are also high, which burns the birds' skin and eyes. To control the spread of diseases in such crowded living conditions, factory-farmed birds are given antibiotics and pesticides to ward off attacks.

A healthy barn will typically have one-fourth of the chickens eating, one-fourth drinking, one-fourth sleeping, and one-fourth walking around and exploring.

Today, many Americans, particularly animal activists, agree that factory-farmed poultry is cruel and inhumane. Factory farms, on the other hand, believe their highly efficient system saves land and food resources while the birds are looked after in state-of-the-art facilities.

Without question, visiting a farm and slaughterhouse is the only surefire way to know exactly how the birds are being raised and processed before they hit your plate.

Air-Chilled Poultry

Air-chilling poultry is a practice that is slowly catching on in the American poultry industry. The words "Air-Chilled Poultry" are appearing on packaged poultry like chicken at various supermarkets. This term refers to an improved process for rapidly reducing the internal temperature of slaughtered birds after they come out of hot water tanks which are used to remove the feathers. Instead of being plunged in ice-water baths after they've been plucked (also a contributing factor to the meat retaining water as often noted on packaging), birds are quickly chilled in air chambers—similar to giant refrigerators—to reduce the growth of bacteria; hence the name *air-chilled poultry*. With less retained water and less chance for salmonella transmission, air-chilled poultry is a step in the right direction.

Behind the Poultry Processing Scene

Presently, there are about three hundred companies with a combined annual revenue of $50 billion that make up the US poultry processing industry. Fifty of the top companies account for more than 90 percent of the revenue.

Once factory-farmed poultry is ready for market, the birds are trucked in crates from the facility to the slaughterhouse regardless of weather conditions. Many birds are injured en route or die from the stress of the journey. At the slaughterhouse, the birds become part of an assembly line. They are shackled upside down by their feet and electrically stunned. Their throats are cut, and they are plunged into scalding-hot water to remove their feathers.

Recently, some slaughterhouses have switched to a more humane way of dispatching the birds: gassing. They use carbon dioxide to gently render the birds unconscious before enduring the conventional slaughter methods. Gassing the birds also protects the meat as there is less stress, bruising, and breaking of wings. According to Petaluma Poultry, the nation's leading natural chicken producer, gassing is a great system.

Perhaps one day other slaughterhouses will update their methods, forcing the poultry industry to gradually switch over so flocks are raised, transported, *and* processed as humanely as possible.

New Animal Welfare Rating System

Recently, Whole Foods Market implemented a new animal welfare system for its meats and other livestock products to help improve the lives of farm animals. In coordination with the nonprofit Global Animal Partnership, Whole Foods's five-step rating system ranges from step 1 (animals aren't crowded in cages or crates) to the highest tier (step 5+), where animals spend their entire lives on the same farm. Color coded tags let shoppers know how various products are rated.

How Does Global Animal Partnership's 5-Step Animal Welfare Rating Standards Program Work?

Each Step builds on the previous one for ever-higher welfare for the animals. In essence, **Step 1** prohibits cages and crates. **Step 2** requires environmental enrichment; **Step 3**, meaningful outdoor access; **Step 4**, pasture-centered production; **Step 5**, an animal-centered approach with all physical alterations prohibited; and, finally, **Step 5+**, animals spend their lives on an integrated farm.

Following is a snapshot of some of the Step-differentiated requirements:

	Cattle Raised for Beef	Chickens Raised for Meat	Pigs	Turkeys
CATTLE RAISED FOR BEEF: 1 NO CAGES, NO CRATES NO CROWDING	• at least 50% vegetative cover on pasture/range • de-horning prohibited	• cages prohibited • all physical alterations, including beak trimming, prohibited	• cages, stalls, and crates prohibited • bedding in all housing • tail docking prohibited	• cages prohibited • toe-clipping and dubbing prohibited
ANIMAL WELFARE RATING: 2 ENRICHED ENVIRONMENT	• objects for grooming and scratching • shade for all animals to rest together at the same time	• enrichments to encourage foraging behavior • cover or blinds	• enrichments to encourage foraging behavior • minimum weaning age of 35 days	• enrichments to encourage foraging behavior • toenail conditioning prohibited
ANIMAL WELFARE RATING: 3 ENHANCED OUTDOOR ACCESS	*There is no Step 3 for cattle.*	• continuous outdoor access during daylight hours	• continuous outdoor access during daylight hours	• continuous outdoor access during daylight hours
ANIMAL WELFARE RATING: 4 PASTURE CENTERED	• removal from pasture/ range only when weather conditions put the animals at risk	• continuous access to foraging areas or pasture • continuous access to indoor foraging areas during inclement weather	• continuous access to foraging areas or pasture • unrestricted access to wallows on pasture	• continuous access to foraging areas or pasture with at least 50% vegetation or cover • beak trimming prohibited
ANIMAL WELFARE RATING: 5 ANIMAL CENTERED: NO PHYSICAL ALTERATIONS	• at least 75% vegetative cover on pasture/range • all physical alterations, including castration, prohibited	• seasonal housing prohibited • perches for all birds to perch at the same time	• litters of piglets stay together • all physical alterations, including castration, prohibited	• seasonal housing prohibited • perches for all birds to perch at the same time
ANIMAL WELFARE RATING: 5+ ANIMAL CENTERED: ENTIRE LIFE ON SAME FARM	• calves weaned naturally • transportation prohibited	• on-farm or local slaughter	• transportation prohibited	• on-farm or local slaughter

Reprinted with permission from Global Animal Partnership, www.globalanimalpartnership.org

Game Birds

There are also farms in America that specialize in raising all-natural and organic game birds for our culinary pleasure, including duck, goose, guinea hen, pheasant, quail, squab, and others. One such company is D'Artagnan from New Jersey. This company, like other sustainable poultry farms, raises its birds on natural foods and fresh clean water, and in open environments that offer protection from poor weather conditions. D'Artagnan does not use antibiotics, growth hormones, artificial preservatives, or animal byproducts. They firmly believe that small farms owned and operated by single families who believe in sustainable farming methods lead to better care and management of their animals.

Some culinary game species such as grouse, partridge, and wood pigeon are truly wild and can be found foraging in natural environments. Through estate hunts organized exclusively for farms like D'Artagnan, these wild game birds are obtained and processed at food inspector–supervised facilities. The birds are then shipped immediately, ensuring the freshest game birds possible.

Well-Raised Game Birds

Ducks should be raised in a large, clean, well-ventilated

Domestic geese are grown commercially for meat due to their large size and fast growth.

and well-lit barn, be fed vegetarian diets, and be given fresh, clean water. They should not be individually caged but allowed to roam free-range outdoors. They should also not be given any antibiotics, steroids, or growth hormones, and they should be allowed the opportunity to fully mature.

Geese should be raised in small flocks in a large, clean, well-ventilated and well-lit barn before being released to free-range outdoors with access to fresh, clean water. Like ducks, geese should be fed a vegetarian-based diet and should not be given any growth stimulants or antibiotics. They should also not be de-beaked or de-toed.

Guinea Hen should be able to roam and nest on the ground, in a free-flight environment, just like they do in their native habitat. They should be given a vegetarian-based diet with fresh, clean water and no antibiotics, steroids, or growth hormones.

Pheasant, like their relative the Guinea Hen, should be raised in an outdoor free-flight environment while being naturally fed on a vegetarian diet with fresh, clean water available.

Similar to the birds above, quail like a large, clean, well-ventilated and well-lit barn as well as being able to free-range/free-fly. They should be given a vegetarian-based diet with fresh, clean water and no antibiotics, steroids, or growth hormones.

Squab, also referred to as baby pigeons, should be farm raised in an all-natural environment, be fed an all-natural vegetarian diet with fresh, clean water, and be given no antibiotics, steroids, or growth hormones.

Wild Turkey, similar to geese, should be raised in a large, clean, well-ventilated and well-lit barn. They should also be able to free-range outdoors, allowing them to grow at their own pace, and they should be given a vegetarian-based diet with fresh, clean water and no antibiotics, steroids, or growth hormones.

Selecting Your Poultry

We ask again, what is the "best" poultry you can buy?

Organic versus Nonorganic. Free range versus factory farmed. Conventional versus air chilled. Vegetarian fed versus non-vegetarian fed. As you can see there are many determining factors that need to be considered. For those who prefer to eat meat that is humanely and sustainably farmed, the answer seems clear—select a bird that is organic and free range as opposed to factory farmed.

But what about quality and taste? If home cooks are being encouraged to change their buying patterns with the hope that consumer demand will support more ecological sound and humane poultry practices, shouldn't there be a noticeable difference in the quality and taste of the birds? Especially when these more environmentally-friendly options are considerably more expensive?

Simple At-Home Taste Test

Curious if one can actually *taste* the difference between environmentally friendly poultry and poultry that is factory-farmed, we conducted a simple, at-home taste test using average boneless skinless fryer breasts chosen at random from various supermarkets. We chose this cut because this is one of the most widely consumed poultry products on the market.

The Chicken Breast Participants:

1. Sweetwater Creek Air-Chilled Organic Chicken distributed by Pitman Family Farms. No added water, no antibiotics, free-range and a vegetarian diet. Price per pound: $11.00.

2. Metropolitan Market 100% Natural Free Range Chicken. No animal by-products, no antibiotics, no growth hormones, no artificial ingredients, minimally processed with a natural all-vegetarian diet. Price per pound: $8.00.

3. Whole Foods Market Fresh Organic Chicken distributed by Draper Valley Farms. Produced exclusively for Whole Foods Market. No antibiotics, no preservatives, vegetarian diet. May contain up to 4 percent retained water. Price per pound: $8.00.

4. Foster Farms All Natural Chicken. No added hormones, no added steroids, no added salt (although it is not a sodium-free food), minimally processed, no preservatives or additives, and may contain up to 2 percent retained water. Foster Farms says they are committed to producing the safest, most wholesome, highest quality and delicious poultry on the market. The fine print on their website, however, reveals their poultry are not fed an all vegetarian diet; they are neither "caged" nor "free-range"; and antibiotics are being used. Price per pound: $6.50.

5. Albertson's Signature All Natural Premium Best Cuts Chicken. No artificial ingredients, no preservatives, no added hormones, minimally processed but may contain up to 3 percent retained water. Price per pound: $5.00.

Here we have five different fresh boneless, skinless fryer breasts ranging from $5.00 per pound to $11.00. Is the $11.00 chicken really the "best" because it's the most expensive? We thought we'd taste and see.

All five breasts were cooked on a hot grill without any salt, pepper, flavoring, or seasonings. All were cooked at the same temperature and removed when properly cooked.

The results are on the following page.

FRESH BONELESS SKINLESS FRYER BREAST	PACKAGING	SMELL	COLOR/APPEARANCE	TASTE
Sweetwater Creek Air-Chilled Organic Chicken (Distributed by Pitman Family Farms) $11.00/lb	Earth friendly packaging. No Styrofoam tray or absorption pad under meat. Vacuum sealed in a pouch. Liquid cannot drain so meat is sitting in minimal residue.	Clean, fresh, no hint of odor.	Meat is clean, very slight pink/rosy hue, very minimal fat along the edges. After cooking, exterior was nice golden brown, crispy around the edges.	Good flavor, texture and juicy.
Metropolitan Market $8.00/lb	Standard Styrofoam tray with absorption pad under meat to absorb excess liquid. (not earth friendly)	Clean, fresh, no hint of odor.	Meat is clean, pink/rosy hue, very minimal fat along the edges. After cooking, meat, exterior had wonderful golden brown color, crispy around the edges.	Great flavor and texture. Expelled the second most juice after slicing into, delicious.
Whole Foods Market (distributed by Draper Valley Farms) $8.00/lb	Earth friendly packaging with tray made from plant fibers	Clean, fresh, no hint of odor.	Meat is much darker than the other breasts – more of a golden brown, which did not affect the flavor or texture.	Great flavor and texture. Very juicy and delicious.
Foster Farms $6.50/lb	Standard Styrofoam tray with absorption pad under meat to absorb excess liquid. (not earth friendly)	Clean, fresh, no hint of odor.	Meat is clean, slight pink/rosy hue, very minimal fat along the edges. After cooking, exterior was nice golden brown, crispy around the edges.	Good flavor, texture and juicy.
Albertson's Signature $5.00/lb	Standard Styrofoam tray with absorption pad under meat to absorb excess liquid. (not earth friendly)	Clean, fresh, no hint of odor.	Meat is clean, slight pink/rosy hue, very minimal fat along the edges. After cooking, exterior was nice golden brown, crispy around the edges.	Expelled the most juice after slicing into. A little bland tasting and slightly chewy.

Our home cooks rated the fresh boneless, skinless fryer breasts, from best tasting to least favorite, and the information was calculated. The top three "best tasting" according to our home cooks are:

• Metropolitan Market
• Whole Foods Market
• Foster Farm

The adage "you get what you pay for" seems to hold up to a certain degree. The least expensive chicken breast, Albertson's in this case, did not make the top three, while the Metropolitan Market, second in price, ranked the highest. The most expensive of the four, Sweetwater Creek Air-Chilled Organic Chicken, didn't make the top three, while the second-lowest-price chicken, from Foster Farms, came in third.

Granted, this was a simple "backyard" test with no lab, test tubes, or microscopes. It was far from scientific, but for the average home cook returning home from a long day's work and stopping at the supermarket to purchase some quick and easy boneless, skinless chicken breasts to cook for dinner, the test proved useful. It proves—from an average home cook's point of view—that paying the most per pound for boneless skinless chicken breasts does not necessarily translate to better tasting poultry. In fact, during our taste test, none of the home cooks were able to *visually* differentiate between which breast came from a free-range bird and which one did not.

Unlike seafood where there are visual and taste differences between certain farm-raised and wild-caught species, there do not seem to be clear indicators in our example (other than price) to help differentiate between various kinds of boneless skinless chicken breasts.

In regards to taste, the price per pound does not appear to be an issue. However, some consumers are more concerned for the birds and are willing to pay a premium to encourage humane treatment. The same holds true for healthier products we put into our bodies. Preferring to avoid poultry that may be laden with antibiotics, steroids, or growth hormones, which may have a negative impact on one's health, consumers find it is worth a little extra money to pay for birds that roam free outside and are fed a better diet, rather than birds injected with chemicals. But does this translate to better-tasting poultry? Perhaps.

Micro-Flocks and Backyard Poultry

For home cooks who are interested in taking "organic, free-range, non-factory–farmed poultry" one step further, consider raising your own "micro-flock," or "backyard poultry." These terms describe the practice of raising a small number of hens (a dozen or fewer) in suburban or urban residential communities. Today, thousands of people across the country are starting their very own backyard flocks (primarily chickens). Even celebrities like Martha Stewart are getting in on the action. Backyard poultry provides families with fresh, nutritious eggs and meat, while poultry manure feeds the soil and is excellent in gardens. Domesticated birds can also help control the insect population around your home, and birds such as chickens will often consume most table scraps and leftover food. There's even a magazine devoted to the subject (*Backyard Poultry*), so you can learn everything you need to know about breed selection, housing, management, health and nutrition, and other topics of interest to better raise poultry on a small scale.

Of course, backyard poultry isn't for everyone, but for those who love to watch their birds forage in the grass, roam outside, bask in the sun and take in fresh air, you cannot get any more traditional, sustainable, and environmentally friendly than eating fresh eggs and meat from poultry you raised yourself.

Closer Inspection: Organic Pioneers

Petaluma Poultry is the nation's leading natural chicken producer and the first certified organic chicken producer. They've been called the "purest, cleanest, antibiotic-free, humanely-raised chicken available today," by San Francisco's Bay Area food press. Their mission: offering healthier chicken choices to consumers.

Founded in 1920, Petaluma Poultry is the brainchild of Allen Shainsky, who grew up in the chicken business and started working on his family's chicken ranch at age six. Taking a break only to attend college and receive a degree in poultry husbandry from the University of California at Berkley, Allen returned to the family farm and eventually grew the backyard company into Petaluma Poultry. During the building of a feed mill to provide the highest quality feed for his chickens, Shainsky and Petaluma Poultry faced stiff competition from rivals Foster Farms and Zackey Farms. But Petaluma prevailed. Allen and his dedicated team were visionaries and far ahead of their time. It's no surprise Allen was a self-proclaimed "poultry king" with a passion for poultry. He spent fifteen years working on an organic chicken farm. He always believed in growing the best tasting poultry by implementing 100 percent organic practices: no antibiotics, no pesticides, and no animal by-products in the feed, and only high-quality animal husbandry—free range, sustainable farming, and a stress free environment. According to Allen, "It's not important to me how much quantity we're putting out. What gets me excited is our flavor and quality." Today, Petaluma Poultry, believing it's their corn-based vegetarian feed that produces the exceptional flavor of its prized chickens, continues to operate just like Allen would want, producing the highest quality and best tasting organic and natural chicken on the market.

"Mom always said you are what you eat, so it makes sense that chickens taste like what they eat," Petaluma Poultry

Proper Handling & Storage

We've all seen the cooking programs on television where the chef is preparing a poultry dish and he or she is washing everything in sight—the knife, the cutting board, the kitchen counter, their hands. Are these chefs germophobes? No, they're simply demonstrating the proper handling of poultry in the kitchen.

Because raw poultry can produce harmful bacteria, such as salmonella, any contact with raw poultry or anything it has touched—the knife, the cutting board, the kitchen counter, other foods, even your hands—can result in cross contaminations, or the transfer of harmful bacteria. The end result can be food poisoning. And anyone who has ever experienced food poisoning will tell you it is not a pleasant experience.

Washing everything that comes in contact with raw poultry with hot soapy water is a must to keep your kitchen area clean and safe from food-borne illness. For example, let's say you're making a chicken stir-fry. You just cut up your raw chicken on a cutting board. It's now time to chop the vegetables. *Do not* chop on the same cutting board using the same knife without washing them (and your hands) with hot soapy water first.

Just as you should be concerned with handling raw poultry, the same is true of cooking and consuming raw poultry. Unlike other meats, such as beef or seafood, there is no such thing as "chicken or turkey tartare." Poultry should never be undercooked or consumed raw because salmonella can still be present. Always cook your poultry completely before eating (internal temperatures should be at least 165°F), and never partially cook poultry with the plan to finish cooking it later.

Here are some other important tips when handling and preparing poultry:

• Do not baste poultry with any marinade the raw poultry was sitting in. After marinating the meat, discard the marinade and do not reuse.

• Do not put cooked poultry on any plate or serving dish that contained raw poultry, unless the plate or platter has been washed with hot soapy water.

• Do not freeze poultry that has been stuffed.

• Do not refrigerate or freeze hot poultry. The meat should cool completely then be wrapped or placed in an airtight container.

It is very important to use good judgment and get yourself into a routine when it comes to handling, storing, and cooking poultry at home. Such efforts will help reduce the growth of bacteria, such as salmonella, keeping your friends and family safe and healthy while enjoying your delicious meal.

If you're like many Americans, you will buy more poultry than you will need for that night's meal. You will plan to prepare some that night while freezing the rest for later. Let's first look at the best ways to freeze poultry.

Freezing Poultry

Packaged poultry, such as boneless, skinless chicken breasts, tenders, or drumsticks, can be frozen in the package. You should do this immediately after unpacking the groceries, or at least forty-eight hours from when you purchase the chicken. If you have a family-size package and live alone, you may want to divide the meat into smaller serving amounts to make thawing more convenient for later meals. There's nothing worse than deciding to defrost some poultry for two, but when you go to retrieve the meat from the freezer, you realized you had frozen the entire family pack of two dozen breasts. And trying to chip off two or three pieces from the frozen block isn't the most efficient method.

Before you portion the poultry, make sure your work area is ready. Have several large pieces of plastic wrap cut and at the ready and have some sealable freezer bags open and ready. (You don't want to have to fumble with the plastic wrap and freezer bags with chicken-y hands.) Portion out the meat on a large cutting board. Tightly wrap as much as you think you'll need for a later meal in plastic wrap. Place the wrapped chicken in a freezer bag. It's best to double wrap for added protection. Make sure all the air is pressed out of the bag. You can roll the bag, use a straw to suck out the air, or you can submerge the bag containing the poultry in water to help "push out the air" before sealing, just make sure no water gets in the bag. It is important you remove as much air as you can, giving your freezer bag a "vacuum sealed" look. The air causes ice crystals to form on the meat, which results in freezer burn and discolored and tasteless poultry. Most freezer bags also have a place where you can write the date, reminding you of when you froze the poultry. Generally, poultry holds up in the freezer for about two months.

Defrosting Poultry

When it comes to defrosting poultry, rushing the process can result in harmful bacteria-riddled meat.

The safest defrosting method is to transfer the poultry to the refrigerator and wait for a day. The cold temperatures (below 40°F) reduce the threat of bacteria while the poultry defrosts at a constant temperature. If you are like most home cooks, though, you may have decided to cook poultry at the last minute. So what can you do if you do not have the time to defrost the meat in the refrigerator?

For starters, never defrost poultry in hot water, in the sun, or on the counter for more than two hours. These methods are unsafe and can result in salmonella poisoning.

When the meat begins to thaw, the internal temperature rises. According to the USDA, anything warmer than 40°F can cause bacteria that may have been present in the poultry before freezing to multiply rapidly.

Instead, the best ways to defrost poultry at the last minute are:

Cold Water Defrosting

Place the frozen poultry in a sealed, watertight plastic bag. If you're cooking a small piece, you can place it under cold running water. Otherwise, submerge the bag in cold water, changing the water about every thirty minutes to ensure the water stays cold. The water must be kept cold at all times. When defrosted, cook the poultry immediately, and do not refreeze.

Microwave Defrosting

Thanks to modern technology, many of the new microwaves on the market have a "poultry defrost" setting. Use the defrost setting if you have one because you want to do exactly that—defrost—and not cook your poultry. Sometimes, areas of the poultry will get excessively warm or even cook during the defrost stage. Because of this, it is important to cook the poultry immediately, and do not refreeze.

Cooking Without Defrosting

This is your last ditch effort if you must cook poultry, and you didn't have time to properly defrost the meat. It is safe, according to the USDA, to cook poultry from the frozen state, but obviously it will take longer.

Fresh Poultry

According to the USDA, fresh poultry is defined as any raw poultry product that has never been subject to temperatures below 26°F. If it has, then the label "frozen" or "previously frozen" must be applied.

Look for the "USDA Grade A" seal or label. It means the poultry was governmentally inspected. The packaging should be unbroken or unsealed.

When purchasing fresh poultry, the package should always feel cold to the touch. When removed from any packaging, the poultry should smell fresh and not feel slimy at all. If your poultry just feels slimy, it may have spoiled. If it feels slimy and smells bad, throw it away.

For poultry you don't intend to freeze, simply store the meat in its original packaging in the refrigerator. If you prefer to remove the poultry from the packaging, tightly wrap the poultry in plastic wrap or place in an airtight container before putting it into the fridge. Also, don't forget to keep an eye on the expiration date.

Helpful Hint: Store the poultry on the bottom shelf of the refrigerator. If any drips of water or juices leak from the package, they won't contaminate other foods. Better yet, store the poultry in a separate drawer in the refrigerator, especially if you have an empty drawer that's not being used for, say, fruit or vegetables.

The Expiration Date

When purchasing poultry from the supermarket, make a point to observe the expiration date on the package. The date is often accompanied by the words "Sell By" or "Use Before." Markets often like to move poultry with the earliest expiration dates to the front of the counter or shelf while placing the later expiration dated poultry in the back. The theory is the hurried shopper will whisk by the poultry aisle, grab some chicken, for example, and move on, never stopping to check the date. If you don't plan on cooking the poultry that night, it's best to take a moment and select a package with a later expiration date, allowing you more time to store the meat before it expires. If you plan on freezing the poultry right away, you don't have to worry so much about the expiration date, as long as it hasn't passed.

Poultry Cooking Methods in This Book

With deliciously photographed food magazines whetting our appetites and television channels devoting themselves to the subject, we're living in a world where cooking is applauded not as a household chore but as a fun and enjoyable event in the kitchen shared by the entire family. That also translates to many exciting methods to use for food preparation. For those of you who have always relied on the microwave or oven, it's time to spread your wings and try some other forms for cooking your bird.

HOME STORAGE OF CHICKEN PRODUCTS

PRODUCT	REFRIGERATOR 40 °F OR BELOW	FREEZER 0 °F OR BELOW
Fresh Chicken, whole	1 to 2 days	1 year
Fresh Chicken, parts	1 to 2 days	9 months
Giblets or Ground Chicken	1 to 2 days	3 to 4 months
Cooked Chicken, Leftovers	3 to 4 days	4 months
Chicken Broth or Gravy	3 to 4 days	2 to 3 months
Cooked Chicken Casseroles, Dishes, or Soup	3 to 4 days	4 to 6 months
Cooked Chicken Pieces, covered with broth or gravy	3 to 4 days	6 months
Cooked Chicken Nuggets, Patties	3 to 4 days	1 to 3 months
Take-Out Convenience Chicken (Rotisserie, Fried, etc.)	3 to 4 days	4 months
Restaurant Chicken Leftovers, brought immediately home in a "Doggy Bag"	3 to 4 days	4 months
Store-cooked Chicken Dinner including gravy	3 to 4 days	2 to 3 months
Chicken Salad	3 to 5 days	Do not freeze if it contains mayonnaise
Deli-sliced Chicken Luncheon Meat	3 to 5 days	1 to 2 months
Chicken Luncheon Meat, sealed in package	2 weeks (but no longer than 1 week after a "sell-by" date)	1 to 2 months
Chicken Luncheon Meat, after opening	3 to 5 days	1 to 2 months
Vacuum-packed Dinners, commercial brand with USDA seal	Unopened 2 weeks; Opened 3 to 4 days	1 to 2 months
Chicken Hotdogs, unopened	2 weeks (but no longer than 1 week after a "sell-by" date)	1 to 2 months
Chicken Hotdogs, after opening	1 week	1 to 2 months
Canned Chicken Products	2 to 5 years in pantry	Do not freeze

Reprinted from the USDA website.

Braising and Stewing

Braising is when you cook a large piece of poultry (such as a breast or half a chicken) over low heat in a sizable pot with enough liquid to partially cover. To add flavor to the food, chopped vegetables such as carrots, celery, and onion (known as *mirepoix*) are often used. While cooking using this method, the pot is covered so the liquid doesn't evaporate. With stewing, the only difference is the meat is cut in smaller pieces and cooked in enough liquid to cover the poultry.

Grilling, Barbecuing, and Broiling

These are very popular cooking methods that use intense direct heat to cook tender cuts of poultry. When grilling or barbecuing, the heat source (often charcoal or briquettes) comes from below, and is considered a somewhat healthy way of cooking since the fat drips off the meat and into the fire. Be careful of flare-ups however, and make sure the cuts of poultry are not too thick or they will char on the outside before the center has a chance to fully cook. One way to avoid flare-ups and charring is to use indirect heat, in which the coals or fire are moved to one side of the grill and the meat is placed on the grate on the opposite side of the grill. This eliminates flare-ups, and the indirect heat allows the meat to cook evenly without the exterior getting burned to a crisp in the process. Although grilling and barbecue are often used interchangeably, a traditional barbecue uses low heat and a lot of smoke and cooks for a much longer period of time than grilling. Broiling, like grilling, uses a high heat, but the primary difference is that the heat source comes directly from above. A broiling pan is a special pan with a grill pan that fits inside. The grill pan has holes in it to allow the fat drippings to fall into the pan below, and, like grilling, you need to continually monitor the poultry as you cook to avoid burning.

Roasting

Roasting is another high-heat cooking method that uses no or little moisture. This method allows poultry, for example, to brown on the outside while retaining the juiciness of the meat on the inside. Once the meat is properly browned, the temperature is lowered so the interior of the meat can cook. Roasting is done in an oven, often using a roasting pan, which is like a broiling pan but is usually larger and with higher sides. Roasting can also be done on an open fire, using a rotating skewer, or rotisserie. This is known as spit-roasting.

Sautéing

This is a quick-cooking method that uses a sauté pan coated with a little oil (olive, vegetable, grapeseed) or fat (butter or lard) over high heat. Like roasting, the meat, often cut in small bite-size pieces, should brown nicely on the outside while the inside cooks through. Two important tips to remember: Do not overcrowd the pan, otherwise the heat will dissolve, and the meat will steam or boil. And keep the meat moving in the pan. This ensures the meat will cook evenly while always keeping the pan hot—important when sautéing.

Shallow and Deep Frying

In shallow frying—as it sounds—food is cooked in a shallow pre-heated pan like a frying or sauté pan with very little stirring as opposed to sautéing. High temperatures are used along with a small amount of fat or oil to cook the food. This method accentuates the flavors of the food while the limited movement of the food offers an enhanced texture through browning. Food is also cooked relatively quickly when shallow fried. When deep frying, the food will be completely submerged in the hot oil or fat. This method is used to cook the food even quicker while creating a moist and juicy inside and a much more pronounced exterior texture through a crunchy, golden brown coating. This delicious coating is often the result from battering or breading the food prior to immersing it into the extremely hot oil (see page 101).

Smoke Points for Various Oils

The smoke point generally refers to the temperature at which a cooking fat or oil begins to break down into glycerol and free fatty acids. The glycerol is further broken down into acrolein, which is a component of the blue-ish smoke. It is the acrolein that causes the smoke to be extremely irritating to the eyes and throat. Once the oil or fat has reached the smoke point both flavor and nutritional values are compromised. So if you are cooking at very high temperatures, such as with deep frying, you will need a fat with a relatively high smoke point.

Considerably higher than the temperature of the smoke point is the flash point; the point at which combustion occurs.

Here are some smoke points:

SMOKE POINTS FOR VARIOUS OILS

FAT	QUALITY (OFTEN NOTED ON LABEL)	SMOKE POINT	
Butter		350°F	177°C
Canola oil	Refined	470°F	240°C
Coconut oil	Refined	450°F	232°C
Corn oil	Refined	450°F	232°C
Flax seed oil	Unrefined	225°F	107°C
Grapeseed oil		420°F	216°C
Lard		370°F	182°C
Olive oil	Extra virgin	375°F	191°C
Olive oil	Virgin	420°F	216°C
Peanut oil	Refined	450°F	232°C
Safflower oil	Refined	510°F	266°C
Sunflower oil	Refined	450°F	232°C
Vegetable shortening		360°F	182°C
Walnut oil	Semi-refined	400°F	204°C

Smoking

This cooking method uses smoke to both cook and flavor the food, such as meat and poultry. The smoke is created typically using alder and oak, although other woods, such as hickory, mesquite, maple, apple, and cherry, can be used to create different flavors. There are two common smoking methods: cold and hot. Cold smoking is where the meat is not exposed to any heat. Using a separate chamber, the aromatic and flavorful smoke enters and saturates the meat over an extensive period of time. Meat or poultry that is hot smoked, on the other hand, is exposed to heat, but it's the smoke that slowly cooks the food at very low temperatures while impregnating the meat or poultry with smoke flavor as it cooks. To accomplish either cold or hot smoking, one will need a smoker designed to properly smoke foods. There are various quality smokers on the market, so do your homework before deciding which smoker is best for you.

Steaming

Steaming uses moist heat in the form of, well, steam to cook the food. In a pot that is equipped with a sieve-like basket, a little water in the bottom evaporates over high heat and converts to steam that circulates around the pot. The lid contains the steam, and the food is quickly yet gently cooked while remaining moist. To achieve such results at home, two essential pieces of equipment are needed: a pot with lid and a metal basket that suspends the food above the water. Bamboo steamers also work well. Unlike some of the earlier methods discussed, food cannot be burned or charred when steaming.

Stir-Frying

Similar to sautéing, stir-frying is just like it sounds, stirring while frying. This Chinese technique is performed in a large heated pan, particularly a wok, over very high heat. This ensures the food will cook quickly while remaining juicy. The food must be continually stirred or tossed so it doesn't burn. Often a little cooking oil is used to prevent sticking and to help brown the meat.

Because the cooking process is very fast, make sure all ingredients have been prepared ahead of time, as there isn't time to do much of anything once the food has been added to the sizzling pan.

The Art of Marinating

Marinades can be as simple as olive oil with a little garlic and some fresh herbs or they can be fancier, more complex, cooked concoctions. Vinaigrettes often make very good marinades. Every cuisine it seems has its own special marinades. We could fill several books with all the possibilities! What I want to do here is to share my own interpretations of some marinades from several cultures to get you started. Soon, you'll be making up your own. In a pinch, it's perfectly acceptable to use bottled marinades, as well as other commercially made products such as Teriyaki sauce or Worcestershire. Just make sure to taste them first. If the flavor isn't appealing straight out of the bottle, it's not likely to improve the taste of your dinner.

All of the recipes make enough to marinate at least a couple of pounds of poultry, fish, or vegetables. You'll note that I've suggested some combinations—a marinade I love with swordfish, another that's great with flank steak—but you should try any marinade with any food that sounds appealing to you.

Caution

1. Always refrigerate meats, chicken, and fishes as they marinate. Bacteria can grow very quickly on room temperature foods. People often ask about reusing marinades, and I don't usually recommend it. If, however, you've got a big batch of marinade that you can't bear to throw away, be sure to bring it to a rolling boil and then immediately refrigerate it. Plan to reuse it within a day or two.

2. If you are going to use some of your marinade as a dipping sauce or drizzle (great idea!), make sure you set aside that quantity before the meat or fish goes in.

You can combine the marinade with the food in almost any container (except cast iron or aluminum, both of which can react with acids and develop off-flavors), remembering that the goal is to have every food surface bathed in the marinade. Perhaps the easiest way to marinate is to put everything into a zip lock bag and close it securely. You can then turn the bag and food easily.

Remove food from the marinade and gently pat it dry. Typically marinated food is then grilled or broiled, but most of these marinades will also work if you prefer to pan roast or sauté. Give special cooking attention to marinades that have sugar, honey, or other natural sweeteners in them. Sugar burns quickly, so moderate the heat accordingly. Finally, remember that we marinate to add flavor not to tenderize as the conventional wisdom suggests. Acid-based marinades actually "denature" proteins over time and make them unappealing.

Marinating Times

You'll see a few exceptions in the recipes ahead and elsewhere in the book, but as a general rule, marinate:

- **Cut up seafood and vegetables** for up to 45 minutes
- **Cut up meat or poultry** for up to 2 hours
- **Whole chickens and fish and large cuts of meat** for up to 6 hours

Sauces and Seasonings
Flavored Butters

Flavored, or compound, butters can be made ahead and are great to have on hand to top and melt over grilled, roasted, or sautéed chicken and other birds. Additionally, they make wonderful flavorings when gently shoved up under the skin of chicken or other birds that you are going to roast whole. Cover and refrigerate for up to a week or roll into logs, wrap tightly in aluminum foil and freeze for later use. Plan to use them up within 6 months. Here is a sampling of some of my favorites:

Maitre d'Hotel Butter

1 pound sweet, unsalted butter
1/4 cup fresh lemon juice
2 tablespoons grated lemon zest
3/4 cup finely chopped parsley

1/2 cup finely minced shallots or green onions
Kosher or sea salt and freshly ground pepper
 to taste

Beat the butter in a bowl until softened. Beat in the lemon juice a tablespoon at a time and then mix in the rest of the ingredients.

Depending on your preference, you can use the shallots raw or sauté them till soft and cool them before beating into the butter. Instead of just parsley you could also use a mixture of fresh chopped herbs of your choice. In the summertime I mix chopped chives, parsley, and basil from my little container garden.

Mustard Tarragon Butter

3/4 cup grainy Dijon mustard
1/3 cup chopped fresh tarragon

1 pound softened unsalted butter
Kosher or sea salt and freshly ground black pepper

Beat the mustard and tarragon into the butter. Season with salt and pepper to taste.

If using dried tarragon, sauté 3/4 cup finely chopped shallots or green onions in 2 tablespoons butter in a skillet until soft but not brown. Add 3 tablespoons dried tarragon along with 3/4 cup dry white wine and reduce over high heat until the liquid has nearly evaporated. Cool and beat into the butter along with the mustard and salt and pepper to taste.

Roasted Garlic Butter

3 large heads garlic, roasted (see page 41)
1 pound softened unsalted butter

Kosher or sea salt and freshly ground black pepper

When garlic roasts it takes on an almost sweet nut-like flavor with none of the hot and funky notes that quickly develop in raw garlic. I usually use 3 large heads of roasted garlic per pound of butter. Squeeze the garlic out of the husks and beat into the butter. Season to taste with salt and pepper.

Blue Cheese Butter

1/3 cup minced shallots
3 tablespoons minced garlic
1 pound softened unsalted butter
1 1/2 cups crumbled creamy blue cheese such as
Roquefort or Gorgonzola

Kosher or sea salt
Freshly ground black pepper
Worcestershire sauce

Over moderate heat sauté the shallots and garlic in the butter till very soft but not browned. Set aside to cool.

When cool, beat the butter with the blue cheese. Add salt and pepper and Worcestershire sauce to taste.

Basil Pesto

This is just a guide. You can add more (or less) of any of the ingredients. Also feel free to substitute your favorite herbs, nuts, oils, or cheeses. Use as is, fold into mayonnaise or crème fraîche, stir into a basic vinaigrette, beat into softened butter to push up under the skin of roast chicken or any bird . . . you get the idea.

MAKES ABOUT 1 CUP
4 cups firmly packed fresh basil leaves
1 to 2 tablespoons chopped roasted, poached, or
toasted garlic (see page 41)
2 tablespoons lightly toasted and chopped pine nuts
or blanched almonds

1/3 cup olive oil
1/4 to 1/2 cup freshly grated Parmesan or Asiago
cheese
Kosher or sea salt and freshly ground black pepper

Plunge the basil leaves into a pan of boiling water for 5 seconds. Immediately drain and plunge into a bowl of ice water to stop the cooking and set the bright green color. Drain and squeeze out all the water that you can. Coarsely chop the basil and add it to a food processor or blender along with the garlic, nuts, and oil and purée. Transfer to a bowl and stir in the cheese. Add salt and pepper to taste. Store covered in the refrigerator for up to 5 days or freeze up to 3 months.

Roasting, Poaching, and Toasting **Garlic**

A simple way of taming garlic's sometimes dominating flavor is to roast, poach, or toast it first. When you cut into raw garlic you break the cell walls and it immediately begins to oxidize. A product of that oxidation is the development of hot, often funky flavors that can overpower a dish. When heated, the enzymes that account for those flavors are neutralized and the garlic will remain sweet and delicate. This is especially important for sauces like pesto, which often are made in big batches and stored refrigerated or frozen for later use. You definitely don't want the garlic to take over down the road. With all these methods garlic can be stored in the refrigerator in a tightly covered container for at least a week.

To Roast Garlic: Slice off the top quarter or so of each garlic head to expose the cloves. Drizzle with a little olive oil and season with salt and pepper. Loosely but completely wrap each head in a piece of foil and roast in a preheated 400-degree oven until the garlic is very soft and lightly browned, about 45 minutes or so. To use, simply squeeze the buttery soft garlic out of the head just like you'd do toothpaste.

To Poach Garlic: Separate but don't peel the cloves. Place the garlic in a small saucepan and cover with at least $1/2$ inch of cold water. Place on the stove over high heat and bring to a boil. As soon as the water boils, drain and repeat the process one more time. Rinse to cool off the cloves and remove the husk.

To Toast Garlic: Separate the cloves and place them unpeeled in a dry sauté pan over moderate heat. Shake and turn them occasionally until the cloves develop toasty brown spots on the skin. Remove, cool, and the skin will easily slip off. The additional benefit of this method is that you've added a lovely toasty flavor to the garlic.

Pan Sauce for Poultry

**MAKES ABOUT ½ CUP (ENOUGH TO SAUCE
4 SAUTÉED CHICKEN BREAST HALVES)**
4 tablespoons unsalted butter, divided
¼ cup finely chopped shallots or green onions
1 cup chicken stock

2 tablespoons fresh lemon juice, or to taste
3 tablespoons finely chopped herbs such as parsley,
  dill, chives, or preferably a combination
Kosher or sea salt and freshly ground black pepper

Heat 2 tablespoons of the butter in a sauté pan over moderate heat and sauté the shallots until softened but not brown, about 2 minutes. Add the chicken stock and lemon juice and bring to a boil over high heat. Continue to cook until reduced by half and lightly thickened, 3 to 5 minutes. Off heat, whisk in the remaining butter to thicken the sauce and then add the herbs and season to your taste with salt and pepper. Serve immediately spooned over chicken.

Romesco Sauce

MAKES 2 CUPS
2 large tomatoes (1 pound), cored
1 large dried ancho chile
⅓ cup extra-virgin olive oil
¼ cup peeled hazelnuts
¼ cup blanched almonds

1 (½-inch-thick) slice firm white bread, cut into
  ½-inch cubes
2 large garlic cloves, sliced
⅛ teaspoon dried hot red pepper flakes
¼ cup drained piquillo or pimento peppers, rinsed
1 tablespoon red wine vinegar, or to taste
Kosher or sea salt and freshly ground black pepper

Place the tomatoes under a hot broiler and roast until lightly charred and softened. Chop them and set aside, saving all the juices.

While the tomatoes are roasting, slice the chile open lengthwise and discard the stem and seeds; then tear the chile into small pieces. Heat the oil in a 10-inch heavy skillet over moderate heat, add the chile, and cook, stirring, until the oil is fragrant and the chile turns a brighter red, about 20 seconds. Transfer the chile with a slotted spoon to a heatproof bowl.

Add the hazelnuts to the skillet along with the almonds, bread, garlic, and red pepper flakes and cook, stirring, until the bread and garlic are golden, 2 to 3 minutes. Add the mixture (including oil) to the chile in the bowl and let cool.

Combine the chile mixture, piquillos, and vinegar in a food processor and purée till smooth. Season to taste with salt and pepper and additional vinegar if needed. Thin with water if desired. Can be made up to 3 days ahead and stored covered and refrigerated. Serve at room temperature.

Garam Masala

There are many variations of this Indian spice blend, which is typically used as a "finishing" spice at the end of cooking.

4 tablespoons coriander seeds
1 tablespoon cumin seeds
1 tablespoon black peppercorns
1½ teaspoons black cumin seeds
¾ teaspoon black cardamom (3 to 4 large pods)

¾ teaspoon cloves
2 (1-inch) sticks cinnamon
¾ teaspoon crushed bay leaves
1½ teaspoons dry ginger

Heat a heavy skillet over medium heat and gently roast all the ingredients (leave cardamom in its pods till later) except the dry ginger, till they turn a few shades darker. Stir occasionally. Do not be tempted to speed up the process by turning up the heat as the spices will burn on the outside and remain raw on the inside.

When the spices are roasted turn off the heat and allow them to cool. Once cooled, remove the cardamom seeds from their skins and mix them back with all the other roasted spices. Add the ginger.

Grind them all together, to a fine powder in a clean, dry coffee or spice grinder. Store in an airtight container in a cool, dark place.

CHICKEN

Today, chicken has become so much a part of our menu that we don't tend to think much at all about these noble little birds. Those of us who are urban dwellers are pretty much disconnected from the farm and any thought or association about how our food is grown, the genetic diversity that exists, and what it means to participate fully in the life cycle of something we eat.

At six years old I joined the FFA (Future Farmers of America). The organization started back in 1928, and its goal was and still is to help youngsters prepare for a life in agriculture and the challenges of feeding a growing population. Their mantra has always been that farming is more than planting and harvesting—it's a science, it's a business, and it's an art! All kids in that part of the world belonged to the FFA. As part of my involvement, I was responsible for raising a chicken, my first real "pet." Colorado was a hot bed for raising poultry. We all searched out the rarest breeds we could find for either egg or meat production. There are thousands of varieties of chickens in the world. If you've never been to a county or state fair and visited the livestock pavilions, definitely put it on your bucket list of things to do. When you go see the poultry, you'll be amazed at the incredible diversity of color, size, shape, sound, and more. The goal for all of us was to raise a blue-ribbon bird and enjoy the bragging rights for a year.

My chicken of choice was a breed commonly known as an "Easter Egger." The name comes from the beautiful blue-green–colored eggs they lay. I can't remember why, but I named her "Bridgie." Most of us don't think of chickens as being particularly lovable or friendly, but Bridgie was different. I had raised her from a tiny chick, and we formed a pretty strong bond. She was a fairly constant companion and would follow me everywhere, even when I went fishing on the stream that ran through the ranch. They never made a movie of "A Boy and his Chicken"—for obvious reasons, no doubt—but I would have been the poster child for that story if they ever did. We had a special bond, and I won two ribbons at the county fair because of her—one for her stately beauty and one for her egg production—both of which I proudly displayed for years.

The chickens on the ranch not only supplied us with eggs and meat, but as a bonus, they provided feathers for bedding and fertilizer in the garden. Additionally, the chickens were our best weather forecasters. You always knew that changes were in the air if the chickens "sang" at night more than usual. If a hen or her chicks refused to leave their coops in the morning, you knew heavy weather was coming. My grandmother also used her chickens as a barometer for when to plant the garden. She believed that when the chickens "molted" (dropped old feathers to be replaced by new ones), it was time to begin planting. If the chickens molted from their heads first, you should sow early (as close to last frost as possible); if they molted from their posteriors first, you should sow late (the *Farmers' Almanac* was our handy guide).

The best chicken I ever ate was in France, in the Franche-Comté, many years ago when I had a chance to dine on the famous Poulet de Bresse. It's a special breed of chicken that has distinctive blue coloring in its legs and comb. It is usually and best served simply roasted with root vegetables. Unlike our commercially grown chickens, which are generally without flavor, a roasted Bresse chicken has an amazing and unique flavor. It doesn't survive well in the huge mass-production farms that we use in the United States, so we don't see it much here. There are, however, a few farms around the country that have started raising strains of the Bresse chicken, and it's worth asking for at your specialty grocer or butcher or farmers' market.

That old saying that "it tastes just like chicken" underscores the versatility of this marvelous bird and its universal taste appeal. In many ways, chicken is a blank canvas with which you can cook and flavor in an almost endless number of ways. It offers so many possibilities—not only in its variety of parts but also in its adaptability to a whole range of cooking techniques and ethnic flavors.

Working a Chicken

Cutting up a chicken is not really difficult. All you are doing for the most part is guiding your knife through the natural separations in the body. It is easier when you become familiar with the physiology of the bird. The following directions apply to all birds in this book.

What do I mean when I say "chicken breast"?

Technically, a chicken has just one breast made up of two pieces, what the French call supremes. When I refer to chicken breast in the following recipes, I'm talking about one of those two pieces or one of the supremes. These can vary greatly in size, as you know—anywhere from four ounces or so up to eight or more.

TO BUTTERFLY OR SPATCHCOCK A CHICKEN

▾ **With poultry shears** or a sharp chef's knife, remove the backbone, cutting or slicing it along each side all the way down to the tail end.

◂ **Splay the chicken** open with the skin side up on a flat surface. Place the heel of your hands, one on top of the other, over the middle of the chicken.

▸ **Press down to flatten** the chicken. You may hear the breast bone crack.

TO CUT UP A BIRD

▼Cut through the skin that connects the legs to the carcass.

◄With shears cut the breast in half along the breast bone and around to the legs for a bone-in breast. For a boneless breast, follow the bones with your knife and separate each breast from the carcass.

▶Splay the legs out to the side and cut through the sockets attaching them to the carcass.

◄Separate legs and thighs if desired. Remove the wings from the carcass and cut off the wing tips. Final result: two breast portions, two thighs, two drumsticks, two wings. Save the carcass and wing tips to make a stock.

TRUSSING

Tie the legs together with cotton twine. Tuck the wings behind the body. There is no need to tie the wings.

Brining and Dry Salting Chicken and Other Birds

Two ways of improving flavor and texture of chicken, turkey, and other birds are brining (wet salting) and dry salting them before cooking. Both rely on the principle of osmosis, which you'll remember from high-school science class, is the movement of elements in liquids across a semipermeable membrane. The effect is to equalize liquid and whatever else is in it on both sides of the membrane. In brining and dry salting, the activator is salt.

My Basic Brine

1/3 **cup kosher salt (Diamond Crystal preferred)**
1/3 **cup brown sugar**
1 **quart cold water**

Simply stir the salt and sugar into the water until they are dissolved. Add the chicken or other bird so that it is covered with the brine. What happens is that the salt and sugar migrate into the flesh (osmosis at work), trying to equalize the concentrations in the pot and inside the meat, which moistens the meat. And sugar is one of nature's best flavor enhancers. Humans are hard wired for sugar from birth. (Ever tasted mother's milk?) The problem with sugar is when we overdo it, as with processed foods that use corn syrup. A little bit, however, is a useful tool with savory foods. Remember the picture of the Italian grandmother standing at the stove and throwing a couple of pinches of sugar into her homemade red sauce? She was doing that for a couple of reasons: First, if the tomatoes were too acidic, the sugar would soften that acidity. Second, being an intuitive cook, she also knew that just a bit of sugar would expand flavor and make the sauce more delicious.

> ### How long to leave the bird in the brine:
>
> - For breasts or whole legs (thigh and drumstick): 2 to 3 hours, refrigerated
> - For whole chickens: 3 to 6 hours, refrigerated
>
> If the chicken tastes salty to you, then cut down the amount of time in the brine the next time you do it.

Dry Salting Here you simply salt the surface of the bird using the amounts below. You need to be sure to allow enough time for this to work before cooking. Again, what happens here is our old friend osmosis. The salt draws moisture from the bird. This moisture dissolves, leaving the surface wet with beads of moisture. (This action is why we are generally told not to salt a steak before cooking—it will dry the meat out.) But then something happens as the bird sits. The salt and moisture are reabsorbed into the flesh and the surface is dry. The meat is more delicious, and the skin is drier and tighter; during cooking, it will crisp much better, and who doesn't like crisp skin? This is especially important for great roast chicken. Once salted, place on a rack on a rimmed baking sheet and refrigerate uncovered for at least 4 and up to 12 hours.

> ### How much dry salt to use:
>
> - 3- to 4-pound whole or butterflied chicken: about 2 teaspoons kosher salt, sprinkled evenly on all sides
> - 4- to 5-pound whole or butterflied chicken: about 3 teaspoons

Smoking Chicken and Other Birds

For the best smoked chicken, brine or dry salt the chicken as described above. You can go directly to the smoker or rub the chicken with a seasoned rub mixture. There are all manner of rubs on the market, but why not make your own? Here's a simple one you can modify to your own taste.

Combine all the rub ingredients and mix well. You can smoke the chicken whole or butterfly it first. Apply the rub generously all over the chicken. Gently push the rub under the skin with your fingers, being careful not to tear the skin. Refrigerate for at least 2 hours and up to 12. Set up your smoker according to the manufacturer's directions. You can also smoke using a kettle grill.

Heat the smoker and get the temperature to 235°F. You'll want to maintain the temperature between 210°F and 235°F the entire time. Place the chicken in the smoker, breast side down to start. After 1½ to 2 hours, turn it over to finish. Total time will be around 4 hours. Chicken is cooked at 165°F, but when smoking, you want to overcook it somewhat. Look for a temperature around 175°F. Test the temperature with an instant-read thermometer inserted into the thickest part of the chicken breast. A good smoked chicken will be very tender and have a late summer tan. The meat will be slightly pink from the brining, and the juices will run clear. Once the bird(s) are the correct temperature, tenderness, color, and the juices run clear, remove it (or them) from the smoker and let rest for at least 10 minutes to allow the juices to redistribute inside the meat.

If you are smoking chicken using a charcoal-fired smoker, soak 3 to 4 cups of wood chips for about an hour. You can use any sort of fruitwood chips you like. Drain them and place directly on the coals once the smoker has reached temperature. This will be sufficient for the entire cooking period even if you add more coals. Too much smoke can create an acrid and bitter flavor. The top vent should always remain open. Use the bottom vents only to maintain the temperature between 210°F and 235°F. Remember that each smoker is different, so experience counts.

Always use tongs and insulated gloves when smoking birds. Avoid using anything pointed, which can pierce the meat and allow the juices to escape. Minimize opening the smoker to maintain the heat. This is especially true if you are using charcoal.

Basic Rub Recipe

¼ cup packed dark brown sugar

¼ cup sweet paprika

1 tablespoon kosher salt

1 tablespoon freshly ground black pepper

1 tablespoon onion powder

1 tablespoon garlic powder

1 tablespoon pure chili powder, such as ancho

½ teaspoon or more cayenne pepper

BASIC CHICKEN STOCKS AND BROTHS

Depending on who you talk to, the main difference between a stock and a broth is the amount of meat, and especially bones, with which it is made. Broths tend to be lighter, while stocks are thicker and gelatinous when cooled because of the collagen that is extracted from the bones and connective tissues while simmering. The gelatinous quality of stocks gives them a richer mouth feel, makes them better for deglazing pans, and enables them to be used in place of butter or cream to make sauces. For our purposes, let's just agree that stocks and broths are basically the same. And in case you were wondering, it's fine to use canned stocks or broths. Just choose those that are defatted and low in salt. See below for a quick recipe to add more flavor to canned stock.

Improving Canned Chicken Stock

Take the basic aromatic vegetables (onions, carrots, celery, plus a little garlic) and sauté until they are lightly browned. Add them along with a bay leaf and one or two whole cloves (the spice) to the canned stock. Figure on about 1½ cups of raw vegetables to 6 to 8 cups of stock along with the bay leaf and clove. Bring this to a boil, then immediately reduce the heat and simmer for 15 to 20 minutes. Strain. Much better!

There are two "geographical" approaches to making your own chicken stock—Asian and European. The traditional European approach that is codified for most of us as the French approach is to use basic aromatic vegetables or *mirepoix* (onions, carrots, celery) along with meat, in this case chicken, to make the stock. In Asia, the stocks are often simpler and rely on just the meat and bones alone or maybe, as they do in China, the addition of aromatics such as ginger and scallion. I provide recipes for both (page 70) and you can decide which you like. The key to good chicken stock is to use all parts of the chicken, including the meat (dark meat preferred), bones, skin, and—if you can get them—the feet (see the following recipe). Bones, skin, and feet contribute not only flavor but also texture to the stock. Also, don't season the stock with salt or pepper. At this point you want to have a basic stock. You may decide to reduce stock for a sauce, and if you season it now to a pleasant level it will be over-seasoned when reduced.

Chicken has a long culinary history. Wild chickens were common in India and East Asia (China, Thailand, and Vietnam) long ago, and that is where chickens were first domesticated, probably around 7000 B.C. For this reason, I've given lots of space

The Recipes

to Asian-influenced dishes since this delicious little bird has been a mainstay on the menu there for such a long time. Also, remember that most of these chicken recipes can be adapted to other birds in the book.

Japanese Fried Chicken

Known as *Kara-age*, this is a classic nibble sold all over Japan and especially at *izakayas*, the Japanese bars that dot Tokyo's nighttime foodscape. Instead of the thick flour-based batters that come from America, this chicken is traditionally marinated, dusted with potato starch, and then beautifully and crisply fried. It's got everything you'd want in a bar snack: crispy, juicy, and salty.

MAKES 4 TO 6 SERVINGS

1 pound (125g) boneless, skinless chicken thighs, trimmed of excess fat
3 tablespoons soy sauce
2 tablespoon mirin*
1 tablespoon sake (optional)
2 garlic cloves, finely minced
1 tablespoon grated fresh ginger
¾ cup (96g) potato starch or cornstarch
Vegetable oil for frying
Kosher or sea salt
1 or 2 lemons, cut into wedges

Cut the chicken into 2-inch pieces. Combine the soy sauce, mirin, sake, garlic, and ginger in a small bowl. Add the chicken, and gently stir to coat the chicken. Marinate in the refrigerator for 30 minutes or so. Pour the cornstarch on a shallow plate.

Add the vegetable oil to a deep, heavy skillet over medium-high heat to a depth of 1 inch or so. Heat to 360°F (182°C). Remove the chicken pieces from the marinade and dredge them in the cornstarch, shaking to remove excess. Add the chicken pieces, in batches if necessary, to the hot oil and cook, turning occasionally, until brown and crisp, about 5 minutes. Drain on paper towels and season immediately with salt. Serve with lemon wedges to squeeze over.

Available at Asian markets

How to **Deep Fry**

There are three important things to think about when deep frying:

1. Good clean oil with a relatively high smoke point. We never want to cook with oil that has been "smoked" because its chemistry changes, and not for the good. If you smoke an oil, and we've all done it, toss it out and start over. See page 35 for the smoke points for various cooking oils. Canola is a good all-purpose oil for frying because of its relatively high smoke point and neutral flavor.

2. The right temperature. The sweet spot for frying is 350°F to 375°F (176°C to 190°C). You don't want to go below 350°F (176°C) because at lower temperatures the food tends to absorb more oil, making it greasy and leaden. If you go higher than 375°F (190°C), the outside will overcook before the inside is done. Use a thermometer. There are all kinds in the market.

3. Cold food into hot fat is best. When cold food hits the hot fat, there is an immediate crisping of the surface, which helps to retard the absorption of oil. It won't make the food impervious to the oil, but it does help to make the food less greasy.

5-Spice Chicken in Rice Paper

Edible rice paper comes in a variety of sizes and has lots of interesting uses. It is available in Asian markets, especially those that feature Thai and Vietnamese ingredients.

MAKES 12 SERVINGS (2 PER SERVING)

3 tablespoons kosher or sea salt

1 tablespoon Chinese 5-spice powder, preferably homemade (recipe follows)

1 (450g) pound boneless, skinless chicken breasts

12 small rice paper rounds or triangles

4 green onions, halved lengthwise and cut into 2-inch batons

2 tablespoons peeled and finely slivered ginger

Canola or other vegetable oil for frying

DIPPING SAUCE

1/2 cup (200g) hoisin sauce

3 tablespoons lime or lemon juice, or to taste

1 tablespoon soy sauce

Combine the salt and 5-spice powder in a small bowl. Cut the chicken breasts into 12 uniform pieces and sprinkle lightly with the seasoned salt, coating all sides.

Place 1 rice paper in a bowl of hot water and soak for 20 seconds or so or until it is nearly softened. Drain briefly and place on a clean hard surface. Place one piece of chicken in the lower third of the paper and top with some of the green onion and ginger. Tightly roll the rice paper over, fold in the sides, and continue rolling to enclose, leaving the top edge unfolded. Repeat with the remaining chicken, green onions, and ginger.

In a large sauté pan, heat 1/4 inch of oil to 360°F (182°C). Cook the rolls in batches for 4 minutes or so or until the rice paper is crisp and the chicken is cooked through. Keep the rolls separated using a chopstick or skewer to prevent them from sticking together, especially in the beginning.

Make the dipping sauce. Combine the hoisin sauce, lime juice, and soy sauce and mix well. Serve the chicken with the dipping sauce and any remaining 5-spice salt.

5-Spice Powder

You can buy 5-spice powder in Asian markets and many supermarkets. It's fine, but when you make your own, the freshly ground spices have lots more fragrance. Spices quickly lose their aromatics after grinding. Add a little cayenne pepper if you're in the mood for more heat.

MAKES ABOUT 1/4 CUP

2 teaspoons Sichuan peppercorns

8 whole star anise

1 teaspoon whole cloves

1 (2-inch) (5cm) stick cinnamon, broken into pieces

1 tablespoon fennel seeds

Toast the spices in a dry skillet over medium heat for 2 minutes or until fragrant. Be careful not to burn. Let cool.

Grind the toasted spices in a coffee grinder, blender, or spice mill to a fine powder. Sift into a small bowl to remove any large particles. Store in an airtight container for up to 4 months.

Grilled Chicken Kebabs with Tzatziki

These are delicious served with freshly grilled flatbreads or pitas. A recipe for flatbread is included below. Many markets also sell ready-made pizza dough, which would also work fine for the flatbread. The tzatziki sauce should be made at least an hour ahead for flavors to bloom. If you are using wooden skewers, soak them in water for 30 minutes before use.

MAKES 4 SERVINGS

TZATZIKI

1 medium (about 12 ounces/340g) English or Kirby
  cucumber, peeled
Kosher or sea salt
1 teaspoon finely chopped garlic
1½ cups (420g) Greek-style yogurt
1 tablespoon chopped fresh mint
2 teaspoons chopped fresh dill
1 tablespoon fresh lemon juice, or to taste
Freshly ground black pepper to taste

KEBABS

2 pounds (900g) boneless, skinless chicken
  breasts or thighs
2 small fennel bulbs
1 red onion
⅓ cup (80mL) extra-virgin olive oil
2 tablespoons lemon juice
1 tablespoon dried oregano, preferably Greek
2 teaspoons chopped fresh rosemary
1 tablespoon kosher or sea salt
1 tablespoon freshly ground black pepper

Prepare the tzatziki ahead of time. Grate the cucumber into a mixing bowl using the medium-sized holes of a box grater. Add a pinch of salt and place in a cheese cloth–lined strainer. Place over a bowl and let drain for a few minutes. Twist and squeeze the cheese cloth to remove as much liquid as you can from the cucumber. Transfer to a bowl and stir in the remaining ingredients. Season to taste with salt and pepper.

For the kebabs, cut the chicken into 2-inch cubes and set aside in a bowl. Cut the fennel and onion into wedges similar in size to the chicken and add to the bowl. In a small bowl, whisk the olive oil, lemon juice, oregano, rosemary, salt, and pepper together. Pour the mixture over the chicken, fennel, and onion, and gently toss to coat. Skewer the chicken and alternate with pieces of fennel and red onion.

Over a medium-hot grill, cook the kebabs until they are nicely browned and just cooked through, about 8 minutes. Serve kebabs with tzatziki sauce and warm pitas or flatbreads.

Shanghai Chicken Wings

This is a typical preparation in Chinese restaurants and in that long forgotten Polynesian "pupu platter," which is making a comeback.

MAKES 4 SERVINGS

²⁄₃ cup (270g) hoisin sauce

¹⁄₂ cup (120mL) rice vinegar

2 teaspoons Chinese chili garlic sauce

1 teaspoon Chinese 5-spice powder (see page 57)

Canola oil or other vegetable oil for frying

2 pounds (900g) chicken wings, tips discarded and drumsticks and wings separated

Kosher or sea salt to taste

Whisk together hoisin sauce, vinegar, chili garlic sauce, and 5-spice powder in a large bowl.

Heat 2 inches of oil in a deep 5-quart saucepan over medium-high heat until a deep-fry thermometer registers 360°F. Working in batches, fry the chicken in hot oil until the skin turns bubbly and golden brown and the meat is cooked through, about 8 minutes.

With a slotted spoon, transfer the cooked chicken to the bowl with the hoisin sauce mixture. Season with salt. Toss until the chicken is fully coated. Serve hot. The cooked chicken can be kept warm in a 180°F oven for up to an hour.

Masa Cakes
with Chicken and Spicy Slaw

These stuffed masa cakes known as *pupusas* are the national dish of El Salvador.

MAKES 12 MASA CAKES

¹⁄₄ cup (60mL) distilled white vinegar

2 teaspoons sugar

1 teaspoon dried oregano, preferably Mexican

2 chiles de árbol, stemmed, seeded, and crushed, or to taste

1 medium carrot, grated (about 1 cup/60g)

1 small white onion, peeled and thinly sliced

¹⁄₄ head green cabbage, shredded

Kosher or sea salt

2 cups (240g) masa harina

8 ounces (230g) chihuahua or Monterey jack cheese, grated

Vegetable oil

2 cups (340g) shredded cooked chicken

Make the slaw by combining the vinegar through cabbage in a bowl. Season with salt.

Combine the masa harina and about 1¹⁄₄ cups water in a bowl; stir to form a soft dough. Let the dough sit for 5 to 10 minutes to hydrate. Pinch off a golf ball-size piece of dough and pat it into a thin disk. Place a couple tablespoons of cheese into the center of the dough; stretch the edges of the dough around the cheese and seal. Pat the dough into a 3¹⁄₂-inch-wide disk. Repeat with the remaining dough and cheese to make 12 pupusas in all.

Heat a few drops of oil in a skillet over medium-high heat. Working in batches, cook the pupusas until golden, about 5 minutes per side. Serve hot topped with chicken and slaw.

Shanghai Chicken Wings

Korean Fried Chicken Wings

Gojujang (also spelled with a K) chili paste is one of the indispensable condiments in the Korean kitchen. It is made by combining powdered red chili peppers, glutinous rice powder, and soybean paste. Note that I am double frying the wings.

MAKES 4 SERVINGS

Canola or other vegetable oil for frying

3 tablespoons pressed fresh garlic

2¹/₂-inch (6.35cm) piece ginger, peeled and finely minced

5 tablespoons (75mL) soy sauce

6 tablespoons (90g) gojujang

3 tablespoons rice vinegar

1¹/₂ tablespoons toasted sesame oil

¹/₄ cup (85g) honey

2 tablespoons fresh lime juice

¹/₃ cup (50g) rice flour

¹/₃ cup (40g) all-purpose flour

¹/₃ cup (40g) cornstarch

16 chicken wings, tips removed and saved for stock (about 1³/₄ pounds)

¹/₄ cup (60mL) green onions, sliced on the bias

Heat 2 inches of canola oil in a 5-quart pot over medium-high heat until a deep-fry thermometer registers 360°F.

Meanwhile, in a small saucepan, make a gojujang sauce. Combine the garlic, ginger, soy sauce, gojujang, vinegar, sesame oil, honey, and lime juice. Bring to a simmer over moderate heat and adjust the seasonings to taste. Keep warm.

In a large bowl, whisk together the flours and cornstarch. Add 1 cup of water and stir to combine. Add the chicken and turn several times to coat thoroughly. Working in batches, fry the chicken in the hot oil until golden, 6 to 8 minutes. Drain on paper towels. Return the oil to 350°F. Fry the chicken until extra crisp, 6 to 8 minutes more. Drain again. Toss the chicken in with the sauce, top with the green onions, and serve hot.

Buffalo Chicken Wings

Chicken Wings became a staple in America back in 1964 at the Anchor Bar in Buffalo, New York. The story goes that a group of friends arrived at the bar late one evening and the only food owner Teresa Bellissimo could find were the chicken wings, which were usually used to make stock. She grabbed them, deep fried them, and whipped up a spicy sauce to coat them, and a legend was born. What are they? They are unbreaded wings deep fried until the skin is crispy and then tossed with a simple sauce of butter or margarine, hot pepper sauce, and vinegar. Sometimes a little garlic powder, celery salt, and other spices are added. According to Buffalo residents, they are always served with carrot and celery sticks, a blue cheese dressing and, of course, a cold beer to cool the hot sauce and chase it all down.

Chicken Liver Parfait

I love the rich velvety texture and taste of this recipe. The addition of the apples offers a little sweetness and texture. One of my favorite uses is to spread it on crackers and then use them to top a crisp salad. This is best made a few hours ahead of time so the flavors can bloom.

MAKES ABOUT 2 CUPS
1 pound (450g) chicken livers, trimmed of any veins and gristle and halved
Milk
5 tablespoons (70g) unsalted butter, divided
1 small tart-sweet apple (such as Fuji), peeled and cut into $\frac{1}{4}$-inch (6mm) dice

$\frac{1}{4}$ cup (60mL) Calvados or other brandy
$\frac{1}{2}$ cup (80g) finely chopped shallots
1 tablespoon finely chopped garlic
Kosher or sea salt and freshly ground pepper
$\frac{1}{4}$ teaspoon ground allspice
2 tablespoons finely grated orange zest

Soak the livers in enough milk to cover for 15 minutes or so.

Meanwhile, heat 2 tablespoons of the butter in a heavy skillet over medium-high heat and sauté the apples until they color a bit but still retain their shape. Add the Calvados and cook for another minute or so and then set aside in a small bowl to cool.

Add the remaining butter to a clean sauté pan over medium heat and cook the shallots and garlic until softened but not brown, about 4 minutes. Drain the chicken livers and pat them dry and season with salt and pepper to taste. Add to the pan and cook, stirring and turning occasionally, until the livers are almost cooked through but still slightly pink inside, about 8 minutes.

Transfer the livers to a food processor. Add any juices from the apples and the allspice and orange zest and purée until very smooth. Season to taste with the salt and pepper. Stir the apples into the mixture and pack into a crock or terrine. Cover with plastic wrap and chill for at least 2 hours. It will keep covered and refrigerated for up to 5 days. Remove from the refrigerator at least 30 minutes before serving.

Note: If you are going to unmold the confit to slice it, be sure to line the mold with plastic wrap to make it much easier to remove. If cutting into slices, use a hot knife.

Smoked Chicken Rice Paper Rolls
With Spicy Dipping Sauce

Edible rice paper makes a wonderful wrap for all kinds of things. In Vietnam, the traditional fillings are salad ingredients along with aromatic herbs such as mint, cilantro, Asian basil known as "holy" basil, fresh cucumber, rice noodles, and some chopped peanuts or dried shrimp. The possibilities are endless, however. The idea is to roll the ingredients tightly without tearing the softened paper. It takes a little practice, but it's really easy to do. For a fun gathering, you might try placing all the ingredients on a table and letting your guests roll their own!

MAKES 8 ROLLS

2 ounces (56g) fine rice vermicelli
8 nine-inch round rice papers
½ cup (12g) gently packed fresh mint
½ cup (12g) gently packed fresh cilantro
½ cup (12g) gently packed fresh Thai or regular basil leaves
1 cup (89g) finely shredded green cabbage

1 cup bean or daikon sprouts, rinsed
1 small cucumber, peeled, seeded, and julienned (about 1 cup, 119g)
1 medium carrot, peeled and julienned (1 cup, 60g)
8 ounces (230g) smoked chicken (see page 50), cut in fine strips
½ cup (75g) dry roasted peanuts, chopped
Spicy Dipping Sauce or Nuoc Cham (recipe follows)

For the chicken paper rolls, place the vermicelli in a bowl, cover with hot water and allow to soak for 15 to 20 minutes or until softened. Drain and place on a cutting board in a tangle and cut once or twice with a sharp knife. Set aside.

Place 2 of the rice papers into a large bowl of warm water and gently turn them for 20 to 30 seconds or so until they are just beginning to soften. Remove from the water and drain for a couple of seconds and then lay them on a flat hard surface such as a cutting board.

Place leaves of mint, cilantro, and basil in a line across the lower third of each wrapper, leaving about an inch on both sides. Top with some of the vermicelli, cabbage, sprouts, cucumber, carrot, smoked chicken, and peanuts. Fold the bottom of the paper snugly up over the filling and roll halfway. Fold each side in on top of the cylinder and "crease" all the way to the top of the wrapper and then continue to roll it up gently but firmly. The paper will seal by sticking to itself. Repeat with the remaining wrappers and filling. Serve the rolls cut into thirds with dipping sauce on the side.

Spicy Dipping Sauce (Nuoc Cham)

½ cup (120mL) fresh lime juice
4 tablespoons (60mL) Asian fish sauce
1 teaspoon minced fresh red chile or to taste

2 teaspoons finely minced garlic
1 tablespoon rice vinegar
5 tablespoons (62g) sugar, or to taste
1 tablespoon fresh cilantro leaves, coarsely chopped

Combine all the ingredients and stir until the sugar is dissolved. Let stand at least 30 minutes before serving for flavors to develop. Adjust salt/sweet/tart/hot flavors to your taste.

Yakitori Chicken

The Japanese term *yakitori* literally means "grilled bird" and refers to skewers of chicken barbecued over a charcoal grill and served in casual, inexpensive *izakayas*, Japanese bars and beer gardens that serve food beyond the usual bar snacks. Traditional yakitori employs a wide range of poultry parts from meat to necks, to offal such as livers, gizzards, hearts, and skin. You could also skewer and grill shiitake mushrooms, small shishito peppers, and more. Traditionally, green onions are part of the mix. It's a quick and easy dish to prepare once you have a batch of *tare* or marinade and basting sauce prepared. If using wooden skewers be sure to soak for at least one hour before using.

MAKES 4 TO 6 SERVINGS

1/2 cup (120mL) soy sauce
1/2 cup (120mL) mirin* or rice vinegar
1/4 cup (55g) sugar
1 tablespoon sliced garlic
1 tablespoon finely chopped ginger
1 pound (450g) boneless, skinless chicken thighs,
  cut into 1-inch (2.5cm) cubes

1/2 pound (230g) shiitake mushrooms,
  stems removed
4 green onions, green and white parts
  cut into 2-inch (5cm) lengths
Sansho or togarashi pepper*
Lemon wedges

Preheat a charcoal or gas grill to moderately high heat. Make sure the grill rack is clean and oil it thoroughly with cooking spray.

In a large bowl, combine the soy sauce, mirin, sugar, garlic, and ginger. Add the chicken and mushrooms and marinate for a few minutes.

Reserving the marinade, remove the chicken and vegetables from the bowl. Separately thread the chicken, mushrooms, and green onions onto skewers. Keeping them separate enables you to control the cooking better.

Pour the marinade into a saucepan to make the *tare* sauce to use as a basting and serving sauce. Boil for 8 minutes or so or until lightly thickened. Strain through a fine sieve and set aside.

Transfer the skewers to the prepared grill rack over direct heat. Cook, basting often with the sauce, 5 minutes per side, until the chicken is starting to brown on the edges and the vegetables are soft and charred at the edges.

Transfer the skewers to a heated platter, drizzle with a little sauce, and serve sprinkled with a little sansho or togarashi pepper and lemon wedges to squeeze over.

Available at Asian markets featuring Japanese ingredients and some supermarkets.

Happy Pancake

Known as *banh khoai*, this is classic Vietnamese street food and can be made with an endless variety of ingredients. It's basically a combination of a pancake and omelet. In street stalls, it's served as is or pieces of the pancake are torn off, wrapped in lettuce or mustard leaves and herbs, and then dipped in a spicy dipping sauce, such as Nuoc Cham (see page 64).

MAKES 6 SERVINGS

1 cup (160g) rice flour
1/2 cup (60g) all-purpose flour
1 teaspoon turmeric
2 cups (475mL) soda water
1/2 cup (120mL) coconut milk, stirred
  before measured
1/2 teaspoon salt
Vegetable oil
2 tablespoons chopped shallots
1/2 pound (230g) ground chicken,
  preferably thigh meat
2 teaspoons chopped garlic
2 teaspoons fish sauce

Freshly ground black pepper to taste
1/2 pound (21-24) shrimp, peeled, deveined,
  and sliced in half lengthwise
6 shiitake mushrooms, stems discarded,
  or cremini mushrooms, thinly sliced
2 cups bean sprouts, rinsed and patted dry
4 scallions, both white and green parts sliced
  thinly diagonally
1 small onion, halved and thinly sliced
3 eggs, beaten
1/2 cup (12g) fresh cilantro, mint, or Thai
  basil sprigs, or a combination
Nuoc Cham (see page 64) or Sriracha to
  drizzle on if desired

Combine the flours, turmeric, soda water, coconut milk, and salt in a blender and blend until smooth. Set batter aside to rest for at least 15 minutes for flours to fully hydrate.

Add 2 tablespoons of the oil to a medium (9-inch) nonstick skillet and heat over medium heat. Add the shallots, chicken, and garlic and cook, stirring until the chicken is cooked through, for about 5 minutes. Season with fish sauce and pepper. Transfer to a bowl.

Wipe out the skillet with a paper towel and add a couple of teaspoons of the oil over moderate heat. Add 1/3 cup or so of the batter to the skillet and quickly swirl around to cover the bottom of the pan. Add a few pieces of shrimp, 1 to 2 tablespoons of the cooked chicken mixture, some mushrooms, bean sprouts, scallions, and onion. Cover and cook for 2 minutes or until the cake is set. Uncover and drizzle about 3 tablespoons of the egg over the pancake and cook until the egg is just set. Fold in half and flip from one side to the other to lightly brown and crisp. Repeat until all the batter and other ingredients are used up. Be sure to stir the batter before making each pancake.

Serve warm topped with fresh herbs and your favorite spicy condiment sauce such as Nuoc Cham or a spicy prepared sauce such as Sriracha.

Chicken Croquetas

Croquetas are common tapas found in bars and are eaten as a snack in homes everywhere in Spain. They have lovely crisp shells with a wonderfully oozy center that comes from the fact that they are made with a classic béchamel sauce base. Anything can be stirred into the base. I've used chicken, cheese, and parsley here. They are completely addictive! Note that the béchamel base needs to be chilled for a couple of hours. These can be done a day ahead covered well with plastic wrap.

MAKES ABOUT 24 CROQUETAS
4 tablespoons (55g) unsalted butter
3 tablespoons (45g) extra-virgin olive oil, divided
$\frac{1}{3}$ cup (50g) finely chopped onion
1 cup (120g) all-purpose flour, divided
1$\frac{1}{2}$ cups (350mL) whole milk
1 cup (170g) shredded cooked chicken

Kosher or sea salt and freshly ground black pepper
Freshly grated nutmeg
3 tablespoons or so finely chopped fresh parsley
$\frac{1}{3}$ cup (30g) freshly grated Gruyere and/or Parmesan cheese
3 large eggs, beaten
2 cups (128g) dry breadcrumbs such as panko
Canola or other vegetable oil for frying

In a large skillet, melt the butter and 2 tablespoons of the olive oil over medium heat. Add the onion and cook until soft but not brown, about 5 minutes. Add $\frac{1}{3}$ cup of the flour and stir to form a smooth mixture, about 2 minutes. Gradually whisk in the milk and cook until the mixture is thick, about 3 minutes. (This is the béchamel sauce base.) Add the chicken and continue to stir for a couple of minutes until the mixture begins to pull away from the side of the skillet. Season to taste with salt, pepper, and nutmeg. Off heat, stir in the parsley and cheese.

With the remaining tablespoon of olive oil, grease a shallow, straight-sided bowl about 8 inches in diameter. Add the chicken mixture and place a sheet of plastic directly on top. Chill until firm, at least 4 hours or overnight. When ready to cook, you can either invert the chilled mixture onto a cutting board and cut into uniform 1-inch cubes or roll 1-tablespoon-size pieces with wet hands into round or cylinder shapes. Return the croquetas to the refrigerator for a few minutes while you set up the breading station with the remaining flour, eggs, and breadcrumbs each in a separate dish.

Lightly dredge the croquetas in the flour, then in the eggs, and then in the breadcrumbs. They can be made a few hours ahead and stored uncovered in a single layer in the refrigerator.

When ready to serve, preheat the oven to 200°F and place a wire rack on a rimmed baking sheet. In a 4-quart saucepan, add 2 inches of oil and heat the oil to 375°F. Working in batches, fry the croquetas until golden brown, about 1 minute per side. Drain on paper towels, and then season lightly with salt. Transfer to the prepared baking sheet and place in the oven to keep warm until ready to serve.

European Chicken Stock

MAKES ABOUT 1 GALLON

6 pounds (2.72kg) meaty chicken parts
 (such as legs, wings, and backs)
2 tablespoons olive oil
3 cups (450g) chopped onion

1 cup (150g) chopped carrots
1 cup (150g) chopped celery
6 large garlic cloves, crushed
1 1/2 (5.7L) gallons water
3 cups (700mL) dry white wine

Rinse the chicken parts and set aside. In a deep stockpot, heat the olive oil and add the onion, carrots, celery, and garlic and sauté until the vegetables just begin to color. Add the chicken, water, and wine and bring just to a boil. Reduce the heat and simmer, partially covered, for 2 to 3 hours, skimming any foam from the surface. (Make sure you do not boil the stock at this stage; if it boils, it will become cloudy. It'll still taste good, but usually you want to have it relatively clear, especially if you want it for a clear soup or sauce.) Remove from the heat, cool, and strain through a fine mesh strainer. Discard the solids. Refrigerate overnight or until the fat has congealed on top. Remove and discard the fat. Store covered and refrigerated for up to 5 days, or frozen for up to 6 months.

Asian Chicken Stock

MAKES ABOUT 3 QUARTS

6 pounds (2.72kg) meaty chicken parts
8 half-dollar-size coins of fresh ginger, crushed
 with the side of a cleaver or knife

6 scallions or green onions, crushed
6 garlic cloves, crushed
2 whole star anise
1 1/2 (5.7L) gallons water

Rinse the chicken parts and place them in a deep pot. Add the rest of the ingredients and bring just to a boil. Immediately reduce the heat and gently simmer partially covered without boiling for 2 to 3 hours, skimming any foam from the surface. Do not boil. Proceed as above. After straining and defatting, return the stock to a clean pot and bring to a boil. Continue to boil uncovered until it is reduced by at least a third. Cool, refrigerate for up to 5 days, or freeze up to 6 months. I like to freeze the reduced stock in standard ice cube trays. When frozen, I pop them out and put them in plastic freezer bags. Two cubes equals about 1/4 cup.

Chicken Feet Stock

The very best chicken stock, in my opinion, is made either partly or wholly from chicken feet. The feet produce a rich, golden broth that is full of all kinds of nourishing nutrients that come from the marrow and the bones. When chilled, it will firm up nicely into a gel, which makes it ideal for sauce reductions as well as soups. You rarely see chicken feet in a supermarket, so you'll have to go to a Mexican or Asian market where they appreciate their gnarly, slightly repulsive (for some of us) appearance. A slow cooker is an ideal tool to use here if you have one.

MAKES 2 QUARTS
2 pounds (.9kg) chicken feet
2 medium carrots, coarsely chopped

1 large onion, quartered
2 celery stalks, coarsely chopped
1 large bay leaf
1/2 bunch fresh parsley

In a large stock pot, bring 3 to 4 quarts of water to a boil over high heat. Add the feet, bring back to a boil, reduce the temperature to medium, and simmer for 5 minutes. Skim and discard any scum that rises to the surface.

Drain the feet completely and rinse in cold water. Using kitchen shears or a sharp knife, chop off the tips of the toes and discard. If there are any rough patches on the claw pad, cut away and discard.

Place the feet back into a large clean stockpot and add enough cold water to cover by 1 1/2 inches (about 1 gallon). Add the carrots, onion, celery, bay leaf, and parsley and bring to a gentle boil over high heat. Reduce the heat to medium low, partially cover, and simmer very gently for 4 to 8 hours, adding more water as desired. Skim any fat that rises to the top. Carefully strain the stock through cheese cloth or a fine mesh strainer. Cool and refrigerate for up to 2 weeks or freeze up to 4 months.

Feet Directly from the Farmer

Chicken feet are usually ready to use; however, if you get them directly from a farmer, you'll need to do a little easy prep. Rub them with coarse salt and then scald them very briefly in boiling water followed by a plunge in ice water. This allows you to easily peel off the yellow membrane. After peeling, chop off the tips of the toes at the first joint. The thought here is that this will help release the gelatin and all the other goodness in the feet.

Chicken Consommé

This is more a technique than a recipe. Consommé is a strong, rich, flavorful soup made by concentrating and clarifying chicken or other meat stocks. The word *consommé* means "completed" or "concentrated" in French and is characterized by its rich flavor and clarity. It's clarified by barely simmering it with a mixture of egg whites and lean ground meat called a "clearmeat." As the consommé simmers, the clearmeat solidifies into a "raft," which floats on top of the liquid. The clearmeat draws proteins and other impurities that cloud a stock out of the liquid, leaving it perfectly clear.

Traditionally, consommé is served as a starter or appetizer course usually with a simple garnish of vegetables cut attractively in brunoise or julienne shapes. Because it is high in gelatin, consommé will jell when it cools, making it a great basis for preparing aspics.

MAKES 1 TO 1½ QUARTS

4 ounces (113g) chicken thigh meat
1 carrot
1 celery stalk
2 garlic cloves

3 egg whites
3 quarts (3L) canned or homemade chicken stock
  (see page 70)
Kosher or sea salt and white pepper to taste

Add the chicken, carrot, celery, and garlic to a food processor and process until very finely chopped. Add the egg whites and process until well combined, and then transfer to a large bowl. Add 1 cup of cold stock and, using your hands, stir until it is combined. Add the remaining stock and mix well. Pour in a large heavy saucepan.

Bring the mixture to a simmer, stirring frequently but gently to keep solids from adhering to the bottom of the pan. Reduce the heat to a bare simmer and cook for 45 minutes or so. Very gently ladle the consommé from the pan, being careful not to disturb the "raft" or coagulated egg mixture (better to leave a little consommé behind than risk clouding the strained consommé).

Strain the consommé through a strainer lined with a couple of layers of rinsed cheese cloth or, alternately, through a coffee filter, into a clean saucepan. Season to taste with salt and white pepper.

Chicken and Shrimp Meatball Soup

Southeast Asian flavors are at work here with the interesting combination of chicken and shrimp meatballs.

MAKES 6 TO 8 SERVINGS

5 ounces (140g) mung bean noodles
$1/2$ pound (230g) peeled and deveined shrimp
$1/2$ pound (230g) boneless, skinless chicken thighs
2 teaspoons finely chopped garlic
3 tablespoons finely chopped green onions, including green tops
2 tablespoons fish sauce
$1/2$ teaspoon freshly ground black pepper
1 teaspoon granulated sugar

8 cups (1.89L) canned or homemade chicken stock (see page 70)
2 tablespoons soy sauce
1 tablespoon (12g) brown sugar
1 teaspoon chili garlic sauce, or to taste
1 (2-inch) (5cm) piece ginger, peeled and julienned
$1/4$ cup (60mL) fresh lime juice
$1/4$ cup (12g) roughly chopped fresh cilantro
Fried garlic or shallots, if desired

Cook the noodles according to package directions. Drain and set aside.

Place the shrimp and chicken in a food processor fitted with the metal blade and pulse until coarsely chopped. Scoop the mixture out into a large bowl and stir in the garlic, green onions, fish sauce, black pepper, and granulated sugar. Using a tablespoon to measure, gently roll each spoonful into a ball and set aside. You should have about 18 balls.

Add the chicken stock, soy sauce, brown sugar, chili garlic sauce, and ginger to a soup pot and bring to a boil. Drop in the meatballs and cook until meatballs are done, about 8 minutes. Keep the soup at a gentle simmer so that it doesn't cloud. Adjust the seasoning to taste. Divide the noodles and lime juice among individual soup bowls, add the meatballs, ladle the broth over the soup, and top with chopped cilantro and fried garlic or shallots.

"Real" Chicken Noodle Soup

You'll never use that little red and white can again! The secret here of course is the fresh vegetables and especially herbs that give this soup its bright clean taste. If you have a stash of frozen pesto on hand, use that in place of the fresh herbs. Use whatever vegetables you like, but shoot for a combination of colors, at least three. As a starting place, I'd suggest broccoli, snap peas, or asparagus for the green; carrots or red bell peppers for the red; and potatoes, parsnips, cauliflower, or the whites of green onion for a white.

MAKES 4 SERVINGS

4 cups (600g) fresh vegetables (such as carrots, celery, zucchini, shallots), cut in bite-size pieces

8 cups (1.9L) canned or homemade chicken stock (see page 70)

8 ounces (230g) dried wide egg noodles or 1 pound (450g) fresh

8 ounces (230g) (2 medium) boneless, skinless chicken breasts, thinly sliced crosswise

¼ cup (12g) chopped mixed fresh herbs (such as basil, parsley, and tarragon)

1 to 1½ tablespoons finely grated lemon zest

Kosher or sea salt

Hot sauce

Heat a 6-quart pot of lightly salted water to a boil and blanch the vegetables individually until crisp tender. Scoop the vegetables out with a strainer and run cold water over them to stop the cooking. Set them aside in one bowl. In a separate pot, heat the chicken stock to a simmer.

Add the noodles to the pot with the vegetable water and cook until they are just tender but still have a little bite to them—*al dente*. While the noodles are cooking, add the chicken to the stock and cook for a minute or two over moderate heat. The stock should just be at a simmer and not boiling. Skim any foam that rises to the surface. Add the cooked noodles, the vegetables, herbs, and lemon zest and heat through. Season to taste with salt and drops of hot sauce and serve immediately. Can be made up to 3 days ahead and stored, covered, in the refrigerator. Heat before serving.

Mulligatawny Soup

The name translates to "Pepper Water," and though we often think of it as an Indian recipe, it's another of those interpretations like Chicken Tikka Masala (see page 107), whose origin was Anglo. One theory is that the English adapted a traditional Indian spiced pea and lentil peasant dish to suit their own love of soup . . . and called it Indian. It's often served with rice and becomes a meal in itself.

MAKES 6 SERVINGS

3 tablespoons (43g) unsalted butter

2 medium white or red onions, chopped (about 3 cups/450g)

2 medium carrots, chopped (about 1 1/2 cups/225g)

2 celery stalks, chopped (about 1 cup/150g)

3 large garlic cloves, chopped (about 2 tablespoons)

1 tablespoon garam masala

2 teaspoons toasted ground coriander

2 teaspoons toasted ground cumin

2 teaspoons ground turmeric

1/2 teaspoon cayenne pepper or to taste

3 large bay leaves

2 cups (300g) dried orange or red lentils, picked over and rinsed

6 cups (1440mL) canned or homemade chicken stock (see page 70)

3 cups (680g) diced cooked chicken

1 cup (240mL) coconut milk

3 tablespoons lime or lemon juice

Kosher or sea salt and freshly ground black pepper

1 1/2 cups (225g) peeled, cored, and finely diced tart-sweet apple (such as Fuji)

Lemon or lime wedges

Heat the butter in a large, heavy soup pot over medium heat. Add the onions, carrots, and celery and cook, stirring occasionally, until golden brown, about 10 minutes. Add the garlic and cook for 2 minutes or so. Add the garam masala, coriander, cumin, turmeric, cayenne, and bay leaves and stir for a minute or two. Add the lentils and chicken stock. Bring the soup to a boil and then reduce the heat to low and simmer, partially covered, until the lentils are tender and very soft, about 20 minutes. Discard the bay leaves.

With an immersion blender, or working in batches with a regular blender, purée the soup until smooth. Stir in the chicken, coconut milk, and lime juice. If you desire a thinner consistency add a little more chicken stock or coconut milk. Season to taste with salt and pepper. Stir in the apples just before serving. Spoon warm soup into bowls and serve with lemon wedges.

Note: Toasting spices helps bring out and amplify their flavor. All you do is heat a pan over moderate heat (no oil), add the spices, and stir until they become fragrant, 2 minutes maximum. Be careful not to burn them.

Chicken Soup with Greens and Shiitake Mushrooms

A whole world of ingredients could be added to this, such as soaked cellophane noodles, cubes of soft tofu, cooked rice, or what have you to make a one-dish meal.

MAKES 6 TO 8 SERVINGS

1/2 pound (230g) fresh shiitake mushrooms
2 tablespoons olive oil
Kosher or sea salt and freshly ground pepper
7 cups (1680mL) canned or homemade chicken stock (see page 70)
1 cup (240mL) dry white wine
1 2-inch (5cm) piece ginger, peeled and cut into thick coins
2 1/2 cups (375g) bias-cut green onions, divided (about 3 bunches)
6 large chicken thighs with skin and any visible fat removed
3 cups packed, thinly sliced Napa or other green cabbage (about 4 ounces/113g)
4 cups (120g) packed young spinach leaves, washed and stemmed (about 1/2 bunch)
2 teaspoons hot pepper sesame oil,* or to taste
1/3 cup (5g) rough chopped fresh cilantro

Remove the stems from the shiitakes and set aside. Heat the olive oil in a sauté pan over medium heat. Slice the shiitake caps thickly and quickly sauté until lightly browned, about 5 minutes. Season with salt and pepper and set aside.

Add the chicken stock, wine, ginger, 2 cups of the onions, and the reserved mushroom stems to a deep pot and bring to a boil over high heat. Reduce the heat to medium low and add the chicken. Slowly simmer until the chicken is just cooked through, skimming off any scum that rises to the surface, about 12 minutes. Do not boil once the chicken is in or the stock will become cloudy.

Remove the chicken from the pot and cut into bite-size pieces, discarding the bones, and set aside. Strain the stock carefully, discard the vegetables, and skim off the fat. Rinse out the pot, pour in the strained stock, and bring to a simmer over medium heat. Add the cabbage and cook for a minute or two so that it is still crisp but just beginning to soften. Stir in the chicken, spinach, and sesame oil. Adjust seasoning with salt and pepper and serve at once, garnished with the cilantro and the remaining 1/2 cup of green onions.

Available at Asian and health food stores. Or you could substitute the Japanese pepper spice mixture called "shichimi togarashi," which contains red pepper, roasted orange peel, yellow sesame seed, black sesame seed, seaweed, and ginger.

Soba and Chicken in Green Tea Broth

Soba noodles are one of Japan's treasures and are made of buckwheat, which is very nutritious. Despite its name, buckwheat is not wheat. It's gluten free and is safe for people with celiac disease. Soba are widely available, and you could also substitute any other fine pasta like angel hair. Soba noodles cook quickly, and the Japanese believe that the cooking should be very gentle because buckwheat has no gluten and can become mushy quickly. I've included their interesting cooking technique for soba in the recipe, which specifies adding cold water at a couple of intervals to ensure the cooking will be gentle. I think it does make a difference, but you can also cook them straight away if you're in a hurry.

MAKES 4 SERVINGS

GREEN TEA BROTH

4 tablespoons genmai cha
  (green tea with roasted rice)
1 1/2 tablespoons (7g) chopped fresh ginger
4 tablespoons (60g) red miso
3 tablespoons (45mL) soy sauce, or to taste
Toasted sesame oil (optional)

CHICKEN

4 ounces (114g) dried soba noodles
Toasted sesame oil
1 tablespoon sugar
3 cups (140g) lightly packed young spinach
  leaves, stemmed
1 pound (450g) poached or grilled boned and
  skinned chicken breast, sliced thinly
4 green onions, sliced on the bias in 1/2 inch
  (13mm) lengths
Japanese pepper blend *shichimi togarashi*
  (available in Asian markets) or cayenne pepper
Soy sauce

To make the green tea broth, place the tea and ginger in a non-aluminum pot and add 8 cups of boiling water. Allow to sit for 2 to 3 minutes and then stir in the miso and soy sauce. Steep for another 3 minutes or so and then strain through a fine mesh strainer. If you want a bright clear broth, place the mixture in a tall, narrow glass container and refrigerate for at least 3 hours or overnight. Miso solids will fall to the bottom, leaving you with a clear top. Carefully pour this off, leaving the solids behind. It can be stored in the refrigerator for up to 5 days. To use: Reheat and add drops of sesame oil to taste, if desired.

For the chicken, in a large pot, bring 6 quarts of lightly salted water to a boil over high heat. Drop the soba noodles in and stir to make sure they separate. When the water begins to boil and foam, add 1 cup of cold water. Return to a boil and repeat the addition of cold water. Bring them back to a boil and test. The noodles should be cooked through but still firm. If not, repeat the process. Immediately drain and rinse with cold water. Gently rub the noodles to remove the surface starch. Toss with a few drops of sesame oil to keep the noodles from sticking together and set aside.

Combine the green tea broth and the sugar in a saucepan and heat to a simmer. Add the spinach and simmer for a minute or two. Place the noodles in deep bowls and ladle the hot broth over the top. Add the chicken and green onions. Pass the pepper and soy sauce for each person to season to taste.

Philadelphia Pepper Pot Soup with Chicken

Known as "the soup that won the war," this is believed to have been invented by a cook in the American Continental Army in 1777. The army had failed to repulse the British, who were in Philadelphia, and George Washington decided to set up winter quarters twenty miles away in Valley Forge. It was a harsh, miserable winter, and the army often went days without bread, or meat, or both. In late December, the absence of meat almost caused a mutiny, and—as the story goes—Washington instructed his cook to make a soup "that will warm and strengthen the body of a soldier and inspire his flagging spirit." Supposedly, he came up with one made from tripe, scraps of meat, and a lot of pepper—the soldiers were warmed and made war-ready, and the British were finally routed. I've done just a little updating to the original recipe, substituting chicken for tripe.

MAKES 6 TO 8 SERVINGS

1 to 2 pounds (450-900g) boneless, skinless chicken thighs

6 ounces (168g) thick-sliced pancetta, diced

2 large onions, diced (about 2 cups/300g)

2 large celery stalks, diced (about 1 cup/150g)

2 to 3 carrots, diced (about 1 cup/150g)

$^1/_2$ pound (230g) leeks, diced (about 1 cup)

2 large poblano chiles, diced (about 2 cups/300g)

8 cups (1.89L) beef or chicken stock (see page 70), or a combination

1 teaspoon dried thyme

1 teaspoon dried oregano

$^1/_4$ teaspoon ground cloves

$^1/_2$ teaspoon crushed red pepper flakes, or to taste

$2^1/_2$ teaspoons freshly ground black pepper, divide

1 bay leaf

1 pound (450g) Yukon Gold potatoes, peeled and diced (about 3 cups)

5 tablespoons (71g) unsalted butter

5 tablespoons all-purpose flour

Kosher or sea salt

$1^1/_2$ pounds (680g) tomatoes, seeded and diced (about 2 cups)

$^2/_3$ cup (40g) chopped fresh parsley or celery leaves (about $^3/_4$ bunch)

Cut the chicken into very thin slices and set aside. In a large heavy soup pot, sauté the pancetta over medium heat until crisp, about 8 minutes. Add the onions, celery, carrots, leeks, and poblanos and sauté until just softened and beginning to brown, about 5 minutes.

Stir in the chicken stock, thyme, oregano, cloves, red pepper flakes, 1¼ teaspoons of the black pepper, and bay leaf. Bring to a boil over high heat. Add the potato and chicken and bring back to a boil. Reduce the heat medium low and cook until both are tender, about 10 minutes.

Prepare a roux by melting the butter in a small skillet over medium heat. When it is melted, stir in the flour and cook for 3 minutes or so, stirring regularly. Stir as much of the roux as you like into the soup to thicken it. Season to taste with salt and the remaining black pepper. Stir in the tomatoes and parsley and adjust the seasoning to taste. The soup should have a nice peppery bite.

Chinese Hot and Sour Chicken Soup

Chinese black vinegar gives this soup a deep, mellow tang that you can't get with white or red vinegar. Black vinegar is widely available at Asian markets.

MAKES 6 SERVINGS

1 pound (450g) boneless and skinless chicken thighs

4 tablespoons (60mL) low-sodium soy sauce, divided

1 tablespoon Chinese rice wine

1 teaspoon toasted sesame oil

1 teaspoon sugar

1 1/2 tablespoons cornstarch

8 cups (1.89L) homemade Asian chicken stock (see page 70)

1 cup (90g) shiitake mushrooms, cut into thin slices

1/2 cup (75g) canned or fresh bamboo shoots, julienned

12 ounces firm silken tofu, cut into 3/4-inch (19mm) cubes

3 tablespoons Chinese black vinegar, plus more as needed

2 teaspoons freshly ground white pepper, plus more as needed

1/4 cup thinly sliced scallions, cut on the bias

Combine the chicken, 1 tablespoon of the soy sauce, and the rice wine, toasted sesame oil, sugar and cornstarch in a large bowl. Mix well to coat each shred of chicken. Let the chicken marinate at room temperature for 10 minutes.

Bring the stock to a boil in a large saucepan over high heat. Add the chicken and stir to separate all the pieces. Let the liquid return to a boil, then reduce the heat to medium and add the mushrooms, bamboo shoots, and tofu. Cook for 3 to 5 minutes, until the chicken is cooked through and the mushrooms have softened.

Season the soup with the remaining soy sauce and the black vinegar and white pepper. Stir, taste, and add black vinegar and/or white pepper as needed. Divide among individual bowls; garnish with sliced scallions.

Hanoi Chicken Noodle Soup (Pho ga)

This is a poultry variation on the famous *pho* soup of Vietnam. It's a simple soup to make and illustrates the love of fresh herbs and greens in that part of the world. You can substitute any green, such as spinach, cabbage, or kale, for the bok choy. Be careful not to overcook.

MAKES 6 SERVINGS

8 cups (1.89L) Asian chicken stock (see page 70)
1/3 cup (50g) coarsely chopped ginger
3 large garlic cloves, peeled and crushed
4 whole star anise
4 whole cloves
1 (3-inch/7.6cm) cinnamon stick
1 teaspoon whole black peppercorns
1 teaspoon whole fennel seeds
2 tablespoons brown sugar, or to taste
3 tablespoons Vietnamese or Thai fish sauce (*nuoc mam*), or to taste

2/3 cup (40g) fresh cilantro sprigs, divided
2/3 cup 40g) fresh mint and/or tender Thai basil leaves, divided
1 pound (450g) chicken breasts or thighs, bone in and skin off
4 ounces (114g) thin rice noodles
8 ounces (229g) baby bok choy, chopped (about 3 cups)
1/4 cup (40g) thinly sliced scallions, cut on the bias
Accompaniments: Vietnamese hot sauce (*tuong ot toi*) or other hot sauce such as Sriracha plus hoisin sauce, bean sprouts, lime wedges, thinly sliced Thai bird chiles

In a medium stockpot, bring the chicken stock to a simmer over medium heat. Add the ginger, garlic, star anise, cloves, cinnamon, peppercorns, fennel, sugar, fish sauce, 1/3 cup of the cilantro, 1/3 cup of the mint leaves, and the chicken. Bring to a simmer, cover, and continue to simmer over medium heat for 5 minutes. Remove from the heat and allow the chicken to cool, covered, for 15 minutes.

Meanwhile, soak the noodles in hot water for 15 minutes or so until they have softened. If necessary, cook them in lightly salted boiling water until just tender, 1 minute or so. Drain and rinse well with cold water to stop the cooking.

Remove the chicken and discard the bones. Thinly slice each chicken breast and set aside. Strain the broth and then return it to the pot and bring to a simmer over medium heat. Add the bok choy and simmer for 2 to 3 minutes.

Divide the noodles and chicken among six bowls. Pour hot broth and bok choy over the noodles and top with the scallions, the remaining cilantro and mint, and accompaniments to taste.

Laksa

Laksa is a popular spicy noodle soup from the Peranakan culture, a merger of Chinese and Malay populations found in Malaysia and Singapore. It's made with a nut-based coconut curry paste. In that part of the world they use candle nuts, which you can find in Asian markets. They are somewhat toxic raw and must be thoroughly roasted before eating, so I'm substituting macadamias or almonds. The laksa paste can be made ahead and refrigerated for three days or frozen for three months and has many delicious uses. I've used zucchini and roasted butternut squash here, but use whatever vegetables you like.

MAKES 4 TO 6 SERVINGS

2 cups (280g) peeled and cubed (1/2-inch) butternut or other hard squash
Olive oil
Salt and freshly ground pepper
1 pound (450g) boneless, skinless chicken breasts
2 tablespoons soy sauce
2 tablespoons rice wine or sake
4 cups (950mL) canned or homemade chicken stock (see page 70)

2 1/2 cups (588mL) coconut milk, well stirred
1 cup (240mL) laksa paste (recipe follows), or to taste
Fresh lime juice to taste
2 small zucchini, julienned
2 ounces (56g) thin rice vermicelli, soaked in hot water for 15 minutes or until soft
Fresh cilantro leaves and green onions thinly sliced on the bias for garnish

Preheat the oven to 425°F. Toss the squash with a bit of olive oil and season with salt and pepper. Place in a single layer on a baking sheet and roast until just tender, about 7 minutes. Set aside.

Trim the chicken breasts of any fat and cut in half lengthwise and then, at a steep angle, cut crosswise into slices about 1/2 inch thick. Stir the soy sauce and rice wine together and toss with the chicken to lightly coat.

Add 2 tablespoons or so of olive oil to a wok or large skillet and heat over high heat. Add the chicken and stir-fry until just cooked through, about 4 minutes. Remove and set aside.

Heat the stock and coconut milk in a deep saucepan and whisk in the laksa paste. Add the lime juice and adjust the seasonings to taste. Divide the zucchini, noodles, and squash among warm bowls. Top with the chicken. Ladle the hot stock over top and serve immediately garnished with cilantro leaves and green onions.

Laksa Paste

MAKES ABOUT 1 CUP

2 tablespoons chili garlic sauce, or to taste
1/3 cup (53g) chopped shallots
1/3 cup (44g) toasted and chopped macadamia nuts or blanched almonds
1/4 cup (24g) peeled and finely chopped ginger
2 tablespoons coriander seeds, ground

2 tablespoons fish sauce or 1 teaspoon shrimp paste, or to taste
Juice and zest from 2 fresh limes
2 teaspoons sugar
2 tablespoons vegetable oil
1 teaspoon toasted sesame oil
1/2 cup (120mL) or so coconut milk

Combine all the ingredients except the coconut milk in a blender and process for 1 to 2 minutes or until very smooth. Store, covered, in the refrigerator for up to 1 week or frozen for up to 3 months.

Posole Blanco with Chicken

A classic Mexican recipe that falls into the soup/stew category and can be made with pork, chicken, or goat. The salsa Colorado can also be stirred into the stew before serving.

MAKES 8 TO 10 SERVINGS

2 small white onions, halved
6 large garlic cloves
2 large bay leaves
Kosher or sea salt and freshly ground black pepper
1 (4-pound/1.8kg) roaster chicken, trimmed of fat
2 (29-ounce) cans white hominy (posole), drained and thoroughly rinsed
Salsa Colorado (recipe follows)

GARNISHES (USE ANY OR ALL):

4 cups (300g) finely shredded green cabbage
2 bunches radishes, finely sliced
4 medium white onions, finely diced (about 2 cups)
¼ cup (7.2g) dried Mexican oregano*
2 large avocados, peeled, seeded, and diced
Cilantro sprigs
Lime wedges

Combine the onions, garlic cloves, bay leaves, 2 teaspoons of salt, 1 teaspoon of pepper, and 3 quarts of water in a large deep pot and bring to a boil. Add the chicken and bring back to a simmer. Skim off the scum for the first 20 minutes or so. Cover and simmer until the meat is very tender, about 1½ hours. Remove the chicken, and when cool enough to handle, discard the skin and bones and coarsely chop or tear the chicken into bite-size pieces. Remove as much fat from the stock as you can, add the hominy, and bring to a simmer. Adjust the salt and pepper to taste and serve with the salsa and other garnishes on the side, so each guest can add what they like.

Salsa Colorado

8 guajillo chiles, seeds and stems removed
6 chiles de árbol, stems removed
3 large garlic cloves, peeled

1 teaspoon ground cumin
1 teaspoon dried Mexican oregano*
2 tablespoons white vinegar
Salt to taste

In a small skillet, toast the guajillos over medium-high heat until lightly toasted and set aside. In the same skillet toast the chiles de árbol until fragrant. Be careful not to burn them or they will become bitter.

Bring 4 cups of water to a boil, add the chiles, and remove the pot from the heat. Let the chiles soak for 15 to 20 minutes. Transfer the chiles to a blender and add the garlic, cumin, oregano, vinegar, salt, and ¼ cup of the soaking water and process until smooth, adding more soaking water as necessary. This can be made ahead and stored in the refrigerator for up to 3 days.

Mexican oregano is a bit different from Mediterranean oreganos. It has a stronger, more floral flavor and is in fact related to lemon verbena. You can certainly use Mediter- ranean oregano in its place.

Chicken Avocado Soup

In this Mexican-inspired soup, we're boosting the flavor of the broth by cooking the chicken in it. You can add whatever vegetables you like to the soup. I like putting fresh spinach in the bottom of the bowl and pouring the hot soup over the spinach.

MAKES 4 TO 6 SERVINGS

2 tablespoons olive oil

1 medium onion, chopped

3 large garlic cloves, chopped

5 cups (1.2mL) canned or homemade chicken stock (see page 70)

1 tablespoon dried oregano, preferably Mexican

1 pound (450g) boneless, skinless chicken breasts or thighs

1½ cups (375g) fresh or canned diced tomatoes in juice

2 small avocados, peeled, pitted, and cut into ½-inch (13mm) dice

3 tablespoons or so fresh lime or lemon juice

Kosher or sea salt and freshly ground pepper

Hot sauce to taste

¼ cup (4g) roughly chopped fresh cilantro leaves

Tortilla strips for garnish (optional)

Sour cream or Cotija cheese for garnish (optional)

Diced zucchini and baby spinach for garnish (optional)

Heat the oil in a large saucepan over medium-high heat and sauté the onions and garlic until lightly colored, about 3 minutes. Add the chicken broth, oregano, and chicken. Bring to a boil and then reduce the heat to medium low and simmer, covered, for 10 minutes. Remove from the heat and let sit for 15 minutes to allow the chicken to finish cooking.

Remove the chicken from the pot and use two forks to shred the chicken. Place the shredded chicken back in the pot. Add the tomato, avocado, and lime juice to the soup. Let the soup sit for 5 minutes before serving. Season to taste with lime juice, salt, pepper, and drops of hot sauce. Stir in cilantro just before serving and garnish with tortilla strips, sour cream, and diced zucchini and baby spinach.

SALADS
Clove-Scented
Poached Chicken Salad
with Apples and Pecans

This is a delicious salad that I love to prepare for picnics. My favorite way to eat it is to roll it up in tender lettuce leaves—similar to a burrito or spring roll! I've also included a simple, basic recipe for poaching chicken breasts, which yields not only a moist, tender breast but also a delicious, rich broth to be used in other recipes.

MAKES 6 SERVINGS

BUTTERMILK DRESSING

1/2 cup (120g) sour cream
2/3 cup (150g) mayonnaise
1/4 cup (60mL) buttermilk
2 teaspoons grated orange zest
2 teaspoons honey, or to taste
2 teaspoons fresh lemon or lime juice
2 to 3 teaspoons curry powder, lightly toasted (see note on page 76)
Kosher or sea salt and freshly ground black pepper

CHICKEN

2 cups (475mL) dry white wine
4 cups (950mL) canned or homemade chicken stock (page 70)
5 whole cloves
1 large bay leaf
1/2 cup (48g) coarsely chopped green onions
3 (8- to 9-ounce) bone-in, skin-on chicken breast halves
2 large tart-sweet apples (such as Fuji), peeled, cored, and sliced (about 2 cups)
1 1/2 cups (225g) fresh fennel or celery, julienned
2 cups (300g) seedless grapes, halved
1 cup (150g) lightly toasted pecans or cashews
Fresh chervil or mint sprigs for garnish

To make the dressing, whisk all the ingredients together and season with salt and pepper to taste. Cover and store refrigerated up to 2 days.

To make the chicken, combine the white wine, broth, cloves, bay leaf, and green onions in a deep skillet or saucepan that will allow the breasts to sit in a snug single layer. Bring to a boil and then reduce the heat and simmer for 3 to 4 minutes. Place the chicken breasts into the simmering broth, which should cover the breasts completely. If it doesn't, add some additional wine and/or broth. Cover the pan and simmer the breasts slowly for 6 minutes (check to be sure the liquid is not boiling). Turn off the heat and allow the breasts to sit, covered, for 20 minutes, until just cooked through.

Remove the chicken from the pan and proceed with the salad or other uses.

Carefully strain the poaching liquid through a fine strainer and store covered and refrigerated for up to 5 days or frozen for up to 3 months. Discard solidified fat layer. This provides a delicious stock for soups, stews, and sauces.

Remove the skin and bones from the chicken and discard. Slice the meat and set aside. Toss the apples and the fennel with half of the dressing and mound on plates. Arrange chicken around the salad along with the grapes and drizzle the remaining dressing over top. Top with the pecans and chervil sprigs.

Lemon-Rice Salad
With Ginger Poached Chicken

This is a simple technique that yields two flavorful ingredients: tender poached chicken and a savory stock that can be used for soups and sauces. The Chinese refer to this method of cooking as "white-cooked or cut," which means it's done without soy sauce and cooked very slowly. It produces a delicate, juicy chicken that is great used in all kinds of ways. The very slow cooking also helps ensure that you have a nice clear stock. I've reduced the stock to concentrate its flavors, but you don't have to. Taste and make up you own mind.

MAKES 4 TO 6 SERVINGS
GINGER POACHED CHICKEN
5 quarts (5L) water
2 large bunches green onions, chopped
1/4 pound (113g) ginger, washed and coarsely
  chopped (no need to peel)
1 star anise (optional)
4 pounds (1.8kg) or so fresh chicken

SALAD
1/4 cup (40g) chopped shallots or green onions
2 tablespoons olive oil, divided
1 cup (210g) basmati or jasmine rice, well rinsed

2 cups (475mL) canned or homemade chicken stock
  (see page 70)
2 teaspoons grated lemon zest
3 tablespoons fresh lemon juice
1/4 cup (12g) roughly chopped fresh cilantro (or
  basil, mint, or a combination)
2 tablespoons finely minced poached garlic
  (see page 41)
1/2 cup (80g) finely diced red onion, soaked briefly
  in cold water and drained
1/2 cup (80g) roasted, diced red bell pepper
1/3 cup (45g) lightly toasted pine nuts, pepitas, or
  chopped cashews

To make the Ginger Poached Chicken, in a pot large enough to hold the chicken and the water, combine all the ingredients. Slowly bring the chicken to a simmer over medium-high heat and skim off any scum that appears. Reduce the heat to low, cover, and cook for 25 minutes. Check occasionally to make sure that the water is just barely moving. Remove from the heat and let stand covered until cool, about 2 hours. Remove the chicken and pull off the meat, reserving the skin and bones for another use.

Strain the stock, discarding the solids, and place in the refrigerator to cool. Remove and discard the congealed fat. Add the stock to a clean pot and reduce over high heat to about 3 quarts. Strain again. Store covered and refrigerated for up to 5 days or frozen for 6 months.

To make the salad, in a deep saucepan over moderate heat, sauté the shallots in 1 tablespoon of the olive oil until soft but not brown. Add the rice and continue to sauté for 3 to 4 minutes longer, stirring regularly. Add the stock and bring to a boil. Reduce the heat to a simmer, cover, and continue to cook until all the liquid is absorbed (10 to 12 minutes). Remove from the heat, allow the rice to cool for 5 minutes, and then gently fluff with a fork and transfer to a large bowl.

Add the chicken stock, lemon zest, lemon juice, cilantro, poached garlic, onion, bell pepper, pine nuts, the remaining 1 tablespoon of olive oil, and 2 cups of Ginger Poached Chicken to the warm rice and gently stir to combine.

Note: A simple way to serve the chicken is to slice it and sprinkle it with one of the flavored salts on the next page.

Flavored **Salts**

Salt has many faces and, believe it or not, many flavors. Most salt sold in markets today is rock salt, which is mined from salt deposits left behind from ancient, extinct seas. You can also buy sea salt, which comes from existing seas and is simply sea water that has been evaporated by the sun.

Some cooks also believe that sea salt is nutritionally superior to rock salt, but unfortunately there is no truth to this. Any extra minerals that may be in sea salt are in such small amounts that they wouldn't make any dietary difference.

OTHER SALT MIXTURES

Herb Salts: Dry herbs combined with salt are now widely available in gourmet food shops. They are easy to put together on your own and allow you to add interesting flavors while cutting down on the amount of sodium in your diet, if that's a concern. These are finishing salts that go on the food just as it's being served. As a result you tend to use less salt because you get its taste "up front." Store flavored salts in airtight containers, especially in humid climates.

Sesame Salt (Gomasio) is a Japanese blend of four or more parts toasted, ground sesame seeds to one part sea salt. It adds a nutty, earthy note when sprinkled on foods. Especially nice on salad greens.

Sour Salt is an Indian blend of six or more parts sea salt with one part citric or ascorbic acid crystals. It adds a tart-salt flavor that I love with fresh tomatoes and on grilled or sautéed fish.

Maccha Salt is a blend of powdered green tea and salt. Try 1 teaspoon of tea to ¼ cup sea salt. The slightly bitter flavor of the tea is delicious on eggs, tofu, and vegetables, and I've even seen it sprinkled on chocolates!

Smoked Paprika Salt: Great on grilled meats and poultry and potatoes; use 2 teaspoons or more of paprika to ¼ cup sea salt.

Lavender Salt: You might want to pulse the lavender a few times in a spice or coffee grinder before adding to the salt. Use 2 teaspoons or more of lavender to ¼ cup sea salt. Delicious on fresh tomatoes and salad greens and especially good on lamb and pork.

Citrus Salt: Stir together 2 tablespoons finely grated citrus zest and ½ cup sea salt so that no lumps exist. Bake on a parchment-lined baking sheet for 60 minutes in a preheated 225°F oven. Use as is or pulse in a food processor for a finer texture. Great on pasta dishes, grilled shellfish, grilled or roasted chicken, and eggs.

Kaffir Lime Salt: Finely mince a fresh kaffir lime leaf, which gives an incredible aroma and limey flavor to anything. I grow kaffir lime trees, so I make this all the time and use it on seafood of all kinds as well as tomatoes, corn, and other vegetables.

Chili Salt is used in Mexico on watermelon and other fruits but is also a delicious condiment to use on poached and roasted chicken and more. Mix two parts fine sea salt with one part pure medium chili powder such as ancho. Try three parts salt to one part chipotle chili powder.

Vietnamese Salad with Chicken

Any crisp vegetables that you like could be added or substituted here. There are several inexpensive tools on the market that make julienning a snap, such as hand-held julienne peelers and slicers. Nuoc cham is a spicy dipping sauce that has as many variations as those who make it. I love serving this in little Asian to-go boxes!

MAKES 4 SERVINGS

NUOC CHAM
½ cup (120mL) fresh lime juice
4 tablespoons (60mL) Asian fish sauce
1 to 2 teaspoons chili garlic sauce, or to taste
5 tablespoons (63g) sugar, or to taste
1 tablespoon fresh cilantro leaves, coarsely chopped

SALAD
1 pound (450g) skinless, boneless chicken thighs
3 tablespoons fresh lime juice
2 tablespoons olive oil
Sea salt and freshly ground black pepper

2 ounces (56g) thin rice noodles, softened in hot water and drained
Toasted sesame oil
2 cups (178g) very finely sliced green or Napa cabbage
1 medium carrot, finely julienned
2 large daikon radishes, finely julienned, crisped in ice water and drained
1 medium red bell pepper, stemmed, seeded, and finely julienned
1 English cucumber, seeded and thinly sliced
¼ cup (12g) or so loosely packed fresh cilantro and/or mint sprigs
2 tablespoons chopped toasted peanuts

For the nuoc cham, combine all ingredients and stir until sugar is dissolved. Let stand at least 30 minutes before serving for flavors to develop. Adjust salty/sweet/tart/hot flavors to taste.

For the salad, gently pound the chicken until it's ¼-inch thick all over. Whisk together the lime juice, olive oil, and salt and pepper to taste and coat the chicken. Grill or pan sear until chicken is just done. Set aside to cool. Slice thinly.

Meanwhile, in a large bowl, toss the softened noodles with a few drops of sesame oil. Combine the cabbage, carrot, daikon, red pepper, and cucumber and gently toss with the noodles. Add the chicken and artfully arrange the salad on a plate or in a small Asian to-go box. Spoon the nuoc cham over and top with cilantro and chopped peanuts. Serve immediately with chopsticks.

Soy-Poached Chicken Salad
With Sweet Chilli Vinaigrette

The technique of poaching chicken in a soy-flavored broth is an old one, and once it is made, the broth can be reused by straining and boiling it for a couple of minutes. It can be stored in the refrigerator for up to two weeks.

MAKES 6 SERVINGS
SOY POACHING LIQUID
3 cups (700mL) water
3/4 cup (180mL) dark soy sauce
1/3 cup sugar
1/3 cup (80mL) Chinese black vinegar (available in Asian markets) or balsamic vinegar
4 tablespoons chopped ginger
4 large garlic cloves, bruised
Juice and half the peel of 1 medium orange
3/4 teaspoon fennel seeds
1 large star anise
1 (3-inch/7.6cm) cinnamon stick
1/4 teaspoon crushed hot chili flakes

CHICKEN
2 pounds (900g) bone-in chicken breasts or thighs
3 cups (140g) mixed young savory greens (such as spinach, arugula, mustard, and cress)
1/2 pound jicama, parsnips, or kohlrabi, peeled and finely julienned
Sweet Chilli Vinaigrette (recipe follows)
Savory sprouts such as daikon radish for garnish

To make the soy poaching liquid, combine all the ingredients in a deep saucepan. Bring to a boil over high heat, reduce the heat to medium low, and simmer for 5 minutes.

To make the salad, remove all visible fat and skin from the chicken and discard. Add to the poaching liquid and bring to a simmer over medium heat. Reduce the heat to medium low and simmer gently for 6 to 8 minutes or until the chicken is just cooked through. Remove from the heat, set aside, and allow the chicken to cool in the liquid for at least 30 minutes to absorb the flavor. (The longer the chicken stays in the poaching liquid, the more flavor and color it will absorb.) The chicken can be prepared a day ahead if desired. Be sure to remove it from the poaching liquid before storing it in the refrigerator.

To serve: Remove the bones from the chicken and shred or thinly slice the meat. Arrange on plates along with greens and jicama. Drizzle the Sweet Chilli Vinaigrette over top and garnish with savory sprouts. Serve immediately.

continued on page 94

Sweet Chilli Vinaigrette

This is a simple, full-flavored sauce based on Thai "sweet chilli sauce," which is widely available in Asian markets. When I don't make it myself (see recipe below), I prefer a brand called *Mae Ploy*. It can be made ahead and is also a delicious dipping sauce. Another virtue is that it's fat free!

MAKES ABOUT 1 CUP

2 teaspoons finely minced ginger
2 teaspoons finely minced garlic
2 tablespoons soy sauce

½ cup (120mL) Thai sweet chilli sauce, or to taste
2 tablespoons fresh lime or lemon juice, or to taste
2 to 4 tablespoons (30 to 60mL) chicken stock or water

Add the first three ingredients to a blender and pulse briefly to combine. Add half the chilli sauce, the fresh lime juice, and enough stock to achieve desired consistency and pulse a couple of times more. Taste and add additional chilli sauce as desired. Store refrigerated in an air-tight container for up to 1 week.

Thai Sweet Chili Sauce, *Nahm Jim Gai*

This is considerably spicier and fuller flavored than what you buy in the bottle.

3 tablespoons finely chopped Thai red bird or other long red chiles with their seeds
1 tablespoon finely chopped garlic
1½ teaspoons kosher salt, or to taste

1¼ (280g) cups sugar
2 tablespoons Thai fish sauce (nam pla)
¾ cup (180mL) distilled white vinegar
½ cup (120mL) water

Combine all the ingredients in a heavy saucepan and bring to a boil. Reduce the heat and simmer, uncovered, until the mixture reduces to a generous cup, about 10 minutes. Cool to room temperature. The sauce will thicken as it cools. Store covered and refrigerated for up to 2 months. Bring back to room temperature when serving or using.

Chicken Waldorf Salad

The original Waldorf salad was created in the late 1890s by Chef Oscar Tschirky for the Waldorf-Astoria Hotel in New York. It was considered the height of sophistication and originally was nothing more than apples, celery, and mayonnaise. Chopped nuts and grapes came later, and a once-popular version for kids contained tiny marshmallows. This is a good place to use some of the Ginger Poached Chicken (see page 89).

MAKES 4 SERVINGS

DRESSING
½ cup (120mL) good quality mayonnaise
1 teaspoon Dijon mustard
⅓ cup (80mL) buttermilk
2 teaspoons fresh lemon or lime juice
½ teaspoon sugar
2 teaspoons roughly chopped tarragon
Kosher or sea salt and freshly ground pepper

CHICKEN
1 pound (450g) chopped cooked chicken
1½ cups (1 small) diced tart-sweet apple (such as Fuji)
1 cup (150g) thinly sliced celery or fennel
1 cup (92g) red seedless grapes, halved
¼ cup (33g) blanched slivered almonds, lightly toasted
1 tablespoon coarsely chopped chives (optional)
12 tender butter lettuce leaves

Whisk the dressing ingredients together, season to taste, and set aside.

Add the chicken to a large bowl along with the apple, celery, and grapes. Stir in the prepared dressing and mound on serving plates. Sprinkle almonds and chives over top. Place the lettuce leaves next to the salad so that guests can use them to roll up and eat the salad. The salad can be made a couple of hours ahead, but it's best the day it's made.

Asian Rotisserie Chicken Salad

This makes good use of leftover rotisserie or roast chicken. You could also add some cucumber or blanched snow peas to this salad.

MAKES 4 SERVINGS

DRESSING

2 cups (100g) lightly packed fresh cilantro leaves
  with tender stems

$1/3$ cup (80mL) fresh lime juice

2 tablespoons brown sugar

1 tablespoon sesame oil

1 teaspoon chili garlic sauce,* or to taste

3 tablespoons (45mL) vegetable oil, such as peanut
  or canola

Kosher or sea salt and freshly ground black pepper

SALAD

3 to 4 cups shredded cooked chicken, skin and
  bones removed

$1/4$ medium red cabbage (about 8 ounces/230g),
  cored and thinly sliced

1 red bell pepper, seeded and thinly sliced

4 scallions, thinly sliced on the bias

1 medium head romaine lettuce, torn into bite-size
  pieces, or 4 cups (224g) mesclun mix

$1/2$ cup (68g) toasted chopped cashews or peanuts

For the dressing: Add the cilantro, lime juice, sugar, sesame oil, chili garlic sauce, and oil to a blender and blend until smooth. Season to taste with salt and pepper.

For the salad: In a large bowl, combine the chicken, cabbage, pepper, and scallions and season with a little salt and pepper. In another bowl toss the lettuce with $1/2$ cup of the dressing and divide among 4 bowls. Top with the chicken mixture, drizzle the remaining dressing over all, and sprinkle with cashews.

Every Asian cuisine has a riff on this very handy condiment. Lee Kum Kee brand from Hong Kong is widely distributed and very good.

Farro Chicken Salad
With Poblanos, Corn, and Tomatoes

Farro, also known as spelt, has a long history in cooking. It's an ancient grain and is believed to have sustained the Roman legions. It is thought to be one of the precursors to our modern wheat. Historically, it was grown extensively in the Middle East, but now we think of it as being Italian, since it continues to be used there in the central and northern regions. It's easy to cook and has all kinds of uses, including soups, risotto, pilaf-like concoctions, and desserts. Of course, it is also ground to make flour for breads and pastas.

MAKES 6 SERVINGS

½ cup (87g) farro

1½ cups (350mL) canned or homemade chicken stock (see page 70) or water

1 large poblano chile, charred and peeled (see Roasting and Peeling Peppers, page 249), and cut into ½-inch (13mm) dice

2 cups fresh corn, preferably grilled or roasted

1½ cups (360g) seeded and diced ripe tomato

¼ cup (24g) green onions, sliced on the bias

½ teaspoon seeded and minced jalapeño pepper, or to taste

¼ cup (12g) coarsely chopped fresh cilantro

2 teaspoons chopped poached or toasted garlic (see page 41)

3 tablespoons lime or lemon juice, or to taste

2 tablespoons fruity extra-virgin olive oil

2 teaspoons honey or agave nectar, or to taste

Sea salt and freshly ground black pepper to taste

⅓ cup (45g) toasted pepitas (pumpkin seeds) or slivered, toasted blanched almonds

1 pound (450g) glazed chicken pieces of your choice (see page 106)

1 medium firm-ripe avocado cut into 6 slices

Fresh cilantro or mint sprigs

Rinse the farro and place it in a saucepan with the chicken stock. Bring to a boil over high heat and then reduce the heat to medium low, cover, and simmer gently until the liquid is absorbed, about 25 minutes. Remove from the heat, uncover, and strain. Allow to cool.

In a large bowl, combine the cooked farro with the poblano, corn, tomato, green onions, jalapeño, and cilantro. Whisk the garlic, lime juice, olive oil, and honey together in a small bowl and season with salt and pepper. Gently stir the dressing into the salad along with the pepitas and chicken. Arrange on plates topped with the avocado and cilantro sprigs.

Chopped Salad
with Smoked Chicken, Melon, and Endive

This puts together some of my favorite flavors that bounce off each other in an interesting way: smoked chicken, sweet melon, bitter endive, and watercress all topped with a creamy, nutty dressing.

MAKES 4 SERVINGS

ORANGE AND WALNUT OIL VINAIGRETTE

1 tablespoon chopped shallots or white parts of green onions

1 large navel orange or three small tangerines, peeled, seeded, and chopped (1 to 2 cups)

2 teaspoons peeled and finely chopped ginger

2 teaspoons smooth Dijon mustard

2 tablespoons toasted walnut oil

1/4 cup (55g) or so olive oil

Kosher or sea salt

SALAD

1 pound (450g) smoked chicken (see page 50)

1 small ripe cantaloupe or other melon, peeled and seeded

3 large Belgian endives

1 bunch fresh watercress, tough stems discarded and snipped into relatively uniform sprigs

For the dressing, combine the shallots, orange, ginger, and mustard in a blender and purée on high speed till smooth. Slowly add the oils in a steady stream until the mixture has thickened. Add a bit more olive oil if you'd like a thicker consistency. Strain, if desired, through a medium mesh strainer and stir in salt to taste.

For the salad, cut the chicken and melon into large dice, about 1/2-inch squares. Wash and cut the endive into halves lengthwise and then across into thirds. Arrange the chicken, melon, endive, and watercress on a large plate. At serving time, drizzle the vinaigrette over the salad and serve.

Steve's "Upper Crust" Southern-Fried Chicken

This is a recipe from my long-time friend and radio co-host Steve Garner. We've been doing a food talk show on Saturday mornings in Northern California (KSRO Good Food Hour, www.ksro.com) for more than twenty-five years. Raised in Kentucky, he has spent his life eating and researching fried chicken. "This method is the result of years of practice, refinement, and serendipity," says Steve. "My recipe is for traditional skillet fried chicken, the texture and flavor of which is heavenly and can't be duplicated in an oven." You will need: a heavy paper bag, two cast-iron skillets, tongs, two wooden spoons, a strainer, a wire rack, and a candy thermometer to measure the oil temperature.

MAKES 4 SERVINGS

4 whole chicken breasts, halved (8 pieces)
½ cup (112g) kosher salt, plus more for seasoning
6 cups (1.4L) buttermilk, divided
Freshly ground black pepper
Canola or other vegetable oil for frying

3 cups (360g) all-purpose flour
2 to 6 tablespoons (30 to 90mL) hot sauce
2 teaspoons lemon pepper or smoked paprika
2 egg whites
1 large onion, peeled and thinly sliced

Rinse the chicken and pat dry. In a large bowl, combine the kosher salt and 4 cups of the buttermilk and stir until dissolved. Add the chicken, cover, and refrigerate for at least 2 hours and up to 4. This ensures great flavor and juiciness. Remove the chicken from the buttermilk and discard the buttermilk brine. Place the chicken on a wire rack on a rimmed sheet pan, season well with salt and pepper, and refrigerate, uncovered, for at least 1 hour.

In two large cast-iron skillets over medium-high heat, add enough oil to reach a depth of ¾ inch for shallow frying, and heat the oil to 375°F. While the oil is heating, place the flour into a heavy paper bag. Pour the remaining 2 cups of the buttermilk into a bowl and add the hot sauce. Be bold here because the coating on the chicken will soften a lot of the heat. Add the lemon pepper or paprika to the buttermilk mixture. Add the egg whites and whisk until well combined.

Remove the chicken from the refrigerator and place it in the buttermilk mixture, coating well. Pull out a piece of chicken with the tongs and allow to drain briefly and then place the chicken, two pieces at a time, into the flour bag, tightly close the bag, and shake vigorously to coat. Remove each piece and gently shake off any excess flour. Place the coated chicken pieces on a wire rack and repeat until they are all coated.

Carefully place each piece of coated chicken, skin side down, into the hot oil, 4 pieces per pan. Turn every 4 or 5 minutes using wooden spoons instead of tongs, which lessens the chance of breaking the crust. There are always hot spots in pans, so gently move the chicken to another part of the pan if some pieces are darkening faster than others.

After 10 minutes, gently divide the onion between the pans. Be careful because this will cause the oil to bubble vigorously. The total cooking time will be between 16 and 20 minutes, depending on the size of the breasts. When the chicken is beautifully golden brown and crisp, remove it and place it on a wire rack with paper towels under it to drain. Remove the crisped onions when they are done and drain on paper towels. Cool for a few minutes and then arrange the chicken on a platter, scatter onions over top, and serve.

Fried **Chicken**

Fried chicken, specifically southern fried chicken, is without question one of America's great dishes. No one seems to know where southern fried chicken came from. According to James Beard in *Beard on Birds* (Warner Books, 1979), its origins go back to English and Viennese cooking. But it is fair to say, I think, that it is generally associated with American slaves who did most of the cooking in the early South, and African-Americans consider it an important part of their soul food repertoire.

There are heated debates that involve every aspect of this seemingly simple dish. Should you salt and pepper only or add paprika or cayenne? What kind of coating: flour only, add cornmeal, flour with an egg wash, bread crumbs? What kind of fat should you use? Should it be accompanied with gravy, and if so, what kind? And, finally, should it be eaten hot, at room temperature, or cold? Personally, I prefer to season my chicken [with salt and pepper], bread it [with flour and cornmeal], cook it in lard and eat it alone and hot.

"Its success depends on the care with which it is cooked. It can be floured, breaded or

dipped in batter; the cooking can be done in lard, lard and butter or vegetable oil. Whatever the variation, it must have a crisp golden-brown coating and a juicy interior, while absorbing a minimum of cooking fat."

Perfect Roast Chicken

Roast chicken is one of the most versatile tools in the cook's repertoire. Terrific as is, one roast chicken can yield enough meat for two meals. It can also be incorporated into a wide variety of dishes.

MAKES 4 SERVINGS

3½- to 4-pound (1.58- to 1.8-kg) roasting chicken, brined (see page 49), if time allows

½ cup (115g) or so flavored butter or pesto (pages 39 to 40)

3 tablespoons unsalted butter, melted

2 tablespoons olive oil

Kosher or sea salt and freshly ground black pepper

1 medium onion, peeled and cut into ½-inch (13mm) dice

1 large celery stalk, cut into ½-inch (13mm) dice

1 medium carrot, peeled and cut into ½-inch (13mm) dice

2 cups (475mL) canned or homemade chicken stock (see page 70)

½ cup (120mL) dry white wine (optional)

If desired and time allows, brine the chicken for at least 4 hours. I highly recommend this step.

Preheat the oven to 450°F.

With your fingers, gently push the compound butter or pesto up under the skin of the chicken. Combine the butter and olive oil and brush half of it over the outside of the chicken.

Place the chicken breast side down on the rack and place it in the middle of the preheated oven. Roast for 15 minutes or so and then turn it breast side up, brush with the remaining butter-olive oil mixture, spread the vegetables in the bottom of the pan, and turn the oven down to 375°F.

After an hour, test the bird for doneness by inserting an instant-read thermometer into the thickest part of the thigh. It should read 165°F to 170°F. Alternately, you can test by lifting the bird with a wooden spoon inserted in the tail opening. If juices that run out are yellow, it's done. If pink, cook a few minutes longer. Also, the leg-thigh should move easily in its socket. Set the bird on a cutting board and allow it to rest for 10 minutes before carving.

5 Steps for Perfect
Roast Chicken

During my training in France, it was often said that the mark of a great chef was his or her ability to do something very simple and do it superbly. The measure was often a roast chicken. It's a simple process, but to do it right, you need to pay attention and follow some basic steps:

1. Brine or dry salt the bird first (see page 49) and then massage it well with butter or olive oil and whatever seasonings you like. Alternately, gently work a flavored butter (see page 39) or pesto (see page 40) under the skin of the bird.

2. Don't truss the bird, but simply bend its wings back under the body and use a V-shaped rack to hold it in the pan. The rack lets air circulate and helps cook the bird evenly.

3. Start with high heat: Preheat the oven to 450°F for the first 15 minutes or so, which helps promote a crisp skin. Then turn the heat down to 375°F to finish the bird. Don't overcook. It's done when the thighs reach 165 to 170°F.

4. Let it rest! Don't cut into the bird for at least 10 minutes after cooking. This allows the juices to redistribute, making it moist and tender.

5. Make a simple and delicious pan sauce while the bird is resting (see page 42).

Basic Tools Needed:
- Heavy roasting pan, at least 9 x 13 inches
- V-rack that fits snugly in the pan
- Instant-read thermometer
- A good sharp knife and a cutting board

Goat Cheese–Stuffed Butterflied Chicken

Gently stuffing a soft cheese or flavored butter (see page 39) up under the skin of any bird adds delicious flavor and helps keep the meat moist.

MAKES 4 TO 6 SERVINGS

1 (3- to 4-pound/1.4- to 1.8-kg) chicken, brined or dry salted if time allows (see page 49)

1 1/2 cups (350g) fresh goat cheese

1/2 cup (50g) freshly grated Parmesan cheese

2 teaspoons finely chopped garlic

1/3 cup (22g) panko bread crumbs

1/2 cup (20g) finely chopped fresh basil

1 tablespoon grated lemon zest

Kosher or sea salt and freshly ground black pepper

Olive oil

Preheat the oven to 400°F.

Rinse the chicken and pat dry. Butterfly the chicken using poultry shears or a sharp chef's knife. Run your fingers under the skin at the neck opening to loosen the skin around the breasts, reaching as far down to include the legs if possible.

In a small bowl, combine the goat cheese, Parmesan, garlic, bread crumbs, basil, and lemon zest. Season to taste with salt and pepper.

Using your hands, gently stuff the cheese mixture into the chicken between the skin and the meat, starting at the breasts. Coax the mixture into an even layer by pressing and pushing it from the outside, above the skin. Place the chicken on a rack, or on several 1/2-inch-thick slices of onion, in a roasting pan, skin side up. Rub it with a tablespoon or two of olive oil and season generously with salt and pepper.

Roast for 1 hour or until the juices run clear from the thigh. To test for doneness with a thermometer, check the thickest part of the breast for an internal temperature of 165°F. Transfer the chicken to a cutting surface and let it sit for 5 minutes or so. To serve, divide the chicken into quarters, and split the two breasts into four pieces.

Lemon and Herb–Roasted Whole Poussins

Whole poussins (baby chickens) weigh about one pound each. This is a good example of another use for a compound or flavored butter (see page 39) to add flavor and moisture.

MAKES 4 SERVINGS

6 tablespoons (85g) unsalted butter, softened
1 tablespoon packed finely grated lemon zest
2 teaspoons finely chopped fresh thyme leaves
1 tablespoon finely chopped chives

Kosher or sea salt and freshly ground white pepper
4 whole poussins
2 medium lemons each cut into 8 wedges
4 large fresh thyme sprigs
Olive oil

Preheat the oven to 400°F. Beat together the butter, zest, thyme, chives, 1 teaspoon salt, and ½ teaspoon white pepper in a small bowl.

Season the cavities of the birds with additional salt and pepper and, working from the cavity end, gently work your fingers under the skin of the breasts and legs to loosen it. Be careful not to tear it. Gently push the lemon butter mixture under the skin and massage the skin to evenly spread the butter over the breasts and legs.

Insert 2 lemon wedges and a thyme sprig into each cavity and then tie the legs together with kitchen string. Tuck the wings behind. Brush the birds with olive oil and season lightly again with salt and pepper.

Place the birds on a rack in a roasting pan and roast for 35 to 40 minutes or until the birds are nicely browned and an instant-read thermometer inserted in the flesh of the thigh registers 165°F. Transfer to a warm platter and remove the string. Allow the poussins to sit for 5 minutes or so before cutting and serving.

Honey Dijon Glazed Chicken

Another technique for cooking chicken (and other birds) that yields moist, tender meat and a sweet, delicious glazed crust is a process that I call "glazing." I have to confess that the original idea for this came from an issue of *Fine Cooking Magazine* a number of years ago. I tried it and loved the result. It's pretty simple. It starts with roasting chicken pieces that have been marinated in a sweet-savory marinade and then finishing with a blast of heat under the broiler to create a crisp, caramelized surface. If you like the result, I'm sure you'll come up with all kinds of interesting glazes on your own. I've included a couple of ideas on the opposite page.

MAKES 4 SERVINGS

¼ cup (85g) honey
2 tablespoons soy sauce
1 to 2 tablespoons ketchup
1 tablespoon Dijon mustard
2 teaspoons Worcestershire sauce

2 teaspoons apple cider vinegar
1 teaspoon Asian chili garlic sauce, or to taste
1 (3- to 4-pound/1.4- to 1.8-kg) chicken cut into 8 or 10 pieces (see page 48)
Kosher or sea salt and freshly ground black pepper

Preheat the oven to 425°F. In a small bowl, whisk together the honey, soy sauce, ketchup, mustard, Worcestershire, vinegar, and chili garlic sauce. Dredge each chicken piece in the glaze to coat completely. Place the glazed chicken pieces skin side down on a rimmed baking sheet.* Pour any left-over glaze over the chicken and season well with salt and pepper.

Roast the chicken on the top rack in the oven until the juices just run clear when you prick the chicken, about 40 minutes. Remove the chicken from the oven and turn the oven to broil. Turn the chicken over and

baste it with the drippings in the pan. If a lot of fat has rendered from the chicken, then spoon some of it off to prevent flare ups. Broil the chicken, basting and turning the pan occasionally so that it will brown evenly, about 6 minutes or so. Drizzle the chicken with the pan drippings before serving.

Don't line the pan with foil or parchment. The glazed chicken has a tendency to stick. Better to soak the baking sheet over night than fuss with peeling off bits of foil or parchment.

Peach-Soy Glaze

2 teaspoons chopped garlic

2 tablespoons peeled and chopped ginger

2/3 cup (210g) peach or apricot preserves

1/3 cup (80mL) soy sauce

3 tablespoons water or dry white wine

2 tablespoons rice vinegar

1/4 teaspoon hot red pepper flakes, or to taste

Add all ingredients to a food processor and process until fairly smooth.

Orange-Balsamic Glaze

1/2 cup (120mL) orange juice concentrate

2 tablespoons brown sugar

3 tablespoons balsamic vinegar

2 teaspoons dry mustard such as Coleman's

1 tablespoon chopped fresh oregano

Mix all ingredients in a small bowl.

Chicken Tikka Masala

This classic Indian dish is achieved by combining chicken *tikka* with a *masala* (mixture of spices) sauce that also commonly contains tomato, cream or coconut milk, and more spices. It is often colored red with food dyes or natural colorants such as turmeric, paprika, or annatto. There are many theories as to how this dish came about. It is however tied directly with Britain, where many believe the dish first appeared. One theory suggests Glasgow (of all places!) as its birthplace. At least one survey has named it England's most popular restaurant dish.

MAKES 4 SERVINGS

4 tablespoons (55g) unsalted butter

3 medium white onions, finely chopped (about 2 cups/320g)

1 teaspoon ground coriander

1 teaspoon ground cumin

1/2 teaspoon fennel seeds

1 tablespoon paprika

1 (28-ounce, 800g) can whole peeled tomatoes with juice, puréed and strained

1 cup (240mL) heavy cream

1 to 1 1/2 cups (240–350mL) chicken stock or water

2 teaspoons garam masala (see page 43), or to taste

2 to 3 pounds (.9 to 1.3kg) Chicken Tikka (see page 122)

Cooked basmati rice

1/4 cup (12g) gently packed fresh cilantro sprigs

Melt the butter over medium heat in a large skillet. Add the onions and cook until soft but not brown. Add the coriander, cumin, fennel, and paprika and continue to cook, stirring, for a couple of minutes to toast the spices. Add the tomatoes and cook for a couple of minutes more. Add the cream and stock and simmer until thickened, about 8 minutes. Stir in the garam masala and chicken. Serve over rice, topped with cilantro sprigs.

Brick Chicken

One of the best ways to cook a chicken (or most other birds for that matter) is to butterfly or spatchcock it, season it well, and then cook it weighted with foil-covered bricks either on the grill or in a heavy skillet. Follow the instructions on page 47 to butterfly the chicken, which means to remove its backbone, flatten the breastbone, and lay it out like a book.

MAKES 2 TO 4 SERVINGS

1 tablespoon fresh pressed garlic

Kosher or sea salt and freshly ground black pepper

1/3 cup (75g) plus 2 tablespoons extra virgin olive oil, divided

2 tablespoons finely grated lemon zest

3 tablespoons finely chopped fresh herbs (such as chives, parsley, and rosemary), divided

3 1/2 pounds or so (1.58kg or so) brined (see page 49) and butterflied chicken

1 to 2 tablespoons all-purpose flour

1 cup (240mL) canned or homemade chicken stock (see page 70) or a combination of stock and dry white wine

2 tablespoons lemon juice

Combine the garlic, 1 tablespoon of salt, 2 teaspoons of freshly ground pepper, 1/3 cup of the olive oil, the lemon zest, and half the herbs in a small bowl. With your fingers, loosen the skin over the breast and thighs and work the garlic mixture as evenly as you can under the skin. Spread any remaining garlic mixture over the bone side of the bird. Place the chicken on a rack set in a rimmed baking sheet and refrigerate for up to 3 hours.

Heat the remaining 2 tablespoons of oil in a heavy 12-inch skillet over high heat. Either wrap two bricks with foil or set another heavy skillet aside. Add the chicken to the skillet, skin side down, and place bricks or the other skillet with a few cans of soup in it on top.

Reduce the heat to medium and cook until the skin is beautifully golden brown and crisp, 15 to 18 minutes. Remove the top weight, turn the chicken over, and pour out all but a couple of tablespoons of fat. Replace the weight on top and continue to cook for another 12 to 15 minutes or until an instant read thermometer inserted into the thigh reads 165°F.

Remove the chicken to a cutting board and allow it to rest for 5 to 10 minutes before carving. Meanwhile, pour off all but 2 tablespoon of fat in the pan, add the flour, and stir to make a roux. Whisk in the stock and lemon juice and whisk until the sauce thickens. Stir in the remaining herbs and serve the chicken with the pan sauce.

Grilled Chicken "Diavola" with Caprese Rigatoni

The marinade and the pasta contain spicy red pepper flakes, hence the "diavola" or "devil-style" title.

MAKES 6 SERVINGS

CHICKEN

3 tablespoons chopped fresh basil
2 tablespoons minced green onion
1 tablespoon minced garlic
1 teaspoon dried oregano
2 teaspoons kosher or sea salt
1/2 teaspoon freshly ground black pepper
1/2 teaspoon red pepper flakes, or to taste
1/3 cup dry white wine
3/4 cup (165g) fruity extra-virgin olive oil
6 chicken breast halves, bone-in or boneless

RIGATONI

1 pound (450g) cherry or pearl tomatoes, halved
1/4 cup (60mL) extra-virgin olive oil, plus more for drizzling
1 teaspoon coarse sea salt
Big pinch red pepper flakes
4 large garlic cloves, peeled
1/2 pound (230g) regular or whole wheat rigatoni
1/2 pound (230g) bocconcini (bite-size fresh mozzarella), halved
1/4 cup (10g) chopped fresh basil leaves

For the chicken, whisk the basil, onion, garlic, oregano, salt, pepper, red pepper flakes, white wine, and olive oil in a large bowl. Add the chicken breasts and marinate, refrigerated, for at least 1 hour.

For the rigatoni, toss the tomatoes, olive oil, salt, and red pepper flakes together in a large bowl. Whack the garlic with the side of a knife and toss it into the bowl. Let it sit at room temperature, tossing once or twice, for 30 minutes, to let the flavors blend.

Remove the chicken from the marinade and grill over moderately high heat until cooked through, 10 to 15 minutes, depending on whether it's bone-in or boneless. At the same time, bring 6 quarts of salted water to a boil over high heat. Stir in the pasta and cook until al dente, about 9 minutes. Remove the garlic from the marinated tomatoes. Drain the pasta, add it to the bowl with the tomatoes, and toss well to mix. Check the seasoning, adding salt and more crushed red pepper if necessary. Gently stir in the bocconcini and basil. Place in a deep bowl, top with the grilled chicken, and serve immediately.

Vietnamese Lemongrass and Chili Grilled Chicken

This simple dish is found at many restaurants and street stalls and captures the fresh and vibrant flavors of the cooking in that part of the world.

MAKES 4 SERVINGS

2 large boneless, skinless chicken breasts or thighs
2 medium lemongrass stalks, tender white parts only, crushed and very finely chopped
2 teaspoons chili garlic sauce, or to taste
2 teaspoons brown sugar

2 teaspoons soy sauce
2 teaspoons fish sauce
2 tablespoons lime juice
3 tablespoons peanut or vegetable oil
Accompaniments: mint leaves, Thai or Vietnamese basil, cilantro, sliced cucumbers, chopped dry roasted peanuts, steamed jasmine rice

Butterfly the chicken breasts by slitting each one horizontally so that it is still joined in one side, and then open it out. Place the butterflied breasts on a cutting board or flat countertop, cover them with plastic wrap, and gently pound flat with a meat mallet or a rolling pin.

Combine the lemongrass, chili garlic sauce, sugar, soy and fish sauces, lime juice, and oil in a large bowl. Mix thoroughly, and then add the chicken, turning to coat. Cover and leave to marinate for at least 1 hour and up to 6 hours.

Place the chicken on a hot grill and cook for about 3 to 4 minutes on each side, until cooked through. Slice and serve with the suggested accompaniments.

Standard Method for Breading Anything

The following recipe shows the standard three-step process for breading or coating almost any protein or vegetable. It has three elements: flour (usually seasoned), beaten eggs, and the coating mixture, which can be bread crumbs, finely chopped nuts, crushed corn flakes, crushed saltine crackers, or whatever. One of my favorites is prepared popcorn that has been coarsely chopped in a food processor. With your left hand, dip whatever you are breading into the flour, shake off the excess, and then place it in the egg. With your right hand, coat the item all over with egg, hold it over the bowl to let the excess drip off and then again with your right hand, coat it with the bread crumbs or whatever you are using. Ideally, place in a single layer on a plate or tray and refrigerate uncovered for at least thirty minutes before cooking. This rest in the refrigerator helps the coating to more securely adhere.

Red Wine–Braised Chicken
With "Little Ears" Pasta

Don't be put off by the number of ingredients here. This is a rich peasant-style chicken stew that can be served with pasta (as it is here) or with rice, polenta, roasted potatoes, or anything you like. Use whatever herbs you prefer, for example, rosemary and savory could substitute for the thyme and basil.

MAKES 6 SERVINGS

3 pounds (1.35kg) boneless skinless chicken thighs
Salt and freshly ground black pepper
2 tablespoons olive oil
1/2 pound (230g) cremini mushrooms, quartered
1 cup (160g) chopped onion
3 tablespoons slivered garlic
1/2 cup (75g) peeled and diced carrots
1/2 cup (75g) thinly sliced celery
2 1/2 cups (595mL) red wine
2 cups (475mL) canned diced tomatoes with juice

2 teaspoons fresh thyme leaves
1/2 teaspoon fennel seeds
5 cups (1.175L) canned or homemade chicken stock (see page 70)
Balsamic vinegar
1/4 cup (15g) finely chopped fresh parsley (preferably flat leaf)
1/2 pound (230g) orecchiette (little ears) or other shaped dry pasta
1/4 cup (10g) chopped fresh basil
1/3 cup (33g) finely shaved Asiago or Parmesan cheese

Season the chicken liberally with salt and pepper. Heat the olive oil in a large, heavy-bottomed saucepan over high heat, and quickly brown the chicken. Remove and set aside. Add the mushrooms, onion, garlic, carrots, and celery and sauté until very lightly browned, about 5 minutes.

Return the chicken to the pan and add the wine, tomatoes, thyme, fennel, and chicken stock and bring to a simmer. Cover and simmer until the chicken is tender, 25 to 30 minutes. Remove the chicken, tear the meat into bite-sized pieces, and set aside. Strain the braising liquid, reserving the vegetables, and return the liquid to the pot. Skim off the fat, bring to a boil, and cook over high heat for 8 to 10 minutes to reduce by half and thicken slightly. (This helps concentrate the flavors.) Taste and adjust the seasoning with salt, pepper, and drops of balsamic vinegar. Add the reserved meat and some of the braised vegetables, if desired, and heat through. Stir in the parsley and keep warm.

Meanwhile, bring a large pot of salted water to a boil and add the pasta. Cook the pasta until just tender, drain, and toss with the chopped basil. Place the pasta in the center of warmed large pasta bowls, ladle the braised chicken sauce over the pasta, and top with fresh basil and cheese.

Coq Au Vin

Here's a simplified version of the French classic. Traditionally, *coq* or rooster was used because these birds contain a lot of connective tissue, which creates a richer broth when cooked. Because they were pretty tough, they were braised a long time to make them tender. This version is much faster but just as delicious. Serve over noodles or rice or with roasted fingerling potatoes. Like all great stews, it's even better reheated the next day.

MAKES 4 SERVINGS

16 small pearl onions
3 ounces pancetta, cut in 1/4-inch (6mm) dice
2 teaspoons olive oil
1/2 cup (60g) all-purpose flour
Salt and freshly ground black pepper
4 large (8-ounce/230g) chicken thighs, skinned but still on the bone
2 shallots or 1 small onion, chopped
3 garlic cloves, chopped
1/3 cup (80mL) brandy

1 1/2 cups (350mL) dry red wine
2 cups (475mL) canned or homemade chicken stock (see page 70)
1 tablespoon tomato paste
1 tablespoon chopped fresh thyme or 1 teaspoon dried
2 bay leaves
16 small cremini or other mushrooms
1 tablespoon cornstarch mixed with 3 tablespoons stock, wine, or water
3 tablespoons chopped fresh parsley

If using fresh pearl onions, put them in a bowl with enough hot water to cover for 20 minutes. Peel and set aside. Alternately, frozen pearl onions are a good substitute.

Meanwhile, gently cook the pancetta in a large nonstick skillet over medium heat until it becomes crisp, about 5 minutes. Remove to a heavy casserole with a cover. Put the oil in the same skillet over medium heat. Mix the flour in a pie plate with 1 teaspoon of salt and 1/2 teaspoon of pepper. Coat the thighs with the flour mixture and shake off the excess. Add the chicken to the skillet and brown well, about 4 minutes on each side. Do not crowd the pan.

Add the shallots and garlic to the chicken and cook, stirring, until both begin to brown, about 3 minutes Add the brandy and carefully ignite with a match. Avert your face! When the flames die down, pour the contents of the skillet into the casserole with the pancetta. Add the red wine, stock, and tomato paste to the skillet. Bring to a boil and stir with a wooden spoon, scraping up any bits on the bottom of the pan (the French call this the *fond*).

Add the wine mixture to the chicken along with the thyme, bay leaves, mushrooms, and pearl onions. Season with salt and pepper to taste and cover. Reduce the heat and simmer for 30 minutes or until the chicken and onions are tender.

Remove the chicken to a platter. Add the cornstarch mixture to the pot and stir well over high heat to reduce and thicken the liquid. Taste for seasoning and remove the bay leaves. Pour the sauce over the chicken, sprinkle with the parsley, and serve.

Chicken and Biscuits

You can use whatever combination of vegetables you like and also substitute turkey or even sautéed or grilled tofu for the chicken.

MAKES 6 SERVINGS

BUTTERMILK BISCUITS
1 cup (120g) all-purpose flour
1 cup (95g) cake flour
2 teaspoons baking powder
1/2 teaspoon baking soda
1 teaspoon sugar
1/2 teaspoon salt
1/4 pound (55g) (1 stick) chilled unsalted butter, cut into 1/4-inch (6mm) pieces
3/4 cup (180mL) buttermilk, plus extra if needed

CHICKEN
1 1/2 cups (350mL) canned or homemade chicken stock (see page 70)
1/2 cup (120mL) dry white wine
1 1/2 pounds (630g) boneless, skinless chicken breasts and/or thighs

2 tablespoons olive oil
1 large white or red onion, finely diced (about 1 cup/160g)
1 1/2 cups (114g) quartered cremini or shiitake mushrooms
3/4 cup (115g) peeled and diced parsnips or potatoes
3/4 cup (100g) diced fennel bulbs
3/4 cup (115g) peeled and diced carrots
4 tablespoons (30g) unsalted butter
1/3 cup (40g) all-purpose flour
1 1/2 cups (350mL) light cream
1 teaspoon whole fresh thyme leaves
Salt and freshly ground black pepper
2 tablespoons Dijon mustard, or to taste
1/4 cup chopped fresh parsley
3/4 cup fresh or frozen peas

For the buttermilk biscuits, mix the dry ingredients together in a food processor with a steel blade. Add the butter and pulse until the mixture resembles very coarse meal. Transfer to a bowl and stir in the buttermilk quickly, using a fork, until it gathers into moist clumps. Do not over mix!

Transfer to a floured work surface and roll out the dough until approximately 1/2 inch thick. Using a round 2- to 3-inch pastry cutter, stamp out 6 to 8 biscuits. (**Note:** The dough can be made up to 2 hours ahead and refrigerated on a lightly floured baking sheet covered loosely with plastic wrap.)

For the chicken, combine the stock and wine in a stock pot and bring to a simmer over medium heat. Add the chicken and return to a simmer. Cover and cook until the meat is just done, about 8 minutes. Strain, reserving the stock, and allow the chicken to cool. Cut the chicken into large bite-size pieces and place them in a large bowl.

Preheat the oven to 400°F. Wash out the pot and return to the stove over medium heat. Add the vegetables and sauté until they are crisp-tender and just beginning to color. Add the cooked vegetables to the reserved chicken. Add the butter to the now-empty pot and melt it over medium heat. Whisk in the flour and cook for 1 to 2 minutes. Whisk in the reserved stock, the cream, and the thyme and bring to a simmer. Continue to cook for a couple of minutes, whisking constantly to form a smooth sauce. Add the chicken and vegetables and stir to combine. Season with salt, pepper, and Dijon mustard to taste. Stir in the parsley and peas. Pour into a baking dish and top with the buttermilk biscuits. Bake until the biscuits are golden and the filling is bubbling, about 30 minutes.

Country Captain Chicken Casserole

If you grew up in the South, then this is probably a familiar dish to you. It's a low-country classic, and its origin is somewhat obscure. The English have a similar dish with a similar name and believe that a British officer brought the recipe back from his station in India. Others maintain that the dish originated in Savannah, Georgia, which was a major shipping port in America for the spice trade. There are probably as many variations on this recipe as there are cooks who prepare it!

MAKES 4 SERVINGS

1 cup (120g) all-purpose flour
1 teaspoon dried thyme
Kosher or sea salt and freshly ground black pepper
3 tablespoons vegetable oil
4 plump whole chicken legs with thighs
6 slices bacon, chopped
2 tablespoons finely chopped garlic
2 cups cored, seeded, and chopped poblano or green bell peppers
3 cups chopped onion

2 tablespoons Madras-style curry powder, to taste
1 (28-ounce) can crushed tomatoes with basil
1 cup (240mL) canned or homemade chicken stock (see page 70) or dry white wine
½ cup (72.5g) golden raisins or currants
2 bay leaves
4 cups (632g) steamed fragrant white rice such as basmati
¼ cup (38g) chopped, dry-roasted peanuts
¼ cup (25g) toasted, dried, and shredded unsweetened coconut (optional)

Combine the flour, thyme, 2 teaspoons of salt and 1 teaspoon of black pepper in a shallow pie plate. Heat the oil in a large Dutch oven or deep skillet over medium-high heat. Dredge the chicken in the seasoned flour and shake off any excess. Add the chicken, skin side down, to the hot oil and cook, turning once, until golden brown, about 10 minutes. Transfer the chicken to a plate and set aside.

Discard all but 1 tablespoon of the oil from the pot; add the bacon and cook, stirring occasionally, until crisp, about 6 minutes. Using a slotted spoon, transfer the bacon to a paper towel–lined plate and set aside.

Add the garlic, peppers, and onions to the Dutch oven and cook, stirring occasionally, until they are soft and just beginning to brown, about 10 minutes. Add the curry and cook, stirring, for another 1 to 2 minutes or until fragrant. Add the tomatoes, chicken stock, raisins, and bay leaves and season to taste with salt and pepper.

Return the chicken to the Dutch oven, nestling it into the sauce; spoon some of the sauce over the chicken. Cover and cook the chicken at a simmer until it's very tender, about 1 hour and 15 minutes. Serve on rice topped with the reserved bacon, peanuts, and coconut.

Chicken Pot Pie

You can use whatever combination of vegetables you like and also substitute turkey or other culinary birds for the chicken. Remember that you'll need to make the pastry at least an hour ahead of time. You can make this in one large baking dish or in individual baking dishes as you choose. Baking time will be less for individual servings.

MAKES 6 SERVINGS

POT PIE DOUGH FOR 1 DOUBLE CRUST

3 cups (360g) all-purpose flour

1 teaspoon salt

1/2 pound (226g) (2 sticks) unsalted butter, chilled and cut into 1/2-inch (13mm) pieces

4 tablespoons (55g) chilled vegetable shortening

4 to 5 tablespoons (60 to 75mL) ice water

POT PIE

2 cups (475mL) canned or homemade chicken stock (see page 70)

1/2 cup (120mL) dry white wine

1 1/2 pounds (680g) boneless, skinless chicken breasts and/or thighs

2 tablespoons olive oil

1 medium onion, diced (about 1 cup/150g)

1 1/2 cups (114g) quartered cremini or shiitake mushrooms

1 small parsnip, diced (about 3/4 cup/100g)

1 small fennel bulb, peeled and diced (about 3/4 cup/65g)

1 medium carrot, peeled and diced (about 3/4 cup/112g)

3 tablespoons unsalted butter

3 tablespoons all-purpose flour

1 cup (240mL) heavy cream

1 teaspoon whole thyme leaves

Salt and freshly ground pepper

1 tablespoon Dijon mustard, or to taste

1/3 cup (20g) chopped fresh parsley

1 cup (144g) fresh or frozen whole peas

1 egg yolk, beaten with 1 tablespoon water

For the pie dough, in a food processor, briefly pulse together the flour and salt. Add the butter and shortening and pulse 3 or 4 times, until crumbly. Add the ice water 1 tablespoon at a time and pulse until the mixture is just moist enough to hold together.

Form the dough into 2 uneven balls: 2/3 for the bottom crust and 1/3 for the top. Flatten them into disks and wrap with plastic. Refrigerate for at least 1 hour before rolling out and baking.

For the pot pie, combine the stock and wine in a stock pot and bring to a simmer over medium heat. Add the chicken and return to a simmer. Cover and cook until the meat is just done, about 10 minutes. Strain, reserving the stock, and allow the chicken to cool. Cut the chicken into bite-size pieces and skim as much fat as you can from the stock.

Wash out the pot and return it to the stove over medium heat. Add the olive oil and vegetables and sauté until the vegetables are crisp-tender and just beginning to color, about 5 minutes. Add to the reserved chicken.

Add the butter to the now-empty pot and melt over medium heat. Whisk in the flour and cook for 1 to 2 minutes. Whisk in 1 cup of the reserved stock and the cream. Cook for a few minutes, whisking constantly to form a smooth sauce.

Add the chicken and vegetables and stir to combine. Season with salt, pepper, and the Dijon mustard to taste. Stir in the parsley and peas.

Preheat the oven to 425°F. Roll out the dough discs on a lightly floured surface and line a deep 9- or 10-inch pie pan or dish with the larger piece of dough. Fill with chicken mixture (you might have extra) and cover with the remaining pastry. Crimp the edges, cut a vent in the top, and brush with the egg wash. Bake for 15 minutes and then reduce the heat to 350°F and continue baking for another 30 minutes, or until the crust is nicely browned.

Chicken "Avgolemono"
With Root Vegetables and Mushrooms

Avgolemono is the classic Greek sauce or soup in which the stock is flavored and thickened at the last moment with a mixture of egg yolks and fresh lemon juice. It's a delicious sauce that you can use with all kinds of delicate meats and fishes. Egg noodles would be a nice addition. This is a dish that you can have ready in less than half an hour. If you prefer dark meat, then substitute thighs. You can use whatever root vegetables you like.

MAKES 4 SERVINGS

2 large chicken breasts

Flour for dredging

4 tablespoons (55g) unsalted butter, divided

2 tablespoons olive oil

Kosher or sea salt and freshly ground black pepper

1 medium carrot, peeled and julienned
(about 1 cup/122g)

1 medium parsnip, peeled and julienned
(about 1 cup/130g)

1 small turnip, peeled and julienned
(about 1 cup/130g)

¼ cup (40g) slivered shallots or green onions

8 ounces (3 cups/216g) thickly sliced cremini,
shiitake, or oyster mushrooms

2 cups (475mL) canned or homemade chicken
stock (see page 70)

½ cup (120mL) dry white wine

1 teaspoon cornstarch

3 large egg yolks

¼ cup (60mL) fresh lemon juice, or to taste

3 tablespoons finely chopped fresh dill

2 tablespoons finely grated lemon zest

Preheat the oven to 425°F. Trim and discard the excess fat from the chicken. Dredge in the flour and shake off the excess. Add 2 tablespoons of the butter and the olive oil to a nonstick skillet and sauté the chicken over medium heat until lightly browned on both sides, about 6 minutes. Depending on your pan, you may have to do this in batches. Season the chicken well with salt and pepper, place it skin side up on the rack in a roasting pan. Roast for 10 to 12 minutes or until just cooked through.

Meanwhile, blanch the carrots, parsnips, and turnips in lightly salted boiling water until crisp-tender, about 3 minutes. Plunge them in cold water to stop the cooking and then drain and set aside.

Add the remaining 2 tablespoons of butter to a deep saucepan over medium heat and sauté the shallots for 1 to 2 minutes or until they just begin to soften. Turn the

heat up to medium high and sauté the mushrooms until they soften, about 3 minutes. Add the chicken stock and wine and boil over high heat until the mixture is reduced by half, about 5 minutes.

In a separate bowl, whisk the cornstarch, egg yolks, and lemon juice together. Whisk in ¼ cup or so of the hot stock mixture to temper the eggs. Turn the heat down to low and stir the egg mixture into the stock mixture in the pan. Continue to stir until the sauce thickens, about 2 minutes. Be careful not to overcook or the eggs will scramble. If they begin to, immediately strain and add a little cold stock or milk to cool down the mixture. Adjust the seasoning with salt and pepper and stir in the dill and zest. Add the root vegetables and cook enough to warm through.

To serve: Place the chicken breasts on warm plates and spoon the sauce and vegetables over and around.

Curry Chicken

This can be done with almost any bird, fish, or vegetable. Adjust the cooking times accordingly. Serve this with steamed basmati or jasmine rice.

MAKES 4 TO 6 SERVINGS

2 dried Thai red chiles
2 teaspoons cumin seeds
1 tablespoon coriander seeds
1-inch piece cinnamon stick
2 whole cloves
6 green cardamom pods
3 tablespoons vegetable oil
1 (3- to 4-pound/1.35- to 1.8kg) chicken,
   cut into 8 to 10 pieces
Kosher or sea salt and freshly ground black pepper
3 medium white onions, sliced (about 2 cups/300g)

3 tablespoons chopped fresh ginger
1 tablespoon chopped garlic
2 teaspoons turmeric
1 cup (240mL) canned or homemade chicken stock
   (see page 70)
2 cups (475mL) coconut milk
Brown or palm sugar
Lemon or lime juice
2 medium tomatoes, diced and seeded (about 1
   cup/240g)
1/3 cup (5g) chopped fresh cilantro or 1/4 cup dried
   fenugreek leaves

In a small skillet, dry roast the chiles, cumin, coriander, cinnamon, cloves, and cardamom by heating them over medium-low heat for 1 to 2 minutes or just until fragrant. Place the spices in a coffee or spice grinder and grind to a fine powder. Set aside.

In a large skillet, heat the vegetable oil over medium-high heat. Season the chicken well with salt and pepper and brown on all sides, about 8 minutes. Set the chicken aside.

In the same pan over moderate heat, sauté the onions, ginger, garlic, and turmeric until the onions are just beginning to brown, about 5 minutes. Scraping up any brown bits on the bottom of the pan, add the onion mixture to a food processor along with the ground spice mixture and the stock and purée. Return the mixture to the skillet, add the reserved chicken and coconut milk and bring to a boil. Reduce the heat and simmer, partially covered, for 35 minutes or until the chicken is cooked through and the sauce has thickened. Stir every 5 minutes or so to make sure the sauce does not burn. Season to your taste with salt, pepper, sugar, and lemon juice. Just before serving, stir in the tomatoes and cilantro or fenugreek and serve hot along with steamed basmati or jasmine rice.

Paella with Chicken, Clams, and Shrimp

This classic saffron-scented dish from Spain is often made outside on the grill, ideally over a wood fire. In Spain they use a special round, often copper, pan that is fairly shallow and allows the smoke to roll over and flavor the food as it cooks. You can do it however you like—on the stovetop or even in the oven. Paella can contain all manner of meats and sausages, along with fish, shellfish, and vegetables, depending on the whim and budget of the cook. The base, however, is the rice. The Spaniards use a variety called Valencia that is available in the United States. Any medium-grain rice such as arborio can substitute nicely. The goal of great paella is to develop a nice toasty and crunchy layer on the bottom of the pan. Using a method called *socarrat*, Spanish chefs crank the heat under the rice really high once it's cooked through, until they smell the rice begin to toast, and then shut it off. When serving, you want to be sure to scrape up a little of that delicious toasty stuff with each portion.

MAKES 6 TO 8 SERVINGS

¼ cup (55g) olive oil

2 pounds (900g) boneless, skinless chicken thighs, cut in half

Salt and freshly ground black pepper

1 large white onion, chopped (about 2 cups/300g)

2 tablespoons sliced garlic

1 medium poblano pepper, diced (about 1 cup)

2 cups (380g) Valencia or other medium-grain rice

½ cup (120mL) dry white vermouth or other dry white wine

4 cups (950mL) canned or homemade chicken stock (see page 70)

¼ teaspoon saffron threads

1 cup (240g) diced fresh or drained canned tomatoes

3 or 4 thyme sprigs or 2 teaspoons dried thyme

1 teaspoon fennel seed

2 pounds fresh (900g) Manila or little neck clams, well scrubbed

1 pound (450g) large (16 to 20) shrimp, peeled and deveined

2 cups cooked fresh or frozen giant lima or fava beans, or garbanzo beans (optional)

Heat a large shallow pan over moderately high heat with the olive oil. Season the chicken generously with salt and pepper and lightly brown it in the pan on all sides, about 5 minutes. Add the onion, garlic, and pepper and stir for another 2 minutes or until the vegetables just begin to color. Add the rice and stir for a minute to coat the grains.

Add the vermouth, chicken stock, saffron, tomatoes, thyme, and fennel and stir gently. Bring to a boil and nestle the clams down in the rice mixture. Cover the pan with foil and cook until the clams open and the rice is tender, about 15 minutes. Nestle the shrimp into the rice mixture, cover, and cook for another minute or so or until the shrimp are pink (they will continue to cook as they sit in the mixture). Remove from the heat and stir in the beans if using. Taste for salt and pepper and serve immediately.

Grilled Tandoori-Style Chicken "Tikka"

In Indian cooking *tikka* refers to chunks of meat threaded onto skewers and then baked in the hot tandoori oven, which can reach temperatures of nine hundred degrees. Here, chunks of chicken are marinated in spices and yogurt. It is traditionally served with *naan*, a tandoori oven bread. *Raita* (a cold yogurt condiment) is often served with Indian food to cut the heat of the spicy dishes. You might also add some aromatic basmati rice on the side.

MAKES 8 TO 10 SERVINGS
CUCUMBER AND MINT RAITA
1 medium unpeeled English cucumber, halved, seeded, and coarsely grated
2 cups (490g) plain whole-milk yogurt
1/2 cup (24g) packed fresh mint, finely chopped
1 teaspoon ground cumin
1/4 teaspoon cayenne pepper, or to taste
Kosher or sea salt to taste

TANDOORI CHICKEN
1 tablespoon toasted ground cumin
2 teaspoons toasted ground coriander
1 tablespoon paprika
1/2 teaspoon cayenne pepper
1 teaspoon garam masala (see page 43)

1 tablespoon ground achiote or a few drops of red food coloring (optional)
1 tablespoon finely chopped garlic
2 tablespoons finely chopped fresh ginger
2 tablespoons vegetable oil
2 cups (475mL) whole-milk yogurt, preferably cream top if you can find it
1/3 cup (80mL) fresh lemon juice
1 tablespoon kosher salt
3 pounds skinless, boneless chicken breasts or thighs, cut into 2-inch (5cm) cubes
3 medium white onions, thinly sliced (about 2 cups/300g)
1/2 cup (24g) roughly chopped cilantro leaves
2 lemons or limes cut into wedges

For the cucumber and mint raita, wrap the grated cucumber in a clean kitchen towel and squeeze dry. Whisk the yogurt, mint, cumin, and cayenne pepper together in a medium bowl. Add the cucumbers and toss to coat. Season the raita to taste with salt and additional pepper. Cover and refrigerate at least 2 hours. This can be prepared a day ahead and stored, covered, in the refrigerator.

For the tandoori chicken, combine the first 12 ingredients (through the salt) in a large bowl and whisk to combine. Add the chicken, stirring or turning to coat, and marinate, covered and chilled, for at least 4 hours and up to 8.

If you are using wooden skewers, soak them in water for 30 minutes. Wipe excess marinade off the chicken and divide chicken among skewers (about 4 cubes per skewer), leaving an 1/8-inch space between cubes. Over a hot grill or under a hot broiler about 4 inches from the heat, cook until the chicken is just cooked through and nicely browned on all sides, about 10 minutes total. Serve immediately with cilantro, lemon wedges to squeeze over, and raita on the side.

Breast of Chicken
With Robiola and Prosciutto

Robiola is considered by many to be Italy's best cheese. It comes from the Piedmont in the north and is a blend of cow, goat, and sheep's milk. You could also use Taleggio or French Affinois with herbs or any creamy soft ripening cheese that you like.

MAKES 4 SERVINGS

4 boneless, skinless chicken breasts, halved

2 cups (128g) dry breadcrumbs such as panko

1 tablespoon finely grated lemon zest

3 tablespoons finely chopped fresh parsley

1/2 cup (50g) finely grated Parmesan cheese

1/4 cup (33g) finely chopped pine nuts

Kosher or sea salt and freshly ground black pepper

2 large eggs

1/2 cup (60g) seasoned all-purpose flour (see note on page 128)

2 tablespoons olive oil

2 tablespoons unsalted butter

4 slices Robiola cheese (about 12 ounces/340g)

4 paper thin slices prosciutto

CHERRY TOMATO SAUCE

2 tablespoons extra-virgin olive oil

2 teaspoons minced garlic

4 cups (556g) ripe cherry tomatoes*, halved

Kosher or sea salt and freshly ground black pepper

3 tablespoons chopped fresh basil

2 tablespoons drained capers

Preheat the oven to 400°F. Lay the breasts between 2 layers of plastic wrap and gently pound with a rolling pin or the bottom of a heavy skillet until uniformly thick, about 1/4 inch thick.

Combine the breadcrumbs, lemon zest, parsley, Parmesan, pine nuts, and salt and pepper to taste on a plate. If you think the mixture is too coarse, you can pulse it once or twice in a food processor.

In a shallow bowl, beat the eggs with a tablespoon or so of water until combined. Set aside.

Dip the chicken breasts in the flour and shake to remove excess. Next, dip them in the eggs, drain briefly, and then press them into the breadcrumb mixture, coating both sides evenly. Place the breaded chicken in a single layer on a baking sheet and set aside. This can be done an hour or two ahead of time and stored uncovered in the refrigerator.

Heat the oil and butter in a large skillet over moderately high heat. Add the breasts in a single layer and cook until the bottoms are nicely browned, about 5 minutes. Carefully flip the chicken and place the pan in the preheated oven. Bake for 5 to 7 minutes or until the chicken is cooked through.

Meanwhile, make the Cherry Tomato Sauce. Heat the olive oil in a sauté pan over medium-high heat. Add the garlic and cook until it is just beginning to brown. Add the cherry tomatoes and season to taste with salt and pepper. Cook for a couple of minutes, until the tomatoes soften just a bit but still hold their shape. Stir in the basil and capers and keep warm.

To serve: Place a slice of the cheese on top of each cutlet, and then return the chicken to the oven for a minute or two, just until the cheese melts. Top with the prosciutto, and serve on warm plates with the Cherry Tomato Sauce on the side.

My favorite cherry variety for this sauce is one called Sun Gold.

Breast of Chicken
With Roasted Tomatillo Sauce

This sauce can be made ahead and stored, covered, in the refrigerator for up to three days. It also makes for delicious enchiladas.

MAKES 4 SERVINGS

TOMATILLO SAUCE

2 tablespoons olive oil, plus some for greasing the roasting pan

1 pound (450g) tomatillos, husked and rinsed

2 large jalapeño or chipotle chiles, or to taste

1 medium white onion, chopped (about 1 cup/115g)

1 tablespoon chopped garlic

2 cups (475mL) canned or homemade chicken stock (see page 70)

2 teaspoons brown sugar

1 cup (16g) finely chopped cilantro

Kosher or sea salt and freshly ground black pepper

CHICKEN

4 (8-ounce/230g) bone-in, skin-on chicken breast halves

Kosher or sea salt and freshly ground black pepper

3 tablespoons olive oil

Crema (Mexican sour cream) or crumbled queso fresco for garnish

1 cup (48g) finely chopped fresh cilantro for garnish

For the tomatillo sauce, lightly oil a rimmed baking sheet or baking pan and roast the tomatillos and chiles under a hot broiler, 4 inches or so from the heat source, until they just begin to char, about 4 minutes. Cool and then transfer to a food processor or blender along with any of the juices on the sheet. Purée until smooth.

Meanwhile, over moderate heat, heat the olive oil in a heavy-bottomed saucepan. Add the onion and garlic and cook, stirring, until golden brown, about 6 minutes. Raise the heat to medium high, add the tomatillo purée, and cook until the sauce is darker and very thick, about 3 minutes. Add the chicken stock, brown sugar, and cilantro, stir, reduce the heat to low, and simmer uncovered for 15 to 18 minutes or until the sauce is thickened. Season to taste with salt and pepper. Set aside.

For the chicken, preheat the oven to 375°F. Season the chicken liberally with salt and pepper. Heat the 3 tablespoons of olive oil in an ovenproof skillet large enough to hold the chicken in one layer over moderately high heat. Add the chicken, skin side down, and cook until the skin is richly browned, about 5 minutes. Flip the chicken and cook on bone side for two minutes or so.

Remove the chicken from the pan and pour out all but 1 tablespoon of fat. Add the tomatillo sauce and bring to a simmer. Nestle the chicken, skin side up, in the sauce, place in the oven, and bake for 15 to 18 minutes, until the chicken is just cooked through. Check with the point of a small knife near the bone.

Place the chicken in shallow bowls and spoon the sauce around. Top with the crema and garnish with the cilantro.

Chicken Enchiladas

A great way to serve the Breast of Chicken (see page 126) is as enchiladas. Prepare the chicken according to the recipe and then follow these directions below.

MAKES 4 SERVINGS
3 tablespoons oil
8 corn tortillas

2/3 cup (160mL) Mexican crema or crème fraîche
2 cups (226g) freshly grated Chihuahua or Monterey
   Jack cheese, plain or with chiles

Preheat the oven to 350°F. Remove the chicken from the roasted tomatillo sauce, remove from the skin and bones, and shred the chicken. Pour the sauce into a saucepan and heat until warm. Spoon a little of the sauce onto the bottom of a 13 x 9-inch baking dish and set aside.

Add the 3 tablespoons of oil to a skillet and heat over moderate heat. Dip both sides of a corn tortilla in the oil to soften and then quickly dip in the sauce in the pan to coat.

Place the tortilla on a plate and fill with 3 or 4 heaping tablespoons of the chicken. (You are dividing the chicken into 8 portions.) Roll the tortilla and place it in the baking dish. Repeat with the remaining 7 corn tortillas.

Cover the assembled tortillas with the remaining tomatillo sauce and dot with dollops of Mexican crema or crème fraîche. Sprinkle the cheese over top, place the baking dish in the oven, and heat until the cheese is melted, about 15 minutes. Serve immediately.

Breast of Chicken "Diane"

This is based on one of those old "war horses" from French bistro cooking that I think is still delicious. Classically, it's done with steaks that are pan roasted. Here I'm using chicken breasts. The approach would work equally well with pork medallions. You might accompany this with quickly sautéed mushrooms and spinach.

MAKES 4 SERVINGS
4 boneless, skinless chicken breasts
Kosher or sea salt and freshly ground black pepper
1 tablespoon olive oil
2 tablespoons unsalted butter
1/4 cup (40g) finely chopped shallots or green onions
   (white part only)

1 1/4 cups (300mL) canned or homemade chicken
   stock (see page 70)
1/4 cup (60mL) brandy (regular, apple, or pear
   would all work)
2 tablespoons Dijon mustard
2 teaspoons Worcestershire sauce, preferably white
2/3 cup (160mL) heavy cream
2 tablespoons finely chopped chives

Gently pound the chicken breasts to even them out a bit. Season liberally with salt and pepper. In a heavy-bottomed sauté pan heat the olive oil and butter over medium-high heat. Add the chicken and cook until golden brown and cooked through, about 4 minutes per side. Set the breasts aside and keep them warm under a tent of foil.

Add the shallots and, over moderate heat, cook the shallots until softened, about 2 minutes. Add the

chicken stock, brandy, and mustard, raise the heat, and bring to a boil. Scrape up any of the delicious browned bits from the bottom of the pan. Reduce by half, about 5 minutes, and then stir in the Worcestershire sauce and cream and reduce to a nice sauce consistency, about 5 minutes. Add any juices from the chicken and season to taste with salt and pepper. Stir in the chives, pour the sauce over the breasts, and serve immediately.

Chicken Melitzana

Melitzana is the Greek name for eggplant, which is probably the most used vegetable in Greek cooking. Halloumi cheese is a cheese from the island of Cyprus that is traditionally made from both goat and sheep milk. Halloumi has a higher melting point than other cheese, which makes it suitable for frying and grilling. It can be found widely in the United States in stores that have good cheese offerings.

MAKES 4 SERVINGS
CINNAMON-SCENTED TOMATO SAUCE
3 medium white onions, chopped
  (about 3 cups/425g)
3 tablespoons extra-virgin olive oil
2 (2-inch/5cm) cinnamon sticks
1 (28-ounce) can of canned crushed tomatoes
  with purée and basil
3 tablespoons ouzo or vodka
2 teaspoons honey, or to taste
Kosher or sea salt and freshly ground black pepper

CHICKEN MELITZANA
1 medium globe eggplant, cut crosswise
  into 4 (¾-inch-thick/19-mm-thick) slices
Extra-virgin olive oil
Kosher or sea salt and freshly ground black pepper
4 bone-in skinless chicken breasts
½ cup (60g) seasoned flour*
4 tablespoons unsalted butter, divided
8 ounces (230g) cremini or other flavorful
  mushroom, thinly sliced
8 ounces (230g) halloumi cheese, cut into 4 slices

To make the tomato sauce, add the onions to a food processor and purée. Heat the olive oil in a saucepan over medium heat, add the cinnamon sticks, and sauté until fragrant, about 3 minutes. Reduce the heat to medium low, add the onion purée, and stir for 10 minutes or so. Add the tomatoes, ouzo, and honey. Simmer gently for 25 minutes or so or until nicely thickened. Season to taste with salt and pepper. Remove and discard the cinnamon sticks before using.

To make the Chicken Melitzana, preheat the oven to 375°F. Brush the eggplant slices with olive oil, season with salt and pepper, and arrange in a single layer on a baking sheet. Roast until they are lightly browned and tender but still holding their shape, about 15 minutes.

Meanwhile, dust the chicken breasts with seasoned flour, shaking off any excess. Heat 2 tablespoons of the butter and 2 tablespoons of olive oil in a heavy skillet over medium heat and cook the chicken for 3 to 4 minutes on each side until golden. Remove the chicken and set aside. (Note: the chicken will not be cooked all the way through at this point.)

Heat the remaining butter and 2 tablespoons more of olive oil in the skillet and sauté the mushrooms over medium heat until they are nicely browned and any liquid has evaporated. Season well with salt and pepper.

Place the eggplant slices in one layer an inch apart in a baking pan or dish. Top each slice with mushrooms and then with a chicken breast. Spoon half the tomato sauce over each pile to cover the breasts. Place the halloumi slices on top and spoon the remaining tomato sauce over the cheese to cover. Bake for 15 to 20 minutes, or until the chicken is cooked through. Serve immediately.

Seasoned flour is simply flour to which you've added salt and pepper and whatever else you like, such as a bit of paprika, to your taste.

Breast of Chicken with Capers and Olives

You could of course do this with thighs if you prefer. Capers typically come packed in brine. They are also available packed in sea salt. Though you have to rinse them well before using, I prefer the salt-packed capers.

MAKES 4 SERVINGS

4 boneless, skin-on chicken breasts
Kosher or sea salt and freshly ground black pepper
¼ cup (55g) extra-virgin olive oil
2 tablespoons thinly sliced peeled garlic
4 or 5 oil-packed anchovies, chopped
½ cup (120mL) dry white vermouth
2 cups (480g) canned petite diced tomatoes
  with juice

2 tablespoons drained capers
½ cup (67g) meaty black or green olives such
  as Cerignola, pitted and chopped
½ teaspoon crushed red pepper flakes
3 to 4 tablespoons fresh lemon juice
2 tablespoons chopped fresh herbs of your choice
  (such as parsley, chives, and/or basil)

Season the chicken liberally with salt and pepper. Heat the oil in a heavy 12-inch skillet over medium-high heat. Add the chicken, skin side down, and cook until the skin is golden and crisp, 6 to 8 minutes. Flip the chicken and continue to cook until just done, 5 minutes or more, depending on thickness. Transfer to a plate.

Pour off all but 2 tablespoons of fat in the pan. Reduce the heat to medium; add the garlic and cook, stirring, until softened and just beginning to brown, about 2 minutes. Add the anchovies and stir until they melt, about 2 minutes. Add the vermouth, raise the heat to high, and cook for 1 to 2 minutes, stirring to scrape up any of the browned bits on the bottom of the pan. Add the tomatoes, capers, olives, pepper flakes, and lemon juice and bring to a simmer. Adjust lemon and red pepper to taste.

Return the chicken breasts and any juices to the pan, nestling them in the sauce. Cover the pan and allow the chicken to heat through, about 5 minutes. Transfer the breasts to a platter, spoon the sauce over them, and sprinkle the herbs over top.

My Favorite Chicken Sandwich

This is more a memory than a strict recipe. If you slice thin little pieces of the chicken and arrange them with the jam and watercress on small croutes (crackers or toasted slices of baguette), you can have elegant hors d'oeuvres with the same ingredients.

MAKES 2 TO 3 SANDWICHES
CARAMELIZED ONION JAM
2 tablespoons olive oil or unsalted butter
2 large white onions, peeled and thinly sliced (about 4 cups/460g)
2 tablespoons (or more) roasted garlic (see page 41)
Big pinch sugar
2 tablespoons balsamic vinegar, preferably white
1 1/2 tablespoons chopped golden raisins

Salt and freshly ground black pepper

SANDWICH
Meat from Ginger Poached Chicken (see page 89)
Whole-grain peasant-style bread, such as Swiss health bread
1 bunch watercress, woody stems removed and discarded

In a large heavy-bottomed sauté pan, heat the olive oil and sauté the onions, stirring, until they are just beginning to color, about 8 minutes. Add the garlic and sugar and continue to cook until the onions are rich golden brown and very soft. This will take another 15 to 20 minutes or so. If the onions are browning too fast, add a tablespoon or so of water and reduce the heat. Stir in the vinegar and raisins and season with salt and pepper. Store, covered and refrigerated, up to 5 days. Serve at room temperature or warmed. Like all jams, this one can be canned using the water bath method.

Pull the chicken meat from the bones or slice it, as you prefer.

Layer the meat on the bread with some Caramelized Onion Jam and watercress, top with another slice of bread. Eat!

Fried Beer-Battered Chicken Sandwich

These are better than anything you'll get at a fast food joint. See page 56 for hints on frying.

MAKES 4 SERVINGS

COLE SLAW

2 cups (140g) finely shredded cabbage

1 small carrot, peeled and finely shredded or
   julienned (about 1/2 cup/55g)

1/2 cup (46g) finely sliced red bell pepper

1/4 cup (24g) finely sliced green onions (1/2 bunch)

2 tablespoons sugar

2 tablespoons champagne or white wine vinegar

2 to 3 tablespoons olive oil

1 tablespoon lime or lemon juice

Kosher or sea salt and freshly ground black pepper

TARTAR SAUCE

1/2 cup (120mL) mayonnaise

1 tablespoon drained chopped capers

1 tablespoon chopped red onion

1 tablespoon sweet pickle relish

1 teaspoon chopped fresh chives or parsley

Kosher or sea salt and freshly ground black pepper

CHICKEN SANDWICH

1 (12-ounce) bottle beer

1 large egg, lightly beaten

2 cups (240g) all-purpose flour

2 teaspoons baking powder

Kosher or sea salt and freshly ground black pepper

4 (5-ounce/141g) boneless, skinless chicken breasts
   or thighs

Vegetable oil for frying

4 onion or Kaiser rolls or other bread of your choice

2 cups coleslaw (recipe follows)

1/2 cup (113g) tartar sauce (recipe follows)

For the coleslaw, combine the cabbage, carrot, bell pepper, and green onions in a large bowl. In a separate bowl, whisk together the sugar, vinegar, olive oil, and lime juice until the sugar is dissolved. Season to taste with salt and pepper and toss with the vegetables. Cover and store the coleslaw in the refrigerator until ready to serve.

For the tartar sauce, mix everything together and season to taste. Cover and store the tartar sauce in the refrigerator until ready to serve.

For the sandwich, whisk together the beer and egg in a bowl. In another bowl, stir together the flour, baking powder, 2 teaspoons of salt and 1/2 teaspoon of pepper. Slowly whisk the flour mixture into the beer mixture to form a smooth batter.

Rinse the chicken and pat it dry. With a meat tenderizer gently flatten the chicken to a relatively uniform 1/2-inch thickness. Season the chicken lightly with salt and pepper.

Heat an inch or so of oil in a deep skillet or saucepan to 360°F. Dip the chicken into the batter and let any excess drain back into the bowl. Fry the chicken in the preheated oil until cooked through, golden brown, and crispy, about 5 minutes. Be sure to turn once or twice for even browning.

Split the rolls in half and slather with tartar sauce on both sides. Add the chicken and slaw to the bottom half of the roll, top with the other half, and enjoy.

Grilled Lime Chicken with Creamed Corn

I'm using thighs here because they have a richer flavor. You could certainly use breasts if you wanted. The creamed corn is a very simple dish, and though you could use frozen corn, I think it's best with fresh sweet corn.

MAKES 4 SERVINGS
$\frac{1}{2}$ cup (120mL) fresh lime juice, divided
3 tablespoons olive oil, divided
2 tablespoons honey, divided
1 teaspoon ground cumin, divided
$\frac{1}{4}$ teaspoon red chili flakes
4 large (6-ounce/169g) boneless, skinless chicken thighs
Kernels from 6 large ears of sweet corn (about 5 cups/820g total)

$\frac{3}{4}$ cup (180mL) canned or homemade chicken stock (see page 70)
$\frac{1}{2}$ pint (1 cup/240mL) cream
Kosher or sea salt and freshly ground black pepper
1 small poblano chile, stemmed, seeded, charred, skin removed, and finely chopped (about $\frac{1}{2}$ cup/75g)
2 tablespoons chopped fresh cilantro
$\frac{1}{2}$ teaspoon finely minced jalapeño, or to taste
Sprigs of cilantro or mint for garnish

Whisk $\frac{1}{3}$ cup of the lime juice, 2 tablespoons of the olive oil, 1 tablespoon of the honey, $\frac{1}{2}$ teaspoon of the cumin, and the chili flakes together and pour the mixture into a shallow dish. Add the chicken, turn to coat, and marinate covered in the refrigerator for at least 1 hour and up to 4 hours.

Meanwhile, put half the corn into a food processor and pulse a few times to finely chop. Place the processed corn in a saucepan with the remaining whole corn kernels, the stock, the remaining $\frac{1}{2}$ teaspoon of cumin, and the cream. Bring the mixture to a simmer over medium heat, stirring constantly, until thick, about

10 minutes. Season to taste with salt and pepper. Stir in the poblano and keep warm.

Remove the chicken from the marinade and season liberally with salt and pepper. On a medium-hot grill, cook until just cooked through, about 5 minutes per side. While the chicken is cooking, stir together the remaining lime juice, olive oil, honey, cilantro, and jalapeño and season to taste with salt and pepper.

Divide the creamed corn among 4 warm soup plates. Place a grilled thigh on top and spoon the cilantro mixture over top. Serve immediately, topped with cilantro sprigs.

Pan-Roasted Asian Chicken Breasts
With Bok Choy Risotto

In this recipe the chicken and bok choy risotto are topped with a *beurre blanc*, as the French call it, or butter sauce. Note that the recipe calls for kaffir lime leaves. These can be found fresh or frozen at many Southeast Asian grocers. If you live in an area where citrus grows, you can also grow your own. Substitute lime zest if you can't find them.

MAKES 6 SERVINGS

CHICKEN

2 tablespoons Asian chili paste (Sriracha or Sambal Olek)

1 tablespoon fish sauce or 2 tablespoons soy sauce

1 tablespoon fresh lime juice

2 kaffir lime leaves, very thinly sliced, or 1 tablespoon finely grated lime zest

6 large bone-in chicken breast halves

4 tablespoons olive oil

BUTTER SAUCE

$1\frac{1}{4}$ cups (300mL) canned or homemade chicken stock (see page 70)

1 teaspoon fish sauce

$\frac{1}{2}$ teaspoon very thinly sliced hot red pepper, or to taste

2 tablespoons softened unsalted butter

2 tablespoons chopped fresh cilantro leaves

2 teaspoons fresh lime juice, or to taste

BOK CHOY RISOTTO

2 tablespoons unsalted butter

$\frac{1}{4}$ cup (28g) chopped shallots or green onions

1 tablespoon chopped lemongrass, white part only

2 teaspoons finely chopped ginger

2 teaspoons finely chopped garlic

$\frac{1}{2}$ teaspoon finely chopped hot red pepper, or to taste

1 cup (150g) Arborio or other risotto rice

$\frac{1}{4}$ cup (60mL) dry white wine

3 to 4 cups (700 to 950mL) canned or homemade chicken stock (see page 70), divided

$\frac{1}{2}$ cup (120mL) coconut milk

8 ounces (3 packed cups/165g) coarsely chopped baby bok choy leaves and stems

1 teaspoon fish sauce

1 teaspoon palm sugar

1 teaspoon lime juice, or to taste

1 kaffir lime leaf, very thinly sliced, or 2 teaspoons finely grated lime zest

Cilantro leaves for garnish

Lime wedges for garnish

Combine the marinade ingredients and rub the chicken breasts with the mixture. Cover and refrigerate for at least 1 and up to 6 hours.

Preheat the oven to 400°F. Heat the olive oil in an ovenproof skillet over medium heat. Brown the chicken breasts, skin side down. Turn the breasts skin side up and place the skillet in the oven for 15 to 18 minutes, or until the chicken is just cooked through. Remove the chicken from the pan, set it aside, and cover with tented foil to keep warm. While the chicken is cooking, prepare the butter sauce and the risotto.

For the butter sauce: In a saucepan, combine the chicken stock and fish sauce and reduce to $1/3$ cup over high heat, about 5 minutes. Add the thinly sliced red chile and, off heat, whisk in the butter to thicken. Stir in the cilantro and lime juice and keep warm.

For the risotto: Add the butter to a deep saucepan and over medium heat sauté the shallots, lemongrass, ginger, garlic, and chile until softened but not brown.

Add the rice, stir to coat with the shallot mixture, and continue to cook for a minute or two. Add the wine and $1/2$ cup of the chicken stock and stir until the stock is nearly absorbed. Add the coconut milk and another $1/2$ cup of the stock and stir until nearly absorbed. Continue adding the stock in $1/2$-cup increments, stirring constantly and allowing each addition to be absorbed before adding the next. You will use about 3 cups of stock in all to get the rice to the stage where it is creamy on the outside and still has a little texture at its core. Add the bok choy and stir until just wilted, about 2 minutes. To finish, stir in the fish sauce, sugar, lime juice to taste, and the lime leaf or zest.

Divide the risotto among 6 warmed shallow soup plates, top with chicken, and spoon butter sauce over top. Scatter cilantro leaves over all and serve immediately with lime wedges for each person to squeeze juice over.

Scallopini of Chicken
With Oyster Mushrooms and Marsala

This recipe combines chicken breast with prosciutto in a kind of *saltimbocca* approach usually done with veal. You could also use boneless thighs for a richer flavor. I've used Marsala wine here, which is traditional, but you could use whatever wine you like, including a sweeter styled sherry or even a *vin cotto**. Any other mushrooms that you like could be substituted, such as chanterelle, hen of the woods, etc.

MAKES 4 SERVINGS

4 (6- to 8-ounce/169- to -230g) boneless, skinless chicken breast halves

4 fresh sage leaves

8 thin slices prosciutto di Parma

4 tablespoons cold unsalted butter, divided

2 tablespoons olive oil, plus more for sautéing if needed

Seasoned flour for dusting (preferably Wondra)

10 ounces (284g) fresh oyster mushroom caps, stems discarded

1 cup (240mL) sweet Marsala wine

1/2 cup (120mL) canned or homemade chicken stock (see page 70)

Kosher or sea salt and freshly ground black pepper

Crisp fried fresh sage leaves for garnish, if desired

Butterfly each breast (or have the butcher do it for you), and with a meat mallet or the back of a small, heavy iron skillet, gently pound each breast until it is about 1/2 inch thick. Place a sage leaf on one side of each breast, season with salt and pepper, and top with 2 slices of prosciutto on each side. Fold the breast over with the prosciutto on the outside. Secure with toothpicks if needed.

Heat 2 tablespoons of the butter and the olive oil in a heavy skillet over medium-high heat. Lightly dust the breasts in seasoned flour and add to the pan. Cook until beautifully browned on both sides, about 3 minutes each side. Remove the chicken from the pan and tent with foil to keep warm.

Add the mushrooms to the pan with a bit more olive oil if necessary and sauté until they are lightly browned and the juices have evaporated, about 6 minutes. Transfer the cooked mushrooms to a plate and cover to keep warm.

Add the Marsala and stock to the pan, scraping up any browned bits, bring to a boil, and reduce by half or until sauce has thickened, about 5 minutes. Whisk in the remaining 2 tablespoons of cold butter and season with salt and pepper.

Place the chicken breasts on warm plates and top with the mushrooms. Spoon the sauce over the mushrooms and garnish with fried sage leaves, if using. Serve immediately

*Vin cotto *translates to "cooked wine" in Italian. You can buy a ready-made one in fancy food stores or make your own by combining 5 cups or so hearty red wine with 1/2 cup or so honey, 2 large cinnamon sticks, and 3 whole cloves in a heavy saucepan and bringing to a boil. Reduce the heat and simmer until reduced to 1 cup, about 20 minutes. Cool and remove the cinnamon and cloves before using.*

Grilled Coconut Chicken
With Peach Chutney

This chicken goes perfectly with the peach chutney, which can even stand on its own for other uses. Note that chutney needs to be made ahead. The dish is still delicious if you decide not to make the chutney. Alternately, you can use a store-bought fruit chutney.

MAKES 4 TO 6 SERVINGS
FRESH PEACH CHUTNEY

$\frac{1}{2}$ cup (120mL) cider vinegar

$\frac{1}{2}$ cup (120mL) dry white wine

$\frac{1}{2}$ cup (100g) loosely packed brown sugar

$\frac{1}{2}$ cup (74.5g) diced red bell pepper

$\frac{1}{2}$ white onion, peeled and diced (about $\frac{3}{4}$ cup/.86g)

$\frac{1}{2}$ teaspoon red pepper flakes, or to taste

$\frac{1}{3}$ cup (48g) golden raisins

1 tablespoon finely chopped garlic

2 tablespoons finely chopped ginger

$\frac{1}{2}$ teaspoon kosher or sea salt

2 pounds (900g) firm, fresh peaches, blanched to remove the skin, pitted, and cut into $\frac{1}{2}$ inch (13mm) dice

CHICKEN

1 (14-ounce) can coconut milk

3 tablespoons chili garlic sauce, preferably Lee Kum Kee brand

3 tablespoons toasted sesame oil

$\frac{1}{4}$ cup (12g) chopped fresh cilantro

$\frac{1}{4}$ cup (12g) chopped fresh Thai purple or regular basil

$\frac{1}{4}$ cup (28g) chopped green onions ($\frac{1}{2}$ bunch)

$\frac{1}{4}$ cup (20g) finely chopped ginger

$\frac{1}{4}$ cup (60mL) Asian fish sauce

$\frac{1}{4}$ cup (50g) packed brown sugar

Juice and grated zest of 4 large limes

1 large butterflied chicken (4 to 4$\frac{1}{2}$ pounds/1.8 to 2.03kg), split, with back bone removed (see page 47)

For the peach chutney, combine the vinegar, wine, and brown sugar in a nonreactive pot over medium heat and bring to a boil. Add the red pepper, onion, red pepper flakes, raisins, garlic, ginger, and salt and simmer for 6 minutes or so. Add the peaches and simmer an additional 5 minutes or until softened but not mushy. Drain the peach mixture, set aside, and return the liquid to the pan. Reduce over high heat until syrupy, 3 to 5 minutes.

Remove the pan from the heat, add the peaches back in, and allow to cool for 10 minutes in the pot. Serve at room temperature. Transfer any remaining chutney to a clean container and refrigerate, covered, for up to three weeks. Makes 2 cups.

For the chicken, combine all the ingredients except the chicken in a large bowl or food storage bag and mix well. Add the chicken and cover or seal the bag. Turn to coat the chicken on all sides. Marinate the chicken, covered and refrigerated, for at least 4 hours, turning a couple of times.

Prepare a grill to medium hot (or preheat the oven to 375°F). Remove the chicken from the marinade, discarding the marinade; grill the chicken on an oiled rack, covered, until the juices run clear and a thermometer inserted in the thickest piece reads 165°F, about 45 minutes, or bake in the oven for about 1 hour. Allow to rest for a few minutes before cutting up and serving.

To serve: Cut the chicken into pieces, serve on warm plates with dollops of the chutney.

Chicken Baked in Parchment
With Asian Flavors

Baking in parchment assures a moist result, and slitting the bag open at the table releases dramatic and delicious aromas.

MAKES 4 SERVINGS

1/2 cup (150g) hoisin sauce
1/4 cup (60mL) soy sauce
2 tablespoons honey
2 teaspoons Asian chili garlic sauce
3 tablespoons rice wine or dry white wine
8 star anise
Juice and zest of 1 large orange (1/3 cup/80mL juice, 2 tablespoons zest)

2 baby bok choy
4 (6- to 8-ounce/169- to -230g) boneless, skinless chicken thighs
4 green onions, cut thinly on an angle
2 tablespoons peeled and finely julienned ginger
Steamed jasmine or basmati rice for serving

Preheat the oven to 375°F. Make the sauce by adding the hoisin, soy, honey, chili garlic sauce, rice wine, star anise, and orange juice to a small saucepan. Over moderate heat, simmer until thickened, about 5 minutes. Set aside to cool.

Cut the bok choy in quarters lengthwise and blanch in salted boiling water for a minute. Drain and refresh under cold water. Set aside.

Cut four sheets of parchment or foil into 12 x 16-inch rectangles. Place two quarters of bok choy in the center of each piece. Brush both sides of the chicken thighs generously with the sauce and place on top of the bok choy. Top with the green onions, ginger, and orange zest and drizzle with any remaining sauce, if desired.

Bring the long sides of the parchment together and fold over twice. Tuck the ends firmly under to form a nice packet. Place on a rimmed baking sheet and bake for 25 to 30 minutes. Serve with rice.

Stir-Fried "Velvet" Chicken

The Chinese technique of "velveting" meat is an interesting one and is as integral to Chinese cooking as pan sautéing meat is to French cooking. The basic ingredients for velveting are cornstarch, egg whites, and salt. These are mixed with the meat and provide a protective layer that keeps it tender and moist. Meat that is stir-fried, boiled, or steamed without the layer of cornstarch can still be tender, but it won't have the silky texture and mouth feel of meat that's been velveted. More likely than not, the meat that you're eating at a Chinese restaurant has been velveted prior to being deep-fried, stir-fried, or steamed. You've probably noticed in Cantonese restaurants that stir-fried meat is almost never browned or seared. Serve this with stir fried vegetables and rice.

MAKES 4 SERVINGS

6 dried shiitake mushrooms

1 pound (450g) boneless, skinless chicken breasts

3 teaspoons cornstarch, divided

1 teaspoon sesame oil

2 egg whites

1/2 teaspoon kosher or sea salt plus more for seasoning

1 cup or so (220g) peanut or other vegetable oil

1/2 cup (120mL) canned or homemade chicken stock (see page 70)

1/2 teaspoon Asian chili sauce, such as Sriracha, or to taste

2 teaspoons soy sauce

2 teaspoons peeled and finely chopped ginger

2 teaspoons finely chopped garlic

1/3 cup (32g) green onions (1/2 bunch), thinly sliced on the bias

In a medium bowl, soak the mushrooms in cold water until soft, about 30 minutes. Remove and discard the stems, thinly slice, and set aside.

Cut the chicken into 1/2-inch cubes. In a bowl, whisk together 2 teaspoons of the cornstarch and the sesame oil, egg whites, and salt. You can add a few drops of water if the mixture is too thick. Mix the chicken with the cornstarch mixture and refrigerate for 20 minutes.

Heat a wok or large skillet over moderately high heat and add the vegetable oil. Drain the chicken briefly and carefully add it to the pan, stirring to prevent the pieces from sticking together. Turn off the heat and allow the chicken to rest in the hot oil for 4 to 5 minutes or until it looks completely white. Mix the remaining 1 teaspoon of cornstarch with the chicken stock, chili sauce, and soy sauce and set aside. Pour the contents of the wok into a strainer set inside a large bowl, reserving the oil.

Wipe the wok clean with paper towels, return 1 tablespoon of the drained oil to the wok, and reheat. Add the shiitake mushrooms and stir-fry for 1 minute. Add the ginger, garlic, and green onions and stir-fry for another minute or so. Add the chicken stock mixture and bring to a boil. Return the drained chicken to the wok and mix to heat through. Season to taste and serve at once.

Buginese Chicken Stew

This recipe is from my good friend and amazing Malaysian cook Mei Ibach. She notes that "in Southern Sulawesi, Indonesia, chicken is part of daily life in villages. Most of the birds roam freely, which contributes to their wonderful flavor. What amazed me was the villagers' warm hospitality to welcome all travelers freely to share their home and indulge in a meal together. This recipe was shared with me by a villager named Rosina during my visit to her house, where she invited me to gather the spices and catch a free-range chicken from her jungle-like backyard." Tamarind is a souring agent like lime and is available in Asian and Mexican markets.

MAKES 6 SERVINGS

3 tablespoons canola oil

2 pounds (900g) boneless, skinless chicken thighs

2 lemongrass stalks

2 teaspoons coarsely chopped garlic

1/2 cup (56g) coarsely chopped shallots

4 quarter-size slices galangal or fresh ginger

2 teaspoons shrimp paste (optional)

3 cups (700mL) canned or homemade chicken stock (see page 70)

2 tablespoons cooking tamarind concentrate or 3 tablespoons lime juice

2 cinnamon sticks

4 whole cloves

1/2 teaspoon ground nutmeg

4 teaspoons Asian fish sauce, or to taste

1 tablespoon palm or brown sugar, or to taste

2 tablespoons rice vinegar

1 cup (240mL) coconut milk

1/4 cup (28g) shallots, peeled and thinly sliced

Cooked jasmine or basmati rice for serving

In a medium stock pot, preheat the oil and pan-sear the chicken thighs for about 5 minutes or until brown. Remove the outer leaves of the lemongrass and cut lengthwise into 2-inch lengths. Lightly bruise with the side of the knife and tie together with a string. Add the garlic, shallot, galangal or ginger, lemongrass, and shrimp paste, and cook for 2 minutes or until caramelized. Add the stock and bring to a boil, then turn to medium-low heat and simmer for 10 minutes, uncovered. Season with the tamarind concentrate, cinnamon sticks, cloves, nutmeg, fish sauce, sugar, rice vinegar, and coconut milk, and continue cooking, turning the chicken from time to time until the meat is cooked (about 30 minutes). Meanwhile, heat 1/2 inch of peanut or vegetable oil in a skillet over medium heat. When hot, add the shallots and cook slowly until golden brown, about 3 minutes. Top the chicken with fried shallots and serve with rice.

Sweet and Spicy Grilled Chicken

This recipe uses a delicious marinade that can also be used with pork or rich fish, such as tuna or salmon. Depending on the number of side dishes, this makes enough to serve up to four people.

MAKES 2 TO 4 SERVINGS

1 (4-pound/1.8-kg) chicken, butterflied
  (see page 47)
Juice and grated zest from 2 large lemons
  (about $^3/_4$ cup/.180mL juice)
$^1/_2$ cup (110g) olive oil
$^1/_3$ cup (114g) honey
2 teaspoons ground cumin

2 teaspoons ground coriander
1 teaspoon ground cinnamon
$^1/_2$ teaspoon cayenne pepper, or to taste
1 tablespoon pure ground chili powder
  such as ancho
2 teaspoons kosher salt
2 tablespoons finely chopped garlic
3 tablespoons chopped fresh mint

Rinse the chicken and pat dry. Combine the remaining ingredients in a blender or food processor and briefly process in 6 to 8 short bursts until combined. Marinate the chicken with the mixture in a covered container for 4 to 6 hours, turning a couple of times to coat thoroughly. Prepare a charcoal or gas-fired grill to medium hot (325 to 350°F) and grill the chicken until done (165°F on an instant-read thermometer in the thickest part of the leg). Make sure the heat is not too high or the honey will burn. Serve immediately.

Chicken and Chickpea Fatteh

This is one of the great dishes from the Eastern Mediterranean. There are endless variations based on meat, birds, eggs, vegetables, and sometimes, just chickpeas.

MAKES 6 SERVINGS

2 cups (475mL) dry white wine

4 cups (950mL) canned or homemade chicken stock (see page 70)

8 whole cloves

1 (3-inch/7.6-cm) cinnamon stick

1 large bay leaf

1 teaspoon whole cumin seeds, crushed

1 teaspoon coriander seeds, crushed

1 cup coarsely chopped green onions

5 large garlic cloves, chopped, divided

3 large (2- to 2½-pound/900- to 1130-g) bone-in, skin-on chicken breast halves

2 cups (328g) cooked chickpeas, drained

Sea salt and freshly ground pepper

3 (8-inch/20-cm round) pita breads

3 tablespoons unsalted butter, melted

1½ cups (420g) thick Greek-style yogurt*

1 tablespoon dried mint

1 teaspoon Aleppo pepper

1½ cups (375g) seeded and chopped ripe tomatoes

¼ cup (34g) lightly toasted pine nuts

Lemon wedges for garnish

Combine the wine, broth, cloves, cinnamon, bay leaf, cumin, coriander, green onions, and half the garlic together in a deep stockpot or saucepan that will allow the breasts to sit in a snug single layer. Bring to a boil and then reduce the heat and simmer for 3 to 4 minutes. Place the chicken breasts into the simmering broth, adding additional wine or broth to cover. Simmer, covered, for 6 minutes. (Check to be sure the liquid is not boiling, just simmering.) Turn off the heat and allow the chicken to cool. Strip the meat from the bones, discarding the skin, and chop the meat into large pieces.

Carefully strain the poaching liquid through a fine strainer into a bowl, discarding the solids. Add the chicken meat and chickpeas to the liquid. Season to taste with salt and pepper and cover the bowl with foil to keep warm.

Meanwhile, preheat the oven to 325°F. Split the pita breads in half, arrange in a single layer on a baking sheet, and brush with melted butter. Toast the pitas until crisp, about 8 minutes. Break them up into fairly large pieces.

Crush the remaining garlic in a bowl with a small amount of salt using the back of a spoon or a wooden mortar to make a smooth paste. Stir a little of the yogurt into the garlic to lighten it and then combine the mixture with the remaining yogurt in a small saucepan. Crumble in the dried mint and pepper and stir to mix well. Gently heat the yogurt mixture but don't let it boil or it will separate.

To assemble, divide half of the crisp pita pieces among six shallow soup bowls. Spoon the chickpeas and chicken with a bit of the broth into each bowl. Top with the remaining pita pieces, spoon tomatoes and a bit more broth over that, and then top with the flavored yogurt mixture. Sprinkle toasted pine nuts over the yogurt mixture and serve immediately with lemon wedges. Remember that you are not making a soup here but more of a brothy stew. You should have poaching liquid left over, which you can certainly find a great use for in other dishes!

If Greek-style yogurt is not available, place 3 cups of regular whole milk yogurt in a fine mesh strainer over a bowl and allow it to drain. The longer you allow it to drain, the thicker it will become.

Jerk Chicken

From Jamaica and the Caribbean, this dish is traditionally grilled, but you could also roast it in a four hundred-degree-oven and finish it under a hot broiler for a couple of minutes to crisp the skin and give it a little char.

MAKES 6 SERVINGS

1/4 cup (55g) vegetable oil
1/2 cup (120mL) lime juice
3 tablespoons packed brown sugar
1 tablespoon dried thyme
2 tablespoons soy sauce
1 cup (96g) chopped green onions
2 tablespoons chopped garlic

3 tablespoons chopped ginger
1 or 2 habanero or scotch bonnet chiles or a
  teaspoon or 2 chipotles in adobo, to taste
2 tablespoons ground allspice
1/2 teaspoon ground cinnamon
1/2 teaspoon ground cloves
Kosher or sea salt and freshly ground black pepper
6 whole skin-on, bone-in chicken legs and thighs

Combine all the ingredients except the chicken in a food processor and process until smooth. Place the chicken in a large baking dish, pour the marinade over it, and massage the marinade into the chicken, making sure to push it under the skin. Cover the chicken with plastic wrap and refrigerate for at least 6 hours or overnight.

Build a medium-hot fire in a charcoal grill or heat a gas grill to medium-high. Place the chicken on the grill over direct heat and cook, turning occasionally, until it begins to brown, about 15 minutes. Transfer the chicken to indirect heat, or reduce the heat to medium low, and continue cooking, turning occasionally, until the chicken is cooked through, about 45 minutes.

Hainan Chicken Rice

The roots of this dish go back to the Chinese island of Hainan in the South China Sea. Considered the landmark dish of Singapore, you'll find this at any shopping mall or food court in Malaysia. The quality of the chicken is all important, so get a good organic, free-range bird for best flavor. The bird is traditionally dipped in an ice-water bath after it is cooked to give it a silky and tender texture. This is known as *bai ji*, or white chicken. Sometimes pandan leaves are added to the cooking pot to make it more fragrant. At a street food stand, a single serving of chicken rice comes with the chicken on rice, slices of cucumber, a bowl of hot stock, chili sauce, and sometimes a ginger sauce. Thick soy or hoisin also accompanies.

MAKES 6 SERVINGS

1 (3½- to 4-pound/1.68- to 1.8-kg)
  chicken, fat removed
Kosher salt
4 green onions, halved
4-inch piece ginger, peeled and smashed

RICE

2 cups (374g) fragrant long-grain white rice, such
  as jasmine or basmati
2 tablespoons vegetable oil
3 tablespoons peeled and finely chopped ginger
2 tablespoons finely chopped garlic
4 cups (950mL) reserved poaching liquid

2 pandan leaves,* tied in a knot (optional)

SEASONING SAUCE

2 tablespoons reserved poaching liquid
1 tablespoon soy sauce
2 tablespoons toasted sesame oil

FOR THE TABLE

Chili Sauce (recipe follows)
Ginger Sauce (recipe follows)
Cucumber slices
Cilantro sprigs
Dark soy sauce or hoisin sauce

Rub the outside of the chicken with a handful of salt to get rid of any loose skin and to firm it up. Rinse it well, inside and out, and season generously with salt inside and out. Stuff it with the green onions and smashed ginger.

Place the chicken in a large pot filled with cold water to cover by 1 inch. Bring to a boil over high heat, and then reduce the heat to low and simmer, covered, for 30 minutes. Check for doneness by inserting a small knife into the flesh of the leg/thigh, where the juices should run clear and the meat should be very tender.

Transfer the chicken to the sink and rinse with cold water for about 2 minutes, until cool. Alternatively, you can put it in an ice bath. Set aside. Strain and reserve the poaching liquid for cooking the rice. You should have at least 6 cups. Season to taste with salt.

To cook the rice: Heat the oil in a deep saucepan over moderate heat and fry the ginger and garlic till fragrant, about 2 minutes. Add the rice to the pan and fry, stirring until it's well coated with the oil. Be careful not to burn the ginger and garlic. Add 4 cups of the reserved poaching liquid, salt to taste, and the pandan leaves, if using, and bring to a boil. Immediately turn the heat down to low. Cover and simmer for 15 minutes or until the liquid is absorbed. Remove from the heat and let it sit with the lid on for 5 minutes or so. Fluff the rice with a fork before serving.

To serve: Heat the remaining 2 cups poaching liquid over medium heat. Cut the chicken into serving size pieces. Spoon rice into deep bowls and top each bowl with the chicken and a ladleful of the hot stock. Mix the seasoning sauce ingredients in a small bowl and drizzle over the chicken. Serve the chicken rice with the chili sauce and ginger sauce, cucumber slices, cilantro, and dark soy or hoisin sauce on the side for each diner to add as they wish.

Look for fresh pandan leaves in Asian markets labeled sometimes as "pandan" or "pandal." Sometimes you can find fresh ones, but more often they'll be in plastic bags of folded leaves among the frozen foods. They are also known as screw pine leaves and are used extensively in Southeast Asian cooking. A couple of bruised lemongrass stalks would be a good substitute.

Chili Sauce

6 red or green fresh jalapeños, or to taste
2 teaspoons chopped garlic
1-inch (2.5-cm) piece peeled ginger, chopped
1 tablespoon or so fresh lime juice

2 teaspoons sugar
2 tablespoons reserved chicken poaching liquid
Salt to taste

Add all the ingredients to a blender and blend until smooth.

Ginger Sauce

3-inch (7.6-cm) piece peeled ginger, grated
2 teaspoons toasted sesame oil

Salt to taste

Mix all together in a small bowl.

Spicy Chicken Wrapped In Banana Leaves

Another recipe from Mei Ibach, whom I admire greatly. She notes, "This is a classic cooking style called Nyonya cuisine, which comes from two vital culinary traditions in Malaysia. The rempah spice here is the mother spice that is used in sauces, soup bases, spreads, condiments, and marinades to flavor meats, sea foods, and vegetables." You can buy toasted macadamias in the market.

MAKES 6 SERVINGS
REMPAH SPICE
10 macadamia nuts, toasted*
1 stalk lemongrass, cut into 1-inch (2.5-cm) lengths
1 teaspoon chopped fresh ginger
2 tablespoons chili powder
4 to 6 red chiles, such as serrano
1 tablespoon vegetable oil
1 tablespoon garlic
¼ cup (28g) chopped shallots
1 tablespoon palm or brown sugar
2 teaspoons fish sauce

1 to 2 tablespoons water
Kosher or sea salt and freshly ground black pepper

CHICKEN
1 whole fryer chicken, about 3 pounds (1.35kg), preferably free-range
Kosher or sea salt and freshly ground black pepper
2 sheets of banana leaves, cut into 14- x 14-inch (35- x 35cm) squares
2 tablespoons sweet dark soy sauce
Cilantro springs
½ cup fried shallots (see directions on page 141)

To make the rempah: Combine all the ingredients in a food processor or blender and purée until smooth. You may need to add a little more water.

Season the chicken well with salt and pepper both inside and out. Rub the rempah spice evenly in the cavity and on the outside of the chicken. Place the chicken in the refrigerator and marinate for at least 30 minutes or up to 8 hours.

Preheat the oven to 375°F.

Wrap the chicken with the banana leaves in two layers and secure with bamboo skewers. Bake the chicken for 1 hour, or until cooked through.

The legs should separate easily and the temperature in the thickest part of the thigh should reach 170°F on an instant-read thermometer.

To serve: Discard the charred banana leaves and transfer the chicken to a platter. Drizzle the soy sauce on the plate around the chicken and garnish with fried shallots and cilantro

To toast the macadamia nuts, place the nuts on a baking sheet in a preheated 375°F oven for 5 to 7 minutes or until fragrant and lightly colored.

EGGS

Eggs have been called nature's most perfect food. One egg has an abundant amount of thirteen essential vitamins and minerals, high-quality protein, unsaturated fats, and antioxidants, all for about seventy-five calories. Egg nutrients can help you with weight control, muscle strength, eye health, brain function, and a healthy pregnancy. Eggs' nutritional value should not be surprising when you remember that an egg contains everything needed for the nourishment of a developing chick.

Particularly important for aiding healthy brain function and pregnancy is choline, of which eggs are a good source. It's estimated that more than 90 percent of Americans are choline deficient. A study of choline intake by Iowa State University researchers found that only 10 percent or less of all older children, men, women, and pregnant women get even close to the recommended amount of choline.

In cooking, eggs are highly prized due to their food chemistry. They serve many unique functions in recipes, including coagulation, foaming, emulsification, and browning.

The history of the egg as food runs parallel with the history of people consuming chickens and other birds as food. Although it is uncertain when and where it began, the practice of raising chickens for food is ancient and so, subsequently, is the consumption of eggs, extending back to the times of early man.

Eggs have always been a symbol of fertility, and beliefs abound that reference its aphrodisiacal powers in many cultures. One of the most widely held food and holiday associations is that of the Easter egg. How the egg became associated with this holiday seems to have roots that are both biological and cultural. Before more modern techniques of poultry raising, hens laid few eggs during the winter. This meant that Easter, occurring with the advent of spring, coincided with the hens' renewed cycle of laying numerous eggs. Additionally, because eggs were traditionally considered a food of luxury, they were forbidden during Lent, so Christians had to wait until Easter to eat them. Interestingly, the custom of painting eggshells was a popular custom among many ancient civilizations, including the Egyptians, Chinese, Greeks, and Persians.

Finding the Right Egg

Conventional egg production in this country has a dark side. Most of the eggs we see in grocery stores today come from hens that are confined inside wire battery cages in which they can barely move. With something like sixty-eight square inches of space in which to live, these hens can't even flap their wings, let alone build nests, perch, dust bathe, or do the other things chickens naturally do.

Numerous experts agree that battery cage confinement contributes to a number of welfare problems, and these concerns have prompted many European countries to ban this system of confinement altogether.

Battery cages continue to dominate egg production in the United States, however, and the egg industry has unfortunately long ignored the allegations of cruelty to animals. But as a growing number of consumers discover the truth about modern egg production, the industry is changing.

Some things to look for when you buy eggs:

Despite the popular notion, the color of the egg shell is not related to the quality or nutritional value of the egg itself.

Organic: Chickens must be fed organic feed without animal byproducts and be "free range," and the use of antibiotics is prohibited. The feed may or may not be processed organically. Read the label.

Cage-free: Instead of the cage system, chickens are kept in large poultry barns. The floor is open and the chickens can sometimes walk around the barn. There is no standard, however, for how much open space is required per bird or what types of antibiotics are permitted. The hens are often de-beaked to prevent pecking. Oftentimes, the temperature and light in the barn is manipulated to mimic the seasons and force the birds into irregular production cycles.

Fertile: These are eggs that can be incubated and developed into chicks. Unfortunately, despite conventional wisdom, fertile eggs are not more nutritious than nonfertile eggs, do not keep as well as nonfertile eggs, and are more expensive to produce. Fertile eggs may contain a small amount of male hormone, but there are no known advantages.

Free-range: Chickens must have access to an outdoor space, which might be dirt, sand, or concrete. Producers who practice this method often have small doors in the coop that open out to a fenced yard.

Vegetarian-fed: Chickens are kept indoors because foraging for food outside might include bugs, which is not considered a vegetarian diet.

Omega-3 enhanced: The chickens are fed ground flaxseed, algae, or fish oil in combination with their feed to enhance the levels of omega-3s.

Day range pastured poultry and pasture pens: This doesn't usually appear on the egg carton, but if it does, it means the chickens have a fenced pasture where they range during the day. At night, they are housed inside a permanent or semi-permanent coop with open floors. Pasture pens are outdoor movable shelters. They have no floors, so the chickens live right on the ground, and a cover protects them from too much sun and rain. The feed is a combination of pasture and commercial, organic, or other feed. Demand this for the eggs you consume. This is a good practice.

Cholesterol and Eggs

Back in the late 1970s and '80s, eggs came under fire from the food police and sales dramatically declined. Medical research linked high levels of cholesterol in the blood to increased risk of heart disease. Egg yolks, of course, are pretty high in cholesterol, and the conventional wisdom was that high cholesterol in food would result in high cholesterol in the blood. The egg white scramble and omelette were born!

The conventional wisdom, we now know, was false. There is no direct link between the amount of cholesterol in food and that found in blood. Lots of studies have found that most people who are not genetically disposed to heart disease can eat eggs every day with no increased risk to their health. Research has shown, however, that blood cholesterol levels are affected by the amount of total fats, especially saturated fats, in the diet. In that scenario, eggs look a whole look more benign. One egg has less than two grams of saturated fat, while a cup of whole milk has five grams and a tablespoon of butter has seven grams. As Julia Child said, "All things in moderation and eat all things." Eggs are a nutritious and inexpensive option that can be regularly consumed by most of us.

Cooking Eggs

There is lots of information and there are many opinions out there about how to cook eggs. My simple recommendations are:

For eggs out of the shell, the overriding requirement is to cook them gently with moderate heat. Eggs are a delicate protein and can become tough and unappealing if the heat is too high.

For perfect hard "boiled" eggs, steam them! Steaming ensures that you don't overcook the egg. If they are overcooked, you get the dreaded green ring around the yolk—a reaction between the sulfur in the egg white and the iron in the yolk, and a sure indication that your eggs are overcooked (and stinky). Use a steamer with a tight-fitting lid. Place the eggs in a single layer in the steamer basket over *gently simmering* water. (Do not let the water boil rapidly.) Cover and cook for ten minutes. Turn off the heat and allow to sit covered for an additional five minutes. Plunge the cooked eggs into cold water, crack the shell and, under a stream of cold running water, peel them. Shells won't stick, and you'll end up with beautiful unblemished whites (for perfect deviled eggs, page 172) and no chalky yolks with grey rings around them. Also, eggs that are a week or so old are best for "hard boiling." As they age, raw eggs become more alkaline, and this makes them easier to peel.

For "soft-boiled" eggs, use the same technique as with the hard-boiled eggs, but cook them for only five minutes, covered, and then crack and serve.

Storing Eggs

The freshness of an egg is not only determined by the date when the egg was laid, but also by the way the egg has been stored. If a freshly laid egg is left at room temperature for a full day, it will not be as fresh as a week-old egg that has been refrigerated between 33°F and 40°F from the time it was laid.

According to the USDA: Many eggs reach stores only a few days after the hen lays them. Egg cartons with the USDA grade shield on them, indicating they came from a USDA-inspected plant, must display the "pack date" (the day that the eggs were washed, graded, and placed in the carton). The date is displayed as a three-digit code that represents the consecutive day of the year (the "Julian Date") starting with January 1 as 001 and ending with December 31 as 365. Though not required, most egg cartons also contain a "sell-by" date. In USDA-inspected plants, this date can't exceed thirty days beyond the pack date, which is within USDA regulations. Always purchase eggs before their sell-by date.

How long are eggs good after the sell-by date?

Refrigerated raw shell eggs will keep without significant quality loss for about 5 weeks beyond the pack date or about four weeks after you bring them home. An obvious rule to follow is that any egg that looks or smells odd should not be used. If an egg is bad, you will know it. Just crack each egg in a small bowl and smell it—your nose will tell you!

What is the best way to store eggs? Buy refrigerated eggs and store them in the refrigerator as soon as you get home. Eggs should be stored in the refrigerator in their carton to help protect them from absorbing odors and also to help prevent them from drying out and to keep them fresh longer. The shell is a porous membrane, and even under refrigeration, eggs slowly lose carbon dioxide, which enlarges the size of the air cell and causes the yolk to flatten and the white to spread. Finally, store your eggs on the middle or lower shelves of the refrigerator, where the temperature is more constant. The door is the worst place to store eggs because temperature varies widely when the door is opened and closed.

Concerns Eating Raw or Soft Cooked Eggs

The American Egg Board warns against consuming raw or lightly cooked eggs on the grounds that the egg may be contaminated with Salmonella. The risk is greater for those who are pregnant, elderly, or very young and those with medical problems that have impaired their immune systems.

Use only properly refrigerated, clean, unbroken, fresh, grade AA or A eggs. Refrigerate any broken eggs, prepared egg dishes, and other foods if you won't be consuming them within an hour.

For summer outings, don't let your egg dishes sit out for very long. Use beds of ice or coolers to keep cold foods cold (40°F or lower). Eggnog and homemade ice cream should be made with a base of pasteurized custard to ensure safety.

A possible solution for concerns about eating raw or undercooked eggs is the process of pasteurizing eggs right in their shell. Using a patented process, a company called National Pasteurized Eggs Inc. produces pasteurized eggs under the Safest Choice brand, www.safeeggs.com. They accomplish this by using a highly controlled time and hot water process. Liquid pasteurized eggs such as Egg Beaters are another option. Though we are not endorsing either product, it is a solution if you are concerned about eating raw or undercooked eggs.

EGG STORAGE CHART

PRODUCT	REFRIGERATOR	FREEZER
Eggs in the shell	3 to 5 weeks	Do not freeze
Egg whites	2 to 4 days	12 months
Egg yolks	2 to 4 days	Yolks do not freeze well
Egg accidentally frozen in shell	Use immediately after thawing	Keep frozen; refrigerate to thaw
Hard-cooked eggs	1 week	Do not freeze.
Liquid egg substitutes, unopened	10 days or 7 days after thawing	12 months
Liquid egg substitutes, Opened	3 days	Do not freeze.
Casseroles with eggs	3 to 4 days	After baking, 2 to 3 months
Commercial eggnog	3 to 5 days	6 months
Homemade eggnog	2 to 4 days	Do not freeze
Pies: Pumpkin or pecan	3 to 4 days	After baking, 1 to 2 months
Pies: Custard and chiffon	3 to 4 days	Do not freeze
Quiche with filling	3 to 4 days	

Source: USDA 2011

Try a Quail Egg!

Although small, quail eggs contain more protein than a chicken egg, and many more essential vitamins and minerals. Quail eggs do not cause allergic reactions, so eating more quail eggs is a great way to boost your immune system and enjoy a healthier life.

Eggs are so versatile and can be used in both savory and sweet dishes, so that's how I've divided this chapter. The focus is on chicken eggs, which make up almost all of

The Recipes

the bird eggs consumed in America. At farmers' markets, you can also find duck eggs (about twice the size of a chicken egg) and goose eggs. Quail eggs are widely available in Asian markets.

The Perfect Omelette

No French cook has completed his or her apprenticeship until he or she can make a perfect omelette. It seems so easy, but timing and temperature along with a little skill make it something that benefits from practice. What you are shooting for is a moist inside (but not runny) and just barely lightly brown outside (but not dry). Auguste Escoffier described an omelette as "scrambled eggs held together in a coagulated skin." Harold McGee puts it perfectly: "If good scrambled eggs demand patience, a good omelette takes panache—a two- or three-egg omelette cooks in less than a minute." Obligingly, butter bubbles as it heats. Wait until the foam is dying down, but not yet beginning to brown, before adding the eggs to the pan.

Omelettes can be stuffed with all kinds of delicious things, such as cheese, asparagus, crab, mushrooms—you name it, but the eggs, after all, are the stars. The toppings are there to support the perfect storm of silky skin holding billowy curds together. My favorite topping for an omelette is crème fraîche and caviar, whatever you can afford.

Perhaps the most famous and popular omelette in France is one called *omelette aux fines herbes*. It is flavored simply with freshly chopped herbs. Dried herbs are no substitute. If all those listed below are not available, use what you like. The technique described below is the same for all omelettes.

MAKES 1 SERVING
2 or 3 large organic eggs, at room temperature
Salt and freshly ground black pepper to taste

1 tablespoon (14.2g) unsalted butter
1 teaspoon finely chopped fresh parsley
½ teaspoon finely chopped fresh tarragon
1 teaspoon finely sliced chives

Break the eggs into a small bowl, add the salt and pepper and whisk with a fork until well beaten.

Heat an 8-inch (20-cm) nonstick sauté pan over medium heat and add the butter and swirl to melt. Pour in the eggs and swirl them in the pan for 5 to 10 seconds, until they are just beginning to set on the bottom. Gently stir the egg mixture, shaking the pan all the while, with a heat resistant rubber spatula (as if you were going to make scrambled eggs) until very soft curds appear. Swirl the eggs in the pan to make a nice round. Reduce the heat to low to avoid browning. Continue cooking for another 30 seconds or so. The eggs will be set on the bottom, but slightly liquid on top.

Remove the pan from the heat and fold the omelette in half while tilting the pan. Add the herbs (or other fillings), then roll the omelette over itself completely. There are lots of ways to fold an omelette, but the simplest way is to add the filling, fold in half and slide out onto a warm plate or serving platter. Classically, if you are using a filling, you make an incision down the whole length with a knife tip to expose a little of the filling and brush it with a little melted butter—sort of gilding the lily!

Apple, Bacon, and Brie Omelette variation: Saute ½ a small apple, finely chopped, with a pinch of sugar in 1 tablespoon of butter for about 3 minutes. Cook a couple slices of bacon until crisp. Cook the omelette according to the directions above using the filling here.

Spinach and Feta Omelette variation: Rinse and steam 3 cups (90g) of baby spinach. Squeeze out the moisture and chop. Mix the spinach with 2 tablespoons of mixed herbs (such as dill, parsley, and mint) and 3 tablespoons of drained and crumbled feta cheese. Cook the omelette according to the directions above using the filling here.

Omelette Soufflé

This is an adaptation from The Good Cook series *Eggs and Cheese* (Time-Life Books, 1980) that brings together two egg techniques: omelettes and soufflés.

MAKES 1 OR 2 SERVINGS
3 large eggs
1 tablespoon crème fraîche or sour cream

Salt and freshly ground black pepper
¼ cup (25g) grated Parmesan or aged goat cheese
1 tablespoon unsalted butter

Preheat the oven to 350°F. Separate the eggs, putting the whites into a medium bowl and yolks into a small bowl. Add the crème fraîche to the egg yolks, season to taste with salt and pepper, and whisk together. Set aside.

Beat the egg whites with a whisk or electric beater until stiff peaks form. Carefully fold the egg yolk mixture and the cheese into the egg whites and set aside.

Melt the butter in a cast-iron skillet or fry pan over medium heat. Pour the egg mixture into the skillet and spread evenly. Cook the omelette, gently shaking the skillet occasionally, until the bottom is golden, 3 to 4 minutes. Lift the edge of the omelette with a spatula and fold in half. Transfer the skillet to the oven and cook the omelette until the center is just set (it will continue to puff while baking), 3 to 4 minutes. Serve immediately.

Baked Eggs with Onions, Peppers, and Prosciutto

Baked, coddled, and shirred eggs are similar in approach. Coddling generally involves a water bath in some way, either in the shell (which is really the same as soft boiling), or in an egg coddler, a charming little individual serving pot with a lid that is placed in a hot water bath. Shirred and baked eggs are placed in ramekins or *cocottes*, as the French would call them, and generally are cooked without the water bath. The results are pretty similar.

MAKES 6 SERVINGS
2 tablespoons (30mL) olive oil
1 medium onion, peeled and sliced lengthwise
1 large red bell pepper, stemmed, seeded, and
  sliced into thin strips
3 garlic cloves, peeled and thinly sliced
½ small fennel bulb, thinly sliced
½ teaspoon fennel seeds

½ teaspoon dried oregano
Salt and freshly ground black pepper to taste
2 cups (72g) finely sliced young chard, center stems
  discarded
6 thin slices prosciutto
6 large eggs
Freshly grated Parmesan cheese

Preheat the oven to 375°F. Heat the olive oil in a large skillet over medium heat. Add the onion, pepper, and garlic and cook until softened, about 5 minutes. Add the fennel, fennel seeds, oregano, and salt and pepper and cook until the vegetables are softened and just beginning to color. Stir in the chard and cook for a minute or two, until it just begins to wilt.

Line six 6-ounce ramekins with prosciutto. Place the ramekins on a baking sheet, divide the onion mixture among them, and crack 1 egg into each ramekin, preserving whole yolks. Bake until the eggs are set, about 12 minutes. Serve immediately with a little sprinkle of Parmesan on top.

Eggs Baked *En Cocotte* with Mushrooms

Adding some dried mushrooms, such as porcini, makes for a richer mushroom flavor. Soak them in warm water, squeeze dry, chop, and add them to the fresh mushrooms.

MAKES 4 SERVINGS

2 tablespoons (28.4g) unsalted butter, plus more for greasing the ramekins

¾ pound (340g) mixed exotic mushrooms (such as oyster, shiitake, chanterelle, or cremini)

3 tablespoons (30g) finely chopped shallots or green onions

½ pint (1 cup, 240 mL) heavy cream, divided

2 tablespoons (6g) chopped fresh parsley

2 tablespoons (6g) chopped fresh basil

2 to 3 drops of lemon juice

Kosher or sea salt and freshly ground black pepper

4 large eggs

¼ cup (27g) freshly grated Parmesan or Gruyere cheese

Preheat the oven to 375°F. Butter four 1-cup (1-240 mL) ramekins and set them on a baking sheet.

Wipe the mushrooms clean with a damp cloth or towel. Remove and discard the stems of the shiitakes, if using. Chop the mushrooms. You should have about 6 cups.

Heat the butter in a large skillet over medium heat and sauté the mushrooms and shallots until they are lightly browned and any moisture has evaporated, about 6 minutes. Stir in ¾ cup (180mL) of the cream and cook for another couple of minutes or until the mixture has thickened. Stir in the herbs and season to your taste with lemon juice and salt and pepper.

Divide the mushroom mixture among the 4 dishes. Break and carefully tip an egg into each dish and pour the rest of the cream over the eggs. Sprinkle each with a little of the cheese. Bake until the whites are just set, about 10 minutes, and serve at once.

Classic Eggs Benedict

Typically served at brunch (especially on Mother's Day in American restaurants) or breakfast, there are many variations on the theme. Classic Eggs Benedict takes two toasted English muffin halves, tops each with a slice of Canadian bacon, a poached egg, and a big spoonful of hollandaise sauce. According to *The Food Lover's Companion* by Sharon Tyler Herbst (Barron's, 1995), the dish originated at Manhattan's famous Delmonico's Restaurant when regular patrons, Mr. and Mrs. LeGrand Benedict, complained that there was nothing new on the lunch menu.

MAKES 4 SERVINGS

HOLLANDAISE SAUCE

4 egg yolks

2 tablespoons (30mL) lemon juice

1 teaspoon Dijon mustard (optional)

12 tablespoons (1½ sticks/ 172g) unsalted butter, melted

Pinch of cayenne pepper or drops of hot sauce to taste

Salt to taste

EGGS

8 large eggs

2 teaspoons vinegar

4 English muffins, split in half

2 tablespoons (28g) unsalted butter, softened

8 thick slices Canadian bacon

Paprika for garnish (optional)

Finely chopped chives for garnish (optional)

Make the hollandaise sauce: with a double boiler or a metal bowl placed over (but not in) barely simmering water, whisk the yolks, lemon juice and optional mustard together. Gradually whisk in the butter, adding it in a small stream until the sauce is thickened. If it is too thick, whisk in drops of hot water to thin it out. Whisk in cayenne and salt to taste. Keep warm. If the sauce curdles or "breaks," whisk in a tablespoon of cold water or put another egg yolk in a bowl and very slowly whisk it into the broken sauce. Keep warm.

Meanwhile, poach the eggs by filling a 10- to 12-inch skillet ¾ full with water and bring to a boil over high heat. Reduce the heat to medium low and add the vinegar. Break the eggs one by one and carefully slide them into the water around the edge of the skillet, which will help keep the eggs together. Poach for 3 minutes or so or until the eggs are just set. You want the yolks to be runny. Alternately, you can add the eggs, turn off the heat, cover the skillet, and let them sit for 4 to 5 minutes.

Meanwhile, toast the English muffin halves and lightly spread with the butter. In another skillet, heat or fry the bacon.

To serve: Place two muffin halves on a warm plate, top each with the bacon and a poached egg and cover with the hollandaise. Garnish, if you like, with a sprinkle of paprika and some chopped chives.

Asparagus, Red Onion, and Goat Cheese Frittata

The word "frittata" derives from the Italian verb "friggere," or "to fry," and in Italy is generally applied to cooking eggs as the main ingredient with other things in a skillet. The main difference between an omelette and a frittata is that the ingredients of an omelette are gently placed into the beaten eggs as they are cooking in the pan, while the eggs in a frittata are folded over to enclose the fillings and then cooked more slowly so it comes out like a cake. Like so many recipes with eggs, there are endless possibilities, so it's a great place to use all those odds and ends and leftovers in your fridge. In Italy, sometimes before serving lunch or dinner, a small portion of the meal is purposely put aside to include in a frittata the next day.

MAKES 4 TO 6 SERVINGS

1/2 pound (230g) fresh asparagus, tough woody ends discarded and cut into 1/2-inch (13-mm) lengths
1 tablespoon each olive oil and unsalted butter
3/4 cup (120g) diced red onion

3 tablespoons (8g) chopped fresh basil
Kosher or sea salt and freshly ground black pepper
8 large eggs
4 ounces (113g) or so crumbled fresh goat cheese

Bring a pot of salted water to a boil, add the asparagus, and cook until crisp-tender and bright green, 3 to 4 minutes. Drain, cool under cold running water, and pat dry with paper towels.

In a large nonstick skillet, heat the oil and butter over medium heat and add the onions. Cook until the onions are translucent but not browned. Stir in the asparagus and basil and season with salt and pepper.

Meanwhile, in a large bowl, whisk the eggs with a little salt and pepper until blended. Reduce the heat to medium low, and add the eggs to the skillet with the onions, and cook until the eggs are set on the bottom and around the edges, about 4 minutes. With a rubber spatula, lift one side of the frittata so that the raw eggs flow under the set edges. Do this 3 or 4 times so that the eggs are evenly cooked and not runny.

Sprinkle the goat cheese over the top, cover, and cook over low heat until the frittata is set and the cheese is nicely softened, 5 to 7 minutes. Alternately, you can slip the pan under a preheated broiler for a couple of minutes to melt the cheese and brown the top.

To serve: Slide the frittata onto a platter and serve hot, warm, or at room temperature, cut into wedges or small squares.

Bacon and Fontina Strata
with Mushrooms and Sun-Dried Tomato

Stratas are basically savory bread puddings. You don't need to do a lot of prep or planning because they are ideal for using up whatever you have in your kitchen. A strata is also a great make-ahead dish. It tastes best when you make it a day ahead and let the custard soak into the bread overnight before baking.

MAKES 8 SERVINGS

Butter for coating the baking dish

10 slices of your favorite bread, cut $\frac{1}{2}$-inch (13mm) thick

6 to 8 slices bacon, cooked and crumbled

2 cups sliced mushrooms, browned in butter

$\frac{1}{2}$ cup (55g) drained and chopped sun-dried tomatoes in oil

$2\frac{1}{2}$ cups (270g) freshly grated fontina, Gruyere, or other semi-soft cheese

10 large eggs

1 quart (950mL) whole milk or light cream

$\frac{1}{2}$ teaspoon freshly grated nutmeg

1 teaspoon dry mustard

Kosher or sea salt and freshly ground black pepper

Grease a 7 x 9-inch baking dish with butter. Layer half of the bread on the bottom of the buttered baking dish, cutting it to fit snugly. Combine the bacon, mushrooms, and sun-dried tomatoes and spread them evenly over the bread along with half of the cheese. Top with the remaining bread cut to fit snugly.

Whisk the eggs, milk, nutmeg, and mustard together and pour over the strata. Season with salt and pepper to taste. Top with the remaining cheese. Cover and refrigerate for at least 4 hours or overnight.

Preheat the oven to 350°F. Uncover the strata and bake for 60 minutes or until it has puffed a bit and is golden brown on top. Shake the dish a little to check; the center shouldn't shimmy. Tent the dish with foil if the top is browning too quickly. When the strata has finished baking, remove it from the oven and set it on a cooling rack for 10 minutes before serving.

Basic Cheese Soufflé

For some reason, soufflés seem to intimidate many cooks, and they really shouldn't. Up on the ranch in the mountains of Colorado where we lived, I can remember my grandmother making them often, usually for what we called supper. Our evening meal was usually lighter and quicker than dinner, or the main meal of the day, which we ate at noontime.

Soufflés are pretty simple. Traditionally, the soufflé is baked in a straight-sided dish that the French call a charlotte. You can use any ovenproof dish that is straight sided and at least four inches deep, with a capacity of six cups (1.4L)or so. Soufflés are made up of two components: a base that is usually a thick, milk-based white sauce (what the French call béchamel) and whipped egg whites. The latter are folded in just before the mixture is baked in the oven and are what give soufflés their unique texture. This is the one to get started with because it brings together all of the individual techniques for putting a soufflé together.

MAKES 4 TO 6 SERVINGS

4 tablespoons (55g) unsalted butter, divided
2 tablespoons finely and freshly grated Parmesan
   or Asiago cheese
3 tablespoons (24g) all-purpose flour
1 cup (240mL) warm milk or light cream

$\frac{1}{2}$ teaspoon freshly grated nutmeg
Salt and freshly ground black pepper to taste
4 large egg yolks
6 large egg whites
1 cup (108g) finely grated Gruyere, Cheddar, or
   other melting cheese of your choice

With your fingers, lightly rub a tablespoon or so of the butter all around the inside of a charlotte or baking dish. Sprinkle the Parmesan inside the dish and roll the dish around in your hands to lightly coat and knock out extra cheese. Set the dish aside in the refrigerator to chill a bit. (A chilled dish seems to keep the butter in suspension better as the soufflé bakes.)

In a saucepan, melt the remaining butter, add the flour, and stir over moderate heat for 2 to 3 minutes without browning. This step cooks the flour so that it doesn't have a raw "floury" taste. Slowly whisk in the warm milk and bring to a boil. Let the mixture boil for 3 to 4 minutes, stirring constantly. The sauce will be very thick. Stir in the nutmeg and salt and pepper and take off the heat. Whisk a little of this warm base slowly into the egg yolks. This tempers or gradually warms the yolks so that they are less likely to scramble. Beat this mixture back into the rest of the base and set aside.

In a clean bowl with a hand or stand mixer, beat the egg whites just until stiff but still shiny and moist looking, about 3 minutes. Preheat the oven to 375°F.

With a spatula, stir a quarter of the whipped egg whites into the base. Do this quickly. This lightens the mixture so that you can fold in the remaining whites. Scoop the rest of the whites on top and with the spatula, cut into the whites, drag it along the bottom, and bring the sauce mixture over the top. Turn the bowl a quarter of a turn, sprinkle on some of the grated Gruyere, and repeat until the whites, cheese, and sauce are just combined. Here, you are doing everything you can to keep as much air as possible in the whites without deflating them.

Spoon the mixture into the prepared dish, gently smoothing the top, and bake for 25 to 30 minutes, or until the soufflé is puffed and golden brown. (For a firmer soufflé, bake in a 325°F oven for 35 to 40 minutes.) If your oven doesn't have a glass window and you're tempted to peek, don't! Keep the door closed for at least the first 20 minutes so that the soufflé can set! When it is done, serve immediately. To maintain as much of the puff as possible when serving, plunge an upright serving spoon and fork straight down into the center of the soufflé and then pull the crust apart and scoop out a serving.

Spinach or Broccoli Soufflé variation: Stir 1 cup (180g) or so cooked and finely chopped spinach or broccoli into the warm sauce base after the addition of the egg yolks. Cut the grated Gruyere quantity to ½ cup (59g).

Shrimp, Crab, Salmon (smoked or otherwise) Soufflé variation: Sauté 3 tablespoons (30g) of finely chopped shallots or green onion in a little butter or olive oil until soft. Add 3 tablespoons (45 mL) of white wine and continue to cook until the wine is evaporated. Remove from the heat, add ½ to 1 cup (68-136g) finely chopped or diced fish, and stir into warm sauce base after the addition of the egg yolks. Cut the grated Gruyere to ⅓ cup (36g).

Mushroom Soufflé variation: Stir 1 cup (145g) of very finely minced oven dried or sautéed cremini mushrooms into the base before the egg whites are added. Cut the Gruyere to ½ cup (54g).

All soufflés can also be prepared in individual ramekins. Cooking time will be 18 to 20 minutes or so, depending on the mixture.

Egg Drop Soup (Stracciatella)

If you've got a rich, good-tasting stock, one of the simplest and quickest recipes that I can think of is egg drop soup. This approach appears in the cuisines of China and the Mediterranean. It's one of those simple peasant dishes to which you can add anything on hand. I'm doing a Roman version here.

MAKES 6 TO 8 SERVINGS

4 eggs
½ cup (50g) freshly grated Parmesan or pecorino cheese
2 teaspoons (1.89g) freshly ground black pepper
8 cups canned or homemade chicken stock (see page 70)
1 tablespoon finely grated lemon zest
4 cups (120g) lightly packed fresh young spinach, watercress, or arugula leaves, stems removed

With a fork, beat the eggs with the cheese and pepper in a medium bowl until well mixed and set aside.

Bring the chicken stock to a boil in a deep saucepan over high heat. Reduce the heat to medium low and stir in the zest. With a large spoon gently swirl the soup in a circle. Gradually pour the egg mixture into the hot soup to form little shreds.

Divide the spinach among warm bowls and spoon the soup over the top. Serve immediately.

Chinese version: Substitute a teaspoon of hot pepper sesame oil for the cheese in the eggs.

Japanese version: Add thinly sliced shiitake mushrooms to the broth and simmer for 2 to 3 minutes before stirring in the eggs. Omit the cheese from the eggs and add 2 teaspoons each of mirin and soy sauce to the eggs.

Italian Garlic and Bread Soup

This is typical of simple peasant-style soups served all around the Mediterranean. It's also the kind of soup your grandmother might have made when you had a bad cold. You could add almost anything else you'd like to the soup depending on what's in season or what needs to be used up in your refrigerator! A good rich stock is required.

MAKES 6 TO 8 SERVINGS

3 large garlic cloves, peeled

$1/2$ cup (110g) extra-virgin olive oil

Kosher or sea salt and freshly ground black pepper

6 slices crusty Italian bread such as ciabatta

6 whole eggs

6 cups (1.42L) canned or homemade chicken (see page 70) or vegetable stock

$1/2$ cup (120mL) dry Marsala or sherry wine, or to taste

3 cups (90g) lightly packed baby spinach or arugula leaves

$2 1/2$ cups (450g) peeled, seeded, and diced ripe tomatoes

Gremolata (recipe follows)

$1/2$ cup (50g) freshly grated Parmesan or pecorino cheese

Preheat the oven to 400°F. In a blender or mini food processor, purée the garlic cloves and olive oil together and season lightly with salt and pepper. Brush the bread slices on both sides with the olive oil mixture and place them on a baking sheet in a single layer. Bake in the oven until lightly browned, about 5 minutes. Set aside.

Poach the eggs in barely simmering water until the whites are just set, about 4 minutes, and then immediately transfer the eggs to a bowl of ice water to stop the cooking. You can prepare both the toasted bread and the eggs 3 to 4 hours ahead if desired.

In a large pot, heat the stock and wine to boiling and season to taste with salt and pepper. Divide the spinach and tomatoes among individual bowls and place a bread slice on top. Using a slotted spoon, place a poached egg on top of the bread and ladle the hot stock over. Sprinkle the Gremolata and Parmesan over top and serve immediately.

Gremolata

3 tablespoons finely minced poached or toasted garlic (see page 41)

$1/4$ cup (15g) chopped fresh parsley

1 tablespoon chopped fresh mint or basil

2 tablespoons finely grated lemon zest

Combine all ingredients in a medium bowl. This can be done an hour or two ahead.

Quiche Lorraine

Although quiche is now a classic dish of French cuisine, it actually originated in the medieval kingdom of Lothringen, which was under German rule and which the French later renamed Lorraine. The original Quiche Lorraine was an open pie with a filling consisting of an egg and cream custard with smoked bacon. It was only later that cheese was added. The bottom crust was originally made from bread dough, but that has since evolved into a short crust or puff pastry crust that is often baked using a tart pan with a removable bottom.

MAKES 6 TO 8 SERVINGS

PIE SHELL

1 ½ cups (180g) all-purpose flour, plus more for
  dusting
½ teaspoon salt
4 tablespoons (55g) chilled or frozen unsalted butter
3 tablespoons (38.4g) chilled vegetable shortening

FILLING

4 large eggs
1 cup (240mL) whole milk
1 cup (240mL) heavy cream
Kosher or sea salt and freshly ground black pepper
6 slices cooked bacon, crumbled
1 cup (170g) finely chopped onion, cooked in butter
  until soft
1 ½ cups (162g) shredded Gruyère or Gouda cheese
1 10-inch (25-cm) prepared tart or pie shell (recipe
  follows)

For the pie shell, combine the flour, salt, butter, and shortening in a food processor and pulse until you have a mixture that looks like coarse oatmeal, 6 to 8 pulses. Add ¼ cup chilled water (60mL) and pulse 3 or 4 times more. Turn out the dough and gather into a ball.

Roll out the dough with a rolling pin on a lightly floured surface into an approximately 12-inch (30-cm) circle. Gently lift the dough into a 9- or 10-inch (23-to 25-cm) tart pan with a removable bottom or a pie pan (preferably glass). Refrigerate until ready to fill.

Preheat the oven to 375°F.

For the filling, beat the eggs in a bowl until smooth and stir in the milk, cream, and salt and pepper to taste. Scatter the bacon, onions, and cheese over the prepared pie shell. Place the pan on a rimmed baking sheet (in case there is a leak) and pour in the egg mixture.

Bake for 35 to 40 minutes or until the quiche is puffed and just beginning to brown. Serve warm or at room temperature, cut in slices.

Note: You can pour the egg filling into the unbaked shell, or you can prebake the crust, which is generally preferred. Cut a square of foil large enough to cover the bottom and sides of the shell. Line the shell with the foil and weight the foil with a cup or so of dried beans or rice. Bake in a preheated 375°F oven for 20 minutes. Lift the foil and weights from the shell and prick any bubbles with the point of a knife; then bake for 5 minutes more. Transfer to a rack to cool before filling.

Chilaquiles

Chilaquiles are a classic Mexican food that is eaten any time of day. You can add whatever else you want to the mix, such as cooked and crumbled chorizo or other sausage, shredded cooked turkey or chicken, or sautéed sliced mushrooms. If you don't have tortillas, a couple of big handfuls of tortilla or corn chips work as well.

MAKES 4 SERVINGS

Vegetable oil
6 day-old corn tortillas, cut into strips
Kosher or sea salt and freshly ground black pepper
1 small white onion, thinly sliced, about 1 cup (115g)
1 medium poblano pepper, stemmed, seeded, and cut into ½-inch (13-mm) dice

8 large eggs, beaten with a tablespoon or so of water or milk
2 to 3 drops of your favorite hot sauce (optional)
⅓ cup (16g) chopped fresh cilantro
1½ to 2 cups (350 to 400g) Pico de Gallo (recipe follows)
¼ to ½ cup (80 to 160g) crumbled queso fresco or Mexican crema

Add ¼ inch (6mm) of oil to a heavy skillet over medium heat. When the oil is hot, add the tortilla strips and toss with salt and pepper to taste. Continue stirring until the tortilla strips crisp, about 2 minutes. At first they'll soften and then become crispy. Set aside and drain on paper towels. Wipe out skillet with paper towels. (Alternately, you can lightly spray the strips with vegetable oil and bake them in a preheated 375°F oven for 10 minutes or so or until crisp.)

Add 2 tablespoons of oil to the pan. Sauté the onion and poblano over medium heat until they just begin to color, about 5 minutes. Stir in the eggs and reserved tortilla strips and cook, stirring, until the eggs are softly scrambled.

Remove from the heat and season to taste with salt and pepper and hot sauce, if using. Stir in the cilantro. Divide among 4 warm plates and top with salsa and queso fresco or a drizzle of crema or sour cream.

Pico de Gallo

Pico de gallo is a classic fresh salsa in Tex-Mex cooking. It translates to "beak of the rooster" because in Mexico, fresh, chunky salsas are often eaten with the forefinger and the thumb that mimics the pecking action of a roster.

MAKES ABOUT 1¼ CUPS

¾ pound (340g) (2 medium) seeded and diced ripe tomatoes
⅓ cup (53g) diced red onion
1 teaspoon minced, seeded serrano chile, or to taste

1 tablespoon minced fresh garlic
3 tablespoons (8g) chopped fresh cilantro leaves
Drops of lime or lemon juice to taste
Pinch of sugar
1 tablespoon olive oil (optional)
Salt and freshly ground black pepper to taste

Combine all the ingredients and allow flavors to blend for at least 30 minutes before using. Store covered in the refrigerator. For best flavor, eat within 3 days, but it can be stored for as long as 5. Can be easily multiplied.

Classic Deviled Eggs

A pastry bag is helpful here to pipe the mashed egg yolk filling attractively back into the whites. If you don't have a pastry bag, then cut off a corner of a zip-top bag and pipe the filling mixture into the egg whites, overstuffing each hole. You can also use a small scoop that is about the size of the egg white cavity. Finally, you can use two spoons to make a quenelle (go to www.finecooking.com for a tutorial). Slice a little bit of the bottom off of each egg to keep it upright and help prevent it from sliding around the plate.

MAKES 8 SERVINGS

4 hard-cooked eggs
1 tablespoon mayonnaise
1 teaspoon Dijon mustard
1 to 2 drops hot sauce, or to taste
Salt and freshly ground black pepper to taste
2 teaspoons finely chopped chives
Paprika or cayenne pepper

Peel the eggs and slice them in half lengthwise. Remove the yolks, combine them with the mayonnaise, mustard, hot sauce, and salt and pepper in a bowl, and mash with a fork until smooth and creamy. Pipe or spoon equal amounts into the hollow of each egg white half. Sprinkle the chives and a little paprika or cayenne on top. They can be made a couple of hours ahead and refrigerated.

Deviled Eggs with Crab variation: Remove the yolks and mash them with 3 tablespoons mayonnaise, 1 teaspoon Dijon mustard, ½ teaspoon Worcestershire sauce, a pinch of cayenne, 1 teaspoon dry sherry, 5 ounces (141g) crabmeat, salt, pepper, and lemon juice, and garnish with paprika.

Pesto Deviled Eggs variation: Remove the yolks and mash them with 1 tablespoon mayonnaise, 3 tablespoons pesto, a dash of hot sauce, and salt and pepper to taste, and garnish with paprika or cayenne.

Bacon and Smoked Paprika Deviled Eggs variation: Cook 3 thick slices of bacon, drain and crumble. Mix with 1 tablespoon parsley. Remove the egg yolks and mash them with the bacon-parsley mixture, 2 tablespoons mayonnaise, a dash of hot sauce, and salt and pepper to taste, and garnish with smoked paprika.

Frisée Salad
With Poached Eggs and Maple Roasted Bacon

A variation on the classic French bistro salad *frisée aux lardons*. The bacon and eggs can be done ahead. To do the eggs ahead, when they are just set, simply place them in ice water and reheat in simmering water for a few seconds at serving time.

MAKES 4 SERVINGS

8 strips thick-sliced bacon
½ cup (120mL) maple syrup
4 large eggs
2 tablespoons white wine vinegar
1 tablespoon finely chopped shallots

1 tablespoon fresh lemon juice, or to taste
2 teaspoons grainy Dijon mustard
3 tablespoons (50g) extra-virgin olive oil
Kosher salt and freshly ground black pepper
6 gently packed cups (226g) of frisée, torn into
  medium-size pieces

Preheat the oven to 425°F. Separate the bacon, blot dry with paper towels, and coat both sides liberally with the maple syrup. Lay the bacon in a single layer on a sheet pan lined with parchment or a silicon baking mat and cook, turning once, until browned and lacquered, about 12 minutes. Transfer to a lightly oiled plate to cool. Break the bacon slices into quarters.

Prepare the eggs for poaching: Bring a 4-quart (3.8L) saucepan of water to a boil, add the vinegar, and reduce the heat to medium low. Crack each egg into its own ramekin and set aside. (Don't cook the eggs yet.)

In a medium bowl, whisk together the shallots, lemon juice, mustard, and olive oil. Season to taste with salt and pepper. In a large bowl, toss the frisée with the vinaigrette. Divide the frisée and bacon among 4 plates.

In the saucepan, slide the eggs into the water and cook until just firm, about 2 minutes. Using a slotted spoon to drain the eggs, top the salads with an egg and season with salt and pepper. Serve immediately.

Grilled Asparagus Salad
with Pancetta and Fried Egg

Everything can be made ahead for this salad except for the eggs, which take just a couple of minutes.

MAKES 4 SERVINGS

1 pound (450g) asparagus, woody ends discarded

Olive oil

Kosher or sea salt and freshly ground black pepper

6 ounces (170g) pancetta cut ¼-inch (6mm) thick and diced

2 tablespoons (28g) unsalted butter

4 large eggs

1 large head (170g) butter lettuce, washed and dried, leaves torn if large

8 breakfast or other radishes, stemmed and sliced lengthwise

Honey Lemon Vinaigrette (recipe follows)

Brush the asparagus with a little olive oil and season with salt and pepper to taste. On a hot grill or in a ridged grill pan, cook the asparagus until nicely marked but still crisp-tender, about 3 minutes depending on thickness. Set aside.

Cook the pancetta in a heavy sauté pan with a little olive oil over medium heat until nicely browned, 5 minutes or so. Remove with a slotted spoon and drain on paper towels. Wipe out the pan and add the butter. Break the eggs into the pan and cook over moderate heat until the whites are set but the yolks are still a little runny.

Toss the lettuce and radishes with the vinaigrette and arrange on plates along with the asparagus. Top each with an egg and a sprinkling of pancetta and serve immediately with a grinding or two of black pepper.

Honey Lemon Vinaigrette

MAKES 1 GENEROUS CUP

2 tablespoons (20g) finely chopped shallots

6 tablespoons (90mL) seasoned rice vinegar

2 tablespoons (40g) honey

4 tablespoons (60mL) fresh lemon juice

4 tablespoons (55g) olive oil

Salt and freshly ground black pepper to taste

Whisk all the ingredients together and season with salt and pepper. Store covered and refrigerated for up to 3 days.

Wilted Greens
with Hazelnut Oil, Eggs, and Fennel
on Sourdough Toast

This is my favorite variation on the Eggs Benedict theme. The hazelnut oil mimics the "meaty" flavor traditionally achieved by Canadian bacon. The end result is lighter and brighter than the heavy hollandaise-topped original. You can substitute any of the other nut oils that you like. This recipe is quick to prepare and perfect for brunch, lunch, or supper. Maybe I'll go fix it right now!

MAKES 4 SERVINGS

4 large eggs
1 large fennel bulb, about 1 pound (450g)
4 tablespoons (60mL) toasted hazelnut oil, divided
Kosher or sea salt and freshly ground black pepper
4 cups (142g) lightly packed water cress leaves, woody stems discarded (2 large bunches)

4 cups (120g) lightly packed young tender spinach leaves, well washed
1 to 2 tablespoons fresh lemon juice
4 thick slices sourdough bread, lightly toasted
1/4 cup (25g) freshly grated Pecorino or Parmesan cheese

Place the eggs in a small saucepan with enough cold water to cover by at least a 1/2 inch (13mm). Bring to a boil and then reduce the heat and simmer gently for 3 minutes. Drain and cool the eggs under running water. Peel and set aside. The whites should be set but the yolks will still be runny when you cut into them.

Trim the fennel of any dark spots and then cut it in half and remove the core and woody base. Slice lengthwise into paper thin slices (if you have a mandoline or similar tool, this is a great place to use it). Toss the fennel with 2 tablespoons of the oil. Over moderately high heat, sauté the fennel in a large sauté pan, stirring constantly until crisp-tender, about 2 minutes. Season with salt and pepper, set aside, and keep warm.

Add the cress and spinach to the pan and toss them with the remaining 2 tablespoons of the oil. Heat the pan again over moderately high heat and sauté the greens until they just begin to wilt, about 1 minute. Season to taste with salt and pepper and lemon juice.

Place the toasts on individual plates and top with the warm greens, fennel, and eggs. Sprinkle the cheese over the top and serve immediately. As you cut into the eggs, the yolks will run and combine with the rest of the ingredients, making a delicious sauce.

Vanilla Custard Sauce

This classic dessert sauce, called *crème Anglaise* in French, is something everyone should know how to make. It can be flavored endlessly and is the base for the best homemade ice cream you'll ever taste.

MAKES ABOUT 1 1/2 CUPS

1/4 cup (55g) sugar
2 large egg yolks

1 cup (240mL) light cream (half-and-half)
1/4 teaspoon pure vanilla extract

Beat the sugar and egg yolks together until lightly colored, about 2 minutes. Heat the cream and zest together in a small saucepan until steaming but not boiling. Slowly beat the hot cream into the yolk mixture, being careful not to scramble the eggs. Return the mixture to pan and cook over moderate heat, stirring constantly, until the sauce just begins to thicken, about 3 minutes.

Remove from the heat and strain the sauce. Stir in the vanilla. If you are not serving the sauce warm, pour it into a bowl and let it cook, stirring occasionally. Place a sheet of plastic wrap directly on the surface of the sauce and refrigerate up to 3 days.

Lemon variation: Add a tablespoon each of grated lemon zest and juice to the eggs and sugar when beating them together.

Mint variation: Add 1/4 cup (12g) roughly chopped mint leaves and stem to the light cream before heating it.

Ginger variation: Add 2 tablespoons chopped candied ginger to the light cream when heating it. Strain it out or leave it in as you desire.

Lemon Curd

This is a classic filling for tarts, sandwich cookies, and lemon meringue pie, a great topping for fresh fruit, and a great spread for biscuits, crumpets, and just about anything! Use this same recipe to make lime or grapefruit curd.

MAKES ABOUT 3 CUPS

1 tablespoon finely grated lemon zest
1 cup (240mL) fresh lemon juice
1 cup (225g) sugar
4 whole eggs

4 egg yolks
$\frac{1}{4}$ teaspoon salt
6 tablespoons (85g) unsalted butter,
  cut in small bits

Place an inch or two of water in the bottom half of a double boiler or similar vessel and bring to a simmer. In a stainless steel bowl, whisk together everything but the butter. Place the bowl over but not touching the simmering water. With a rubber spatula (preferably) or a whisk, stir constantly until the mixture thickens, about 5 minutes. Be careful not to overcook or the eggs can scramble. Remove from the heat and whisk in the butter. Cover and store, refrigerated, for up to 3 weeks.

Note: Lemon curd is a wonderful filling for a sweet blueberry omelette. Prepare the omelette as described in the basic recipe on page 158. Spread 3 to 4 tablespoons (45-60mL) of lemon curd on the bottom half of the omelette, sprinkle $\frac{1}{4}$ cup (37g) berries on top, fold, and finish the omelette as directed. Place on a plate and dust with powdered sugar.

Chocolate Soufflé

This soufflé is a little denser then traditional versions. Its great attribute, however, is that it can be made ahead and held in the refrigerator for up to a day before baking. Allow a little longer baking time if you are taking it straight from the refrigerator.

MAKES 1 (1½-QUART) OR 8 (6-OUNCE) SOUFFLÉS
3 tablespoons (40g) unsalted butter, divided
¼ cup plus 1 tablespoon sugar (67g)
5 ounces (141g) finely chopped bittersweet chocolate
1 tablespoon all-purpose flour
⅓ cup (80mL) milk

1 teaspoon vanilla
4 eggs, separated
2 teaspoons finely grated orange zest
⅛ teaspoon cream of tartar
Garnish: powdered sugar, purée of strained, lightly sweetened raspberries or blackberries, if desired

Preheat the oven to 375°F. With 1 tablespoon of the butter, lightly butter one large (1½-quart) soufflé or eight (6-ounce) individual soufflé dishes and sprinkle with 1 tablespoon of the sugar, turning the dish(es) to coat evenly. Set the dish(es) in the refrigerator to chill while you make the soufflé mixture.

Place the chocolate in a double boiler and melt over barely simmering water, stirring occasionally, about 2 minutes. (Alternately, you can melt it in the microwave: Place the chocolate in a glass bowl and heat for 1 minute at half power. If necessary, give it 10-second doses at half power until it is just beginning to melt.)

In a separate saucepan, melt the remaining 2 tablespoons of butter, add the flour, and cook and stir over low heat for 3 minutes. Add the milk and whisk until the mixture is smooth and lightly thickened, about 2 minutes. Continue to cook for 5 minutes, until the mixture thickens nicely. Remove from the heat, gently stir in the melted chocolate, vanilla, egg yolks, and zest until thoroughly combined, set aside, and cool to room temperature.

In a separate bowl, beat the egg whites with the cream of tartar until soft peaks form. Sprinkle the remaining ¼ cup sugar in gradually and continue to beat until the whites are stiff but not dry. Stir ¼ of the whites into chocolate mixture to lighten it and then carefully fold in the remaining whites. Pour the mixture into the prepared soufflé dish(es) and place on a baking sheet.

Bake for 30 to 35 minutes if using one large dish or 12 to 14 minutes for individual dishes, until a wooden skewer inserted in the center comes out moist but not gooey. Soufflés will puff and crack before they are done.

Remove from the oven, dust with powdered sugar, and garnish with a spoonful or two of fresh berry purée, if using.

Traditional Eggnog

Eggnog is descended from a hot British drink called posset, which consists of eggs, milk, and ale or wine. The basic recipe for eggnog is eggs beaten with sugar, milk or cream, and some kind of spirit. In the American South, bourbon replaced ale (though nog, the British slang for strong ale, stuck). There is a similar traditional English dessert called Syllabub, which is made with milk, sugar, and wine, straddling the line between drink and liquid dessert. I've used bourbon and brandy here, but you could use either one alone or substitute dark rum.

MAKES 6 SERVINGS
3 cups (10mL) whole milk
7 large eggs
1 cup (225g) sugar
1 pint (2 cups, 475mL) heavy cream

⅓ cup (80mL) bourbon
⅓ cup (80mL) Cognac or other brandy
1 teaspoon vanilla
Freshly grated nutmeg

Bring the milk just to a simmer in a heavy saucepan. Whisk together the eggs and sugar in a large bowl and then add the hot milk in a slow stream, whisking all the time. Pour the mixture into the saucepan and cook over moderately low heat, stirring constantly with a heatproof spatula, until the mixture registers 170°F on an instant-read thermometer, 5 minutes or so.

Pour the custard through a fine-mesh strainer into a large bowl and stir in the cream, bourbon, brandy, and vanilla. Cool completely, uncovered, and then chill, covered, until cold, at least 3 hours and up to 48. The flavor of eggnog improves when it is made a day ahead to allow the alcohol to mellow and the flavors to marry.

Classic Crème Brûlée

Crème brûlée can be flavored endlessly, but this simple classic version is the best, I think.

MAKES 6 SERVINGS
1 pint (2 cups, 475mL) heavy cream
1 (3-inch, 7cm) vanilla bean, split lengthwise,
   or 2 teaspoons vanilla extract

6 large egg yolks
1/2 cup plus 6 tablespoons sugar (200g)
2 teaspoons Grand Marnier or other brandy
   (optional)

Pour the cream into a medium saucepan, scrape the seeds from the vanilla bean into the cream, and add the vanilla pod. Bring the cream just to a simmer over moderate heat. Remove from the heat and let cool to room temperature. Remove the vanilla pod and scrape any remaining seeds into the cream. If using extract instead, add it now.

Preheat the oven to 325°F. In a medium bowl, whisk the egg yolks until pale in color, about 1 minute. Whisk in 1/2 cup of the sugar until dissolved. Gradually whisk in the cream. Stir in the Grand Marnier if using.

Place six 6-ounce ovenproof ramekins in a baking pan. Divide the custard mixture among the dishes. Pour hot water into the pan to come halfway up the sides of the dishes.

Bake in the oven for 35 to 40 minutes, or until the center of each custard still jiggles slightly. Remove from the oven and lift the dishes from the hot water. Let the custard cool, then cover each, and refrigerate for at least 2 hours or up to 2 days.

When ready to serve, place the dishes on a baking sheet. Evenly sprinkle 1 tablespoon of sugar over each ramekin. Using a handheld blowtorch, caramelize the sugar by holding the torch about 4 inches from the surface of each custard and moving the torch to brown and caramelize the sugar evenly. Alternately, preheat the broiler and place the pan about 4 inches from the heat source; watching carefully, broil until the sugar turns golden brown, 1 to 2 minutes.

Jasmine variation: Add 2 rounded teaspoons of jasmine tea leaves to the cream when heating it and use only 1 teaspoon vanilla extract.

Lavender variation: Add 1 teaspoon dried culinary lavender flowers to the cream when heating and use only 1 teaspoon vanilla extract.

TURKEY

Domestication of the turkey began more than two thousand years ago by Aztecs and Mayans in Mexico and Central America. In the early 1500s, Spanish explorers to the Americas found both wild and domesticated varieties. They took them back to Spain, where several European varieties were developed. By 1600, turkeys were found throughout Europe, where they were widely used in celebrations and holiday feasts. American folklore says that the colonists cooked turkey as the main course for the first Thanksgiving, which was celebrated at Plymouth Rock in 1621. This is probably apocryphal, and it is more likely that other birds (such as goose or duck), fish (such as cod), clams, lobsters, and certainly venison made up the main course.

Turkey has become inextricably bound to Thanksgiving, when most of them are harvested and consumed. It all began on October 3, 1789, when George Washington declared a day of Thanksgiving. Ben Franklin wanted the turkey to be our national bird because of its beauty and intelligence, but it lost out to the bald eagle. On October 3, 1863, Abraham Lincoln officially

This male turkey is proud of his caruncle, the red-pink fleshy growth on the head and upper neck.

proclaimed Thanksgiving a national holiday. In 1941, FDR made that day a federal holiday.

Until about the middle of the last century, most of the turkeys eaten on Thanksgiving were what we now call "heritage breeds," including the Standard Bronze, Bourbon Red, White Holland, Narragansett, and Jersey Buff varieties. These turkeys are gorgeous, hardy creatures developed in Europe and America over hundreds of years, and they are rich in flavor. They are the ancestors to the Broad-Breasted White, a breed that arose in the 1960s with the advent of industrial turkey farms. Though related to their heritage ancestors, the

Broad-Breasted White birds bear little resemblance to heritage birds in either taste or texture.

Today, more than 99 percent of the 270 million turkeys sold in America each year are Broad-Breasted Whites and almost all come from factory farms. These birds are bred to be so literally broad-breasted that by the time they are eight weeks old, they are often too "breasty" to walk, much less procreate. Every Broad-Breasted White (BBW) on the market is the product of artificial insemination. They are kept inside in giant flocks, given antibiotics to prevent disease, and fed constantly so that they reach maturity in almost half the time it takes a heritage turkey. The result is bland, mushy meat that we have come to equate with tenderness, but in reality processors often inject the dressed birds with saline solutions and vegetable oils to improve "mouth feel" and keep the voluptuous breasts from drying out. It's no doubt why culinary magazines at Thanksgiving offer up their latest techniques for adding flavor like brining, stuffing flavored butters under the skin, constant basting, and more. It's all aimed at getting the BBWs to taste like something.

Heritage breeds, however, are making a comeback. Heritage birds are leaner and will take less time to cook. Usually they will be done in three-fourths the time of the Broad-Breasted Whites. They have been championed by a group of producers, ranchers, and breeders such as the American Livestock Breeds Association, Slow Food, Local Harvest, and others (see Resources, page 310). Though still a tiny part of the turkeys produced in the United States, they are becoming more readily available. I suggest that next Thanksgiving, you give one a try.

In the recipes that follow I'm assuming the use of the BBWs. The guidelines for selecting a good turkey

A turkey has excellent vision and hearing.

are the same as those for chicken, such as making sure it's organic and free range (see page 22).

Does Eating Turkey Make You Sleepy?

One of the most widely believed food myths is that eating turkey can make you sleepy. This is often used as an excuse not to eat turkey, or a justification for why you may often feel sleepy after a big Christmas or Thanksgiving meal. While this myth isn't true, there is some scientific basis for the belief. Turkey contains an essential amino acid called L-tryptophan, which is a precursor for serotonin, a neurotransmitter that controls mood and regulates sleep. It works only in the absence of other amino acids and on an empty stomach. The actual reason for your drowsiness probably has more to do with the massive caloric intake after the egg nog and wine you've been sipping all morning.

The
Recipes

Turkey Kafta

Kafta is a mixture of ground meat (usually lamb) and spices that is formed into small sausage shapes, skewered, and grilled. They are typical street food in the Middle East. Here, I'm using ground dark meat turkey, but you could use any bird. You will need twelve ten-inch skewers for this recipe. If using wooden ones, be sure to soak them in water for at least thirty minutes before cooking.

MAKES 12 SKEWERS

TZATZIKI

1 medium (about 12 ounces) English or Kirby
  cucumber, peeled
Kosher or sea salt
1 teaspoon finely chopped garlic
1½ cups (420g) Greek-style yogurt
1 tablespoon chopped fresh mint
2 teaspoons chopped fresh dill
1 tablespoon fresh lemon juice, or to taste
Freshly ground black pepper to taste

KAFTA

1 pound (450g) ground turkey leg or thigh meat
3 tablespoons (12g) finely chopped fresh parsley
⅓ cup (50g) finely chopped sun-dried tomatoes
3 tablespoons (23g) Aleppo pepper or pure chili
  powder, such as ancho
½ teaspoon ground allspice
1 teaspoon dried mint
½ teaspoon ground cumin
½ teaspoon ground coriander
¼ teaspoon ground cinnamon
2 tablespoons finely grated lemon zest
⅓ cup very finely chopped onion
Kosher or sea salt and freshly ground black pepper

Prepare the tzatziki ahead of time. Grate the cucumber into a mixing bowl using the medium-sized holes of a box grater. Add a pinch of salt and place in a cheese cloth–lined strainer. Place over a bowl and let drain for a few minutes. Twist and squeeze the cheese cloth to remove as much liquid as you can from the cucumber. Transfer to a bowl and stir in the remaining ingredients. Season to taste with salt and pepper.

Prepare a hot grill (425 to 450°F, 218 to 230°C). In a large bowl, stir all of the ingredients together and season to taste with salt and pepper. Allow the mixture to sit, refrigerated, for at least 30 minutes to allow the flavors to bloom. Pinch off 1 to 2 teaspoons of the sausage and sauté to check the seasoning level; adjust to your taste. Divide the mixture into rounded tablespoon-size balls and form each ball into a log shape on the end of each of 12 skewers. Grill, turning, until lightly charred, about 5 minutes. Serve with tzatziki sauce.

Turkey Tortilla Soup

This is a rendition of the famous soup of the Southwest. I'm using turkey legs here, but you could use the whole legs of any bird. The pork adds deeper flavor to the soup stock.

MAKES 6 SERVINGS

2½ pounds (1.13kg) bone-in, skin-on turkey legs and/or thighs

1 pound (450g) meaty pork bones, such as spare ribs or fresh hocks

1 large onion, peeled and quartered

1 head garlic, halved across the equator (don't peel)

1 tablespoon Mexican oregano

⅓ cup (75g) vegetable oil

4 corn tortillas

Kosher or sea salt and freshly ground black pepper

2 tablespoons chopped canned chipotle chiles in adobo, or to taste

⅔ cup (30g) chopped fresh cilantro, divided

2 medium avocados, peeled, pitted, and cut in large dice

6 ounces (170g) melting cheese (such as shredded mozzarella, Oaxaca, or Jack),

Lime wedges for serving

Put the turkey, pork bones, onion, garlic, and oregano in a large soup pot. Add water to cover (about 12 cups) and bring to a boil over high heat. Reduce the heat to low and simmer, partially covered, until the turkey is very tender, about 1 hour. Be sure to skim the surface of the stock occasionally, as scum will rise to the top. Remove the turkey and pork from the stock and place the meat on a cutting board. When cool enough to handle, shred the turkey using your fingers, discarding the skin and bones. If there is any meat on the pork, do the same. Strain the stock, discarding the solids, and set aside.

Meanwhile, put the vegetable oil in a large skillet over medium heat. When the oil is hot but not smoking, fry 2 of the tortillas (one at a time if necessary), turning once, until crisp and golden, 2 to 3 minutes per tortilla. Drain on paper towels. Cut the 2 remaining tortillas into thin strips and add them to the hot oil, stirring to separate them until they are crisp and golden, 3 minutes or so. Drain on paper towels and lightly salt them while they are still warm. Set aside.

Add 2 cups of the reserved stock to a blender with the chipotles and ⅓ cup of the cilantro. Crumble the 2 whole fried tortillas, add to the blender, and purée until the mixture is smooth, adding more stock as necessary.

Pour the purée and remaining stock back into the pot, bring to a simmer, and cook for a few minutes. Add salt and pepper to taste. Stir in the shredded turkey. Divide the avocados, cheese, and remaining ⅓ cup of cilantro among six bowls. Ladle the soup into the bowls and garnish with the fried tortilla strips. Serve immediately with lime wedges to squeeze over top.

Tortillitas with Turkey

A little-known savory pancake from Spain that makes a delicious little tapas. Any chopped poultry meat could be used here. Serve this with Romesco Sauce.

MAKES 4 TO 6 PANCAKES
TURKEY
1/2 cup (113g) ground dark meat turkey
1/2 teaspoon ground cumin
1/4 teaspoon ground coriander
1/2 teaspoon ground black pepper
Olive oil
Salt

BATTER
1/2 cup (46g) chickpea flour
1/2 cup (60g) all-purpose flour
1/2 teaspoon baking powder
Kosher or sea salt and freshly ground black pepper
1/3 cup (33g) chopped scallions, white and
   green parts
2 tablespoons mixed chopped fresh herbs (such as
   rosemary, parsley, thyme, cilantro)
Romesco Sauce (see page 42)

For the turkey, combine the turkey with the cumin, coriander, and black pepper and mix. Add 1 to 2 tablespoons of olive oil to a small skillet over medium heat and cook the turkey until lightly browned and cooked through, about 3 minutes. Season to your taste with salt and set aside.

For the batter, in a bowl, combine the flours, baking powder, and salt and pepper to taste. Add 1 cup of water and stir to combine; consistency should resemble pancake batter (if batter is too thick, add more water, a tablespoon at a time). Stir in the scallions, cooked turkey and any juices, and the herbs.

Add 1 to 2 tablespoons olive oil to a 9- or 10-inch nonstick skillet over medium-high heat. When the oil is hot, pour one-third of the batter into the center of the pan and tilt to form a pancake, spreading the batter gently with a spatula if necessary.

Cook until the pancake is set around the edges, about 1 minute. Flip the pancake and continue cooking for another couple of minutes, then flip it again and cook for another 30 seconds or so, until it is crisp on the outside but still moist inside. Remove from the pan and serve immediately, cut into wedges, with Romesco on the side to spoon over top. Cook the remaining pancakes in the same way and serve warm.

Italian Wedding Soup

This is a classic soup preparation. If you don't have the cheese rind, you can substitute a quarter cup more of grated cheese.

MAKES 8 SERVINGS

MEATBALLS

1 1/4 pounds (563g) ground dark meat turkey
2/3 cup (30g) fresh white breadcrumbs
2 teaspoons minced garlic
1/4 cup (15g) chopped fresh parsley
1/2 cup (113g) freshly grated pecorino Romano cheese
1/4 cup (25g) freshly grated Parmesan cheese, plus extra for serving
2 tablespoons milk
2 large eggs, lightly beaten
2 teaspoons kosher salt
1 teaspoon freshly ground black pepper
Olive or vegetable oil for frying

SOUP

3 tablespoons (42g) olive oil
2 medium yellow onions, chopped (about 3 cups)
2 large carrots, peeled and diced (about 2 cups)
2 celery stalks, thinly sliced (about 1 cup)
1 (3-inch, 7.6-cm square) piece Parmesan or pecorino cheese rind
12 cups (2.8L) canned or homemade chicken stock (see page 70)
1 1/2 cups (350mL) dry white wine
1 cup (115g) uncooked small pasta, such as stellini or stars
8 ounces (227g) kale, chopped (about 5 cups)
1/4 cup minced fresh dill
Kosher or sea salt and freshly ground black pepper

For the meatballs, combine the turkey, breadcrumbs, garlic, parsley, pecorino, Parmesan, milk, eggs, salt, and pepper in a bowl and gently mix with a fork. Heat 1/4 inch or so of oil in a large, heavy skillet over medium heat. With a teaspoon, drop 1-inch meatballs into the hot oil and cook until brown on all sides and cooked through, about 8 minutes. You may need to do this in a couple of batches. You should have about 40 meatballs. Drain on paper towels and set aside.

For the soup, heat the olive oil in a large heavy-bottomed soup pot over medium heat. Add the onion, carrots, celery, and cheese rind and sauté until the vegetables are softened, about 5 minutes. Add the chicken stock and wine and bring to a boil. Reduce the heat and simmer for 5 to 10 minutes. Add the pasta and kale to the simmering broth and cook until the pasta is just tender, about 5 minutes. Add the dill and meatballs to the soup and simmer for 1 to 2 minutes. Season to taste with salt and pepper. Remove the cheese rind if desired and eat it or save it for another soup. Ladle the soup into warm bowls and sprinkle each serving with extra grated Parmesan.

Turkey Confit

Classic confit is traditionally made with duck or goose legs. The meat is seasoned well, cooked very slowly in its own fat, and then chilled to "cure" and develop flavor. When removed from the fat, a marvelous transformation occurs. The meat has a deep rich flavor and a silky texture that literally melts in your mouth. It's really very simple to do. Because turkey is much leaner than duck or goose, you'll have to add fat to make the dish. Happily, olive oil works fine and tastes great. The key is to make sure not to brown the meat as it's cooking in the oil. What to do with the oil after using the confit? It's fantastic! It picks up all the flavor of the bird and seasonings. Simply strain it and keep it refrigerated. Then use it the next time you sauté potatoes, eggs, or almost anything, to add delicious flavor.

MAKES ABOUT 2 POUNDS MEAT
PLUS LOTS OF DELICIOUS FAT

1 teaspoon rubbed sage
2 teaspoons dried thyme
1 medium bay leaf, crumbled
3 to 3½ pounds (1.35–1.58kg) bone-in, skin-on
   turkey thighs (or legs and wings)

2 tablespoons kosher or sea salt
2 teaspoons freshly ground black pepper
5 whole cloves
5 large garlic cloves, peeled
2 quarts (1.9L) extra-virgin olive oil

In a spice grinder, finely grind the sage, thyme, and bay leaf. Rub the turkey with the herbs and season with the salt and black pepper. Poke a clove into each of the garlic cloves and nestle them into the turkey thighs. Chill for at least 6 hours or overnight, uncovered.

Remove the turkey from the refrigerator and quickly rinse off most of the salt and seasonings. Pat dry with paper towels. Reserve the clove-studded garlic.

Place the thighs in a deep ovenproof saucepan or Dutch oven just large enough to hold them in a single layer along with the garlic. Cover with the olive oil and slowly heat the oil over medium until a few bubbles begin to appear. You'll want to pay attention for the first fifteen minutes or so until you stabilize the temperature at around 190°F on an instant-read thermometer.

You can now cook the turkey, covered, on top of the stove or in a preheated 225°F oven, checking to make sure that the oil stays around 200°F. Cook, turning once or twice, for about 2½ hours or until the meat is very tender but not falling off the bone.

Gently place the meat in a container and pour oil over it so that the meat is completely covered. Cover and store in the refrigerator for at least 3 days and up to 2 weeks before using. Though confit can be used immediately, it really benefits from a mellowing in the refrigerator for a few days. Don't forget to save and use the delicious oil!

Rachael Sandwich

A Reuben, as you probably remember, is corned beef on grilled rye with sauerkraut and Swiss cheese. Though I like corned beef, it's nice to change it up with this version using turkey breast. It's one of my favorites, tryptophan notwithstanding. There are, of course, lots of variations.

MAKES 1 SANDWICH
RUSSIAN DRESSING
1/4 cup (60g) mayonnaise
1/4 cup (60g) sour cream
2 tablespoons ketchup
2 tablespoons prepared chili sauce, such as Heinz
1 tablespoon Worcestershire sauce
2 teaspoons lemon juice
1 tablespoon horseradish
Kosher or sea salt and freshly ground black pepper

SANDWICH
2 slices rye, whole grain, or pumpernickel bread
1 tablespoon Russian dressing
1/3 pound (150g) sliced roasted turkey
1/4 cup (40g) coleslaw or drained and rinsed sauerkraut
2 slices Swiss cheese
2 tablespoons softened unsalted butter or olive oil

To make the Russian dressing, combine all of the ingredients and adjust the seasonings to taste. (Makes about 3/4 cup.)

Assemble the sandwich by spreading one side of each bread slice with the dressing. Layer the turkey, coleslaw, and cheese on one of the dressed sides. Cover with the remaining bread slice, dressing side down. Spread top bread slice evenly with half the softened butter. Heat a skillet over moderate heat and place the buttered side down in the skillet. Spread up-facing side with remaining butter. Cover; grill slowly on each side until golden brown. Serve hot or at room temperature.

Deep-Frying Turkey

Most of us have heard about deep-frying turkey, which originated in the South and is often called "Cajun Fried Turkey." When I finally tried it, I have to admit the results were outstanding. The turkey was crisp, moist, not greasy and took a whole lot less time to cook. However, I must say that having a big pot of hot bubbling fat over an open flame can be risky. Underwriters Laboratory (UL) notes that an overheated turkey fryer can explode. And, if the oil ignites, it can become what they describe as "a vertical flame thrower." A number of homes and other buildings (such as garages) are destroyed each year due to the unsafe use of a turkey fryer. UL has refused to list turkey fryers as safe. They have a very graphic video on YouTube that shows the dangers. There is another option, however, and to be completely transparent, I have to say that I have no connection with this product or company: Char-Broil, *www.charbroil.com*. The company makes a product called "The Big Easy," a propane-powered infrared roaster oven that gives you foods that look and taste like they were fried. Anything you can lower into the cooking chamber can be cooked quickly (turkey at about 10 minutes a pound). It's also great for chicken and other larger birds.

Hot Brown

If you have ever lived in or near Louisville, Kentucky, then you'll know about this famous hot turkey sandwich, which originated in the Brown Hotel in downtown Louisville. This recipe comes from Beverly Swetnam, whose grandfather got the original recipe from Chef Fred K. Schmidt, who created the sandwich in 1926. She notes that "Chef Schmidt created this as a late-night menu item to serve guests that had been out late drinking and dancing. Something different than ham, bacon, and eggs. You can find The Hot Brown on almost every menu in restaurants all over Kentucky. Everyone has their own version."

MAKES 4 SANDWICHES
SAUCE
¼ pound (1 stick) unsalted butter
6 tablespoons (47g) all-purpose flour
2 cups (475mL) canned or homemade chicken stock (see page 70)
2 cups (475mL) milk or half-and-half
Kosher or sea salt and white pepper
1 cup (100g) freshly grated Romanocheese, divided

SANDWICH
4 slices good bread, toasted
12 ounces (340g) sliced turkey
4 cups (950mL) sauce
Paprika
8 slices half-cooked bacon

To make the sauce, melt the butter in a saucepan over medium heat and then whisk in the flour to make a roux. Do not brown. In a medium saucepan, heat the broth and milk just to the boiling point. Whisk the hot milk mixture into the roux, beating vigorously with a wire whisk until the sauce thickens, about 4 minutes. Season to taste with salt and white pepper and stir in half of the cheese. Simmer and stir until the cheese melts, about 2 minutes.

To make the Hot Brown, preheat the oven to 375°F. Trim the toast and place the slices on 4 individual ovenproof platters. Arrange turkey slices over the toast and divide the sauce over each serving, covering the turkey and toast completely. Sprinkle with the remaining grated Romano cheese and dust with paprika. Place two slices of bacon in an X pattern on top of each serving. Place the plates in the oven for 12 minutes or until bubbly. Serve immediately.

Turkey Tetrazzini

This dish purportedly was named for Luisa Tetrazzini, an Italian soprano who was popular in America in the early 1900s. Beautifully plump, she supposedly once said, "I must not diet. If I diet my face sag." She loved rich pasta with chicken or turkey and mushrooms, and this dish was created for her by an unknown chef. All kinds of variations exist, including with peas, toasted slivered almonds, and more. This is a wonderful dish to make with leftover Thanksgiving turkey. Chicken can be substituted for the turkey.

MAKES 4 TO 6 SERVINGS

4 cups (about 12 ounces, 340g) sliced button or cremini mushrooms

6 tablespoons (85g) unsalted butter, divided

2 tablespoons all-purpose flour

2 cups (475mL) canned or homemade turkey or chicken stock (see page 70)

1/2 pint (1 cup, 240mL) heavy cream

3 to 4 tablespoons (45 to 75mL) medium-dry sherry, such as amontillado

1/4 teaspoon freshly grated nutmeg

Kosher or sea salt and freshly ground black pepper

1/2 pound (230g) dry cavatelli or pennette pasta

3 to 4 cups (500 to 680g) chopped or shredded cooked turkey

1/2 cup (50g) freshly grated Parmesan or other hard grating cheese

1/3 cup (15g) dry breadcrumbs, preferably panko

Sauté the mushrooms in 2 tablespoons of the butter in a heavy 4-quart saucepan until lightly browned and all liquid has evaporated, about 5 minutes. Set the pan and mushrooms aside.

Melt 3 tablespoons of the butter in a small saucepan over medium heat. Add the flour and cook, stirring, for 2 to 3 minutes to make a roux. Gradually whisk in the stock, cream, and sherry. Bring the sauce to a boil and then reduce the heat to a simmer and cook for 5 minutes, whisking the whole time. Stir in the nutmeg and season to taste with salt and pepper.

Meanwhile, cook the pasta in boiling salted water until al dente, about 9 minutes (or according to package directions). Drain well. Grease an 8-cup baking dish or casserole. Preheat the oven to 375°F.

In a medium bowl combine half the sauce with the turkey, and in another bowl combine the other half with the mushrooms and the pasta. Transfer the pasta mixture to the prepared baking dish or casserole and make a well in the center. Spoon the turkey mixture into the well.

Combine the Parmesan with the bread crumbs and sprinkle evenly over the top of the casserole along with the remaining tablespoon of butter cut into small bits. Bake for 30 minutes or so or until it is bubbling and the top is lightly golden brown.

Turkey Piccata

This quick, classic Italian recipe could be done with any poultry breast. Veal piccata, done similarly, was one of the most famous dishes in Italian restaurants in the 1950s. Unscrupulous chefs and restaurant owners sometimes substituted inexpensive turkey breast for expensive veal since the two are so similar when cooked. We don't see veal piccata so much now since questionable husbandry practices made this meat a controversial choice a number of years ago.

MAKES 6 SERVINGS

2 pounds (900g) skinless turkey breast, sliced into 6 cutlets
Kosher salt and freshly ground black pepper
½ cup (60g) all-purpose flour

2 tablespoons olive oil
4 tablespoons (57g) unsalted butter, divided
3 tablespoons (45mL) fresh lemon juice
2 tablespoons drained capers
1 tablespoon chopped chives
2 tablespoons chopped fresh parsley

Cover the cutlets with a piece of plastic wrap and, using a meat pounder or the bottom of a small heavy skillet or saucepan, flatten each to an even ¼-inch thickness. Sprinkle the turkey on both sides generously with salt and pepper. Put the flour in a shallow bowl. Dredge each cutlet in the flour and shake off any excess.

In a large sauté pan over medium-high heat, heat the oil and 2 tablespoons of the butter. When the foaming subsides, add the turkey and cook until golden brown on one side, 2 to 3 minutes. Turn and brown the other side, 1 to 2 minutes. When done, remove the turkey cutlets from the pan, sprinkle with a little more salt and pepper, and set aside on a plate.

Remove the pan from the heat and whisk in the lemon juice, capers, and chives, scraping up any brown bits and pieces left on the bottom. Whisk in the remaining 2 tablespoons of butter.

Return the turkey to the pan along with any juices, place the pan over medium heat, and warm gently for 30 seconds or so. Place the cutlets on a warm serving platter, top with the sauce and the parsley, and serve immediately.

Turkey Picadillo Tacos

Picadillo roughly translates to "mincemeat" in Spanish. Picadillo is traditionally made with beef or pork, but it can also be made with turkey. Usually made with tomatoes and served with rice it's also delicious as a filling for tacos, savory pastries such as empanadas, or even as an appetizer served with chips and guacamole.

MAKES 6 SERVINGS

4 tablespoons (55g) olive oil, divided

1 1/2 pounds (680g) ground dark meat turkey

1 large onion, chopped

3 garlic cloves, finely minced

1 large poblano chile, cut in 1/4-inch (6-mm) dice (about 1 1/2 cups, 115g)

1 tablespoon ancho chili powder

2 teaspoons ground cumin

1 teaspoon ground cinnamon

1/4 teaspoon ground cloves

1/2 cup (120mL) red wine, plus additional as needed

1 (15-ounce, 424g) can diced tomatoes

1/2 cup (120mL) golden raisins, plumped in hot water and drained

10 pitted green olives, slivered (about 1/4 cup, 27g)

Salt and freshly ground black pepper to taste

12 flour or corn tortillas

Accompaniments: cilantro sprigs, shredded cabbage, sliced radishes, lime wedges, sliced avocados, queso fresco or crema

Heat 2 tablespoons of the olive oil in a large skillet. Add the ground turkey and brown over high heat. Set aside. Heat the remaining olive oil in the skillet and add the onion, garlic, and poblano and cook for 10 minutes, stirring occasionally, over moderate heat.

Return the turkey and its juices to the pan along with the ancho chili powder, cumin, cinnamon, cloves, wine, tomatoes, raisins, and olives. Reduce the heat and simmer, uncovered, for about 15 minutes. If too dry, add a little red wine, a bit at a time. Season to taste with salt and pepper.

Spoon warm picadillo into fresh corn tortillas and top with any or all of the accompaniments.

Spice-Rubbed Grilled Turkey Tenderloins
with Summer Succotash Salad

Note that you'll need to make the succotash salad ahead for this recipe.

MAKES 4 SERVINGS

2 tablespoons brown sugar
1 teaspoon salt
1 teaspoon ground cumin
Pinch cayenne pepper

$1/8$ teaspoon ground ginger
$1/8$ teaspoon ground coriander
$1 1/2$ pounds (680g) turkey tenderloin
2 tablespoons (28g) olive oil

In a small bowl, combine the brown sugar, salt, cumin, cayenne, ginger, and coriander and mix well. Brush the turkey tenderloin with olive oil and rub with the brown sugar mixture.

Prepare a grill to 350°F to 400°F (medium-high heat). When it is hot, place the turkey on the grill, cover with the lid, and cook for 8 minutes on each side or until a meat thermometer inserted into the thickest portion registers 165°F. Let it stand at least 5 minutes before slicing and serving.

Summer Succotash Salad

Succotash has many variations depending on where you are from, but its basic components are beans and corn.

MAKES 6 SERVINGS

2 tablespoons (20g) finely chopped shallot
4 tablespoons (60mL) lemon juice, plus more to
   taste
$3/4$ teaspoon kosher or sea salt
10 tablespoons (140g) fruity extra-virgin olive oil,
   divided
2 cups (226g) diced summer squash

1 cup (150g) diced red onion
3 cups (600g) fresh corn kernels (from 4 large ears)
$1 1/2$ cups (177g) cooked fresh or frozen shelling
   beans, or edamame
$1 1/2$ cups (237g) cherry or grape tomatoes, halved
$1/4$ cup (12g) chopped fresh basil
2 tablespoons chopped fresh chives
Freshly ground pepper

In a small bowl, combine the shallot, lemon juice, and salt and let sit for a few minutes. Whisk in 6 tablespoons of the olive oil and season the vinaigrette to taste.

In a sauté pan over medium-high heat, add 2 tablespoons of the olive oil and sauté the squash and onion until they just begin to soften and lightly colored, about 3 minutes. Set aside to cool. Add another 2 tablespoons of oil to the pan and then add the corn and cook quickly until lightly colored and tender, about 3 minutes. Set aside to cool with the squash.

In a large bowl, add the cooled cooked vegetables along with the shell beans, tomatoes, basil, and chives and toss gently with the vinaigrette. Season to taste with salt, pepper, and additional lemon juice if desired. Can be made ahead and stored in the refrigerator for up to 2 days. Bring back to room temperature before serving.

Turkey Tenderloin
with Wild Mushrooms, Pancetta, and Spinach

Turkey tenderloins are the best choice for making uniform cutlets. Although they vary in size according to the breast they accompany, you'll usually find them in the twelve to fourteen-ounce range. Wondra flour, suggested below, is great for lightly coating foods that are going to be sautéed. It's very fine and browns quickly, but all-purpose flour will work if that's all you have.

MAKES 6 SERVINGS

1 (1½-pound, 680g) turkey tenderloin
½ cup (60g) Wondra flour
Kosher salt and freshly ground black pepper
½ teaspoon smoked or regular paprika
4 tablespoons (55g) olive oil, divided
3 ounces (84g) pancetta, cut into a small dice (about ½ cup)

1 pound (450g) cremini mushrooms, stems trimmed and sliced ¼-inch (6-mm) thick
1 teaspoon coarsely chopped fresh thyme leaves
¼ cup (60mL) Marsala wine
1 tablespoon white wine vinegar
½ cup (120mL) heavy cream
2 tablespoons unsalted butter
10 cups (500g) gently packed baby spinach

Cut the tenderloin into 6 cutlets of the same size. Gently flatten the cutlets with a rolling pin or the bottom of a heavy skillet. Combine the flour, salt and pepper to taste, and paprika in a shallow bowl. Lightly flour the cutlets on both sides and set aside.

Heat 2 tablespoons of the olive oil in a large sauté pan over medium heat. Add the pancetta and cook till crisp and browned, about 8 minutes. Using a slotted spoon, remove the pancetta to paper towels to drain, leaving the fat in the pan.

Increase the heat to high; add the mushrooms and thyme and cook, stirring occasionally, until the mushrooms are golden brown, about 8 minutes. Add the wine and vinegar and scrape up any brown bits on the bottom of the pan. Reduce the heat to low, stir in the cream, and cook until the sauce thickens nicely, about 2 minutes. Add the pancetta and stir to combine. Season to taste with salt and pepper. Set aside and keep warm.

Wipe out the pan and add the butter and 1 tablespoon of the olive oil and heat over moderate heat. Sauté the turkey cutlets until golden brown on each side, about 4 minutes total depending on thickness. You may have to do this in batches.

Wipe out the pan, add the remaining 1 tablespoon of olive oil and, over moderately high heat, wilt the spinach briefly, seasoning to taste with salt and pepper.

To serve: Place the turkey on warm plates. Top with spinach and then the mushroom mixture and serve immediately.

Pan-Seared Turkey Breast
with White Wine, Mustard, and Crème Fraîche Sauce

This is a simple recipe based on the classic French pan sauce technique (see page 42). You could substitute some crushed green peppercorns for the mustard and any fresh aromatic herb for the tarragon.

MAKES 4 SERVINGS

2 tablespoons olive oil
2 tablespoons butter
1 1/4 to 1 1/2 pounds (563 to 680g) skinless turkey breast or tenderloin, cut in 4 cutlets
Kosher or sea salt and freshly ground black pepper
2 tablespoons finely chopped shallots

1/2 cup (120mL) dry white wine, such as sauvignon blanc
1/2 cup (120mL) canned or homemade turkey or chicken stock (see page 70)
2 teaspoons grainy Dijon mustard
2/3 cup (160g) crème fraîche, preferably Kendall Farms
2 teaspoons chopped fresh tarragon

Heat the oil and butter in a large sauté pan over moderately high heat. Add the turkey, season with salt and pepper, and cook on both sides until the turkey is golden and just cooked through. Transfer the turkey to a plate, set aside, and keep warm tented with foil.

Add the shallots to the pan and cook over moderate heat until softened but not brown. Add the wine, stock, and mustard and cook for 2 to 3 minutes, until the liquid is reduced by half. Whisk in the crème fraîche and tarragon along with any juices from the turkey. Season to taste with salt and pepper and serve on warm plates topped with the sauce.

Crème Fraîche

Crème fraîche ("fresh cream") is matured, thickened cream with a tangy flavor and velvety texture. Its great virtue is that it doesn't separate like sour cream will when heated. The thickness of crème fraîche can range from that of commercial sour cream to almost as solid as room-temperature margarine. In France, where crème fraîche is a specialty, the cream is unpasteurized and therefore contains the bacteria necessary to thicken it naturally. In America, where all commercial cream is pasteurized, fermenting or culturing agents are added.

To make your own (it may not be quite as stable as a commercial brand when heated): Combine 2 cups of heavy cream and 1 cup of cultured sour cream or 1/2 a cup of cultured buttermilk in a deep saucepan. Warm gently to about 90°F (barely warm to the touch). Remove from the heat and pour into a clean jar. Cover the opening with a clean tea towel or cheesecloth and allow the mixture to sit at room temperature (75°F to 80°F) for 6 to 8 hours or overnight, until the cream is very thick. Stir it gently, cover, and refrigerate for up to 2 weeks. The crème fraîche will become more tart as it ages.

Turkey and Poblano Chili

Other birds could be substituted here.

MAKES 4 TO 6 SERVINGS

3 tablespoons olive oil

2 pounds(900g) boneless, skinless turkey legs and/or thighs cut into 1-inch cubes

2 large white onions, chopped (about 2 cups, 300g)

8 garlic cloves, chopped (2 tablespoons)

1 teaspoon fennel seed

1 tablespoon ground cumin

2 teaspoons fresh oregano, preferably Mexican

¼ teaspoon ground cinnamon

Kosher or sea salt and freshly ground black pepper

1 (28-ounce, 784g) can petite diced tomatoes, with juice

2 medium poblano peppers, charred, peeled (see Roasting and Peeling Peppers, page 209), and chopped (about 2 cups, 280g)

3 cups (700mL) canned or homemade turkey or chicken stock (see page 70)

Cilantro rice (recipe follows)

In a large Dutch oven or soup pot, heat the oil over medium-high heat. Add the turkey and cook, stirring occasionally, until it is just beginning to brown, about 5 minutes. Transfer the turkey to a platter, add the onion and garlic, and cook until the onion is translucent, about 5 minutes. Add the fennel, cumin, oregano, and cinnamon and cook, stirring, for another minute or so. Season lightly with salt and pepper.

Add the tomatoes, poblanos, and turkey stock and simmer for 5 to 8 minutes to thicken the mixture. Adjust seasonings to taste and serve over hot cilantro rice.

Cilantro Rice

1 tablespoon olive oil

2 teaspoons chopped garlic

1 cup (230g) fragrant rice such as basmati or jasmine

1¾ to 2 cups (420 to 475mL) canned or homemade turkey or chicken stock (see page 70)

Kosher or sea salt and freshly ground black pepper

Zest and juice from 1 large lime

½ cup (8g) chopped cilantro

Add the oil to a saucepan over medium heat. Add the garlic and rice and sauté for a couple of minutes, stirring frequently. Add the turkey stock, salt and pepper to taste, and lime zest and bring to a boil. Reduce the heat, cover, and cook on low for 15 minutes or until the rice has absorbed all the liquid. When the rice is done, stir in the lime juice and the cilantro. Serve immediately.

Note: If you are using regular long grain rice, follow the cooking directions on the package regarding the amount of liquid to use and the cooking time.

Turkey Saltimbocca
with Lemon Egg Sauce and Butter-Braised Spinach

The literal translation of saltimbocca is "jump in the mouth." This is an interesting approach to the holiday turkey that can be done relatively quickly and makes a great presentation. I've poached the turkey here, but you could also slowly sauté the turkey rolls (without the plastic wrap of course) as an alternative. The Lemon Egg Sauce here is based on the Greek *avgolemono* soup.

MAKES 4 SERVINGS

2 (12-ounce, 340g) turkey tenderloins
8 thin slices prosciutto
8 large fresh sage leaves
4 ounces (113g) smoked mozzarella, sliced as thinly as possible

2 tablespoons olive oil
16 cherry or grape tomatoes
Kosher or sea salt and freshly ground black pepper
Butter Braised Spinach (recipe follows)
Lemon Egg Sauce (recipe follows)
Fresh sage or mint sprigs

Butterfly the tenderloins and gently pound out until approximately ¼ inch thick. Place even layers of prosciutto, sage leaves, and smoked mozzarella on each cutlet, leaving a ½-inch border all around. Place each cutlet on a square of plastic wrap and roll up tightly lengthwise to form a sausage shape. Twist the ends tightly and tie with kitchen twine.

Place the rolls in simmering water and poach for 20 minutes to cook the meat through (160°F on an instant-read thermometer). Remove the rolls from the water, unwrap and discard the plastic, and slice into medallions.

In a small sauté pan, heat the oil over moderately high heat and add the tomatoes. Cook for 1 to 2 minutes or until they are just beginning to collapse. Season to taste with salt and pepper.

To serve: Place the spinach on warm plates, arrange the medallions on top, and ladle the sauce around. Garnish with tomatoes and herb sprigs and serve immediately.

Butter Braised Spinach

1 large bunch spinach
2 tablespoons butter
1 tablespoon minced shallots or green onions

Pinch of fresh grated nutmeg
Kosher or sea salt and freshly ground black pepper to taste

Wash the spinach thoroughly and remove thick stems. Heat the butter in a sauté pan and sauté the shallots until they are soft but not brown, about 2 minutes. Turn up the heat and add the spinach all at once.

Stir and cook for a minute or two, until the spinach is just wilted. Remove from the heat and season with nutmeg and salt and pepper. A nice little addition here would be a tablespoon or two of crumbled goat cheese stirred into the spinach at the last moment.

Lemon Egg Sauce

MAKES ABOUT 1 CUP

1½ cups (360mL) canned or homemade chicken stock (see page 70)

⅓ cup (80mL) dry white wine

1 teaspoon cornstarch softened in 2 tablespoons stock, wine, or water

2 large egg yolks

3 tablespoons (45mL) fresh lemon juice, or to taste

3 tablespoons (45mL) heavy cream (optional)

1 teaspoon finely grated lemon zest

Kosher or sea salt and freshly ground white pepper

1 tablespoon minced chives

Bring the stock and wine to a boil in a small saucepan and reduce by half, about 4 minutes. In a separate bowl, whisk together the cornstarch, eggs, lemon juice, cream, and zest. Slowly whisk the reduced stock into the egg mixture, being careful not to scramble the eggs. Return the mixture to the saucepan, place over moderate heat, and cook, stirring constantly, until sauce thickens, about 2 minutes. Immediately strain, season to taste with salt and pepper and additional lemon juice if desired, and stir in the chives just before serving.

Pesto-Stuffed Turkey Breast

You could use a traditional pesto (see page 40) or the pistachio pesto that I'm suggesting here. Some finely chopped and sautéed mushrooms would also make a nice addition. Note that I suggest chilling the prepared breast overnight before cooking if you have time.

MAKES 8 TO 10 SERVINGS
PISTACHIO PESTO
1½ cups (50g) packed fresh basil leaves
⅔ cup (82g) chopped unsalted and lightly toasted pistachios
⅓ to ½ cup (80 to 120mL) extra-virgin olive oil
1 tablespoon poached or toasted garlic
3 tablespoons (15g) freshly grated Parmesan cheese
2 tablespoons chopped fresh mint
Zest and juice of 1 small lemon
Kosher or sea salt and freshly ground black pepper to taste

TURKEY
1 (4- to 5-pound, 1.8 to 2.25kg) skin-on, boneless turkey breast
Kosher or sea salt and freshly ground black pepper
Olive oil
⅓ cup (20g) finely chopped fresh parsley
2 tablespoons finely chopped poached garlic (see page 41)
3 tablespoons finely grated lemon zest
¼ pound (1 stick, 113g) unsalted butter, melted

To make the pistachio pesto, blanch the basil in boiling salted water for 3 seconds, drain immediately, and plunge into cold water to stop the cooking and preserve the green color. With your hands, squeeze as much of the water as you can from the basil. Chop it roughly, add it and the rest of the pesto ingredients to a blender or food processor, and purée, scraping down the sides, about 2 minutes. The mixture should be thick, so use a minimum amount of olive oil. Season to taste with salt and pepper.

For the turkey, arrange the turkey skin side down on a cutting board. Remove the tenderloins and reserve for another use. Make a lengthwise cut about ¾ inch deep down the middle of each breast. Be careful not to cut all the way through. Cover the breasts with plastic wrap. Using the smooth side of a meat mallet or the bottom of a heavy skillet, gently pound the breasts evenly to 1½-inch thickness. Season lightly with salt and pepper and smear the pesto over the breasts, leaving a 1-inch border around the edges.

Starting with one long side of each breast, tightly roll into a cylinder with the skin facing out. Tie the breast at 1-inch intervals with kitchen twine and then tie the length of the breast with twine to secure it. The objective here is to create uniform log shape so that the breast will cook evenly. Rub the exterior of the breast with olive oil and season with salt and pepper. Combine the parsley, garlic, and lemon zest in a small bowl and sprinkle evenly over the breast. Wrap the breast in plastic wrap and chill for at least an hour and preferably overnight.

Preheat the oven to 375°F. Unwrap the turkey and discard the plastic. Line a rimmed baking sheet with foil and set a rack inside the baking sheet. Place the turkey on the rack and bake for 1 to 1¼ hours, basting the turkey with the butter and turning every 20 minutes or so. The thickest part of the turkey should register 145°F on an instant-read thermometer. Increase the heat to 500°F and continue cooking, turning once, until the turkey is nicely browned, about 10 minutes more. Transfer the turkey to a serving platter and let it rest for at least 15 minutes, tented loosely with foil. Remove the twine and slice the turkey crosswise into ½-inch slices to serve.

Turkey Mole

Mole recipes can include a ton of ingredients. Here is one that is a little simpler but still has great flavor.

MAKES 6 TO 8 SERVINGS

12 dried ancho chiles

1 (6- to 8-pound, 2.7 to 3.6kg) turkey, cut into serving pieces

3 tablespoons vegetable oil

2 medium onions, chopped

4 large garlic cloves, peeled and chopped (about 2 tablespoons)

1 teaspoon fennel seeds

2 tablespoons sesame seeds, divided

1 day-old tortilla, roughly chopped

1 pound (450g) tomatoes, seeded and chopped

3/4 cup (109g) toasted blanched almonds

2/3 cup (96g) raisins

1/2 teaspoon ground cloves

1 teaspoon ground cinnamon

1 tablespoon ground coriander seeds

1 teaspoon ground black pepper

3 ounces (84g) Mexican chocolate (such as Ibarra), chopped

Salt to taste

Fresh lime juice

Fresh tortillas, queso fresco, and cilantro sprigs, for serving

Toast the chiles in a dry frying pan over medium heat until puffed and fragrant, about 30 seconds. Be careful not to burn them or they will be bitter. Tear off the stems, shake out the seeds, and tear the peppers into pieces. Put them into a bowl with hot water to cover and soak for 30 minutes. Drain and set aside.

Put the turkey pieces into a large, heavy pan, cover with cold, salted water, and simmer very gently, covered, for 1 hour. Drain, reserving the stock. Pat the turkey pieces dry with paper towels. Heat the vegetable oil in a large frying pan and sauté the turkey pieces in batches until lightly browned on all sides. Transfer the turkey to a large saucepan, reserving the oil in the frying pan.

In a food processor, combine the onions, garlic, fennel seeds, 1 tablespoon of the sesame seeds, the tortilla, tomatoes, almonds, raisins, cloves, cinnamon, coriander seeds, pepper, and chiles and process to a coarse purée. If necessary, do this in batches.

Heat the remaining oil in the frying pan over medium heat and cook the purée, stirring, for 5 minutes. Add 2 or so cups of the reserved turkey broth, the chocolate, and salt to taste. Cook, stirring, over very low heat, until the chocolate has melted, about 4 minutes. The sauce should be thick. Pour the sauce over the turkey pieces in the saucepan and cook, covered, over low heat (so sauce just barely simmers) for 30 to 40 minutes, or until the turkey is tender. Remove the turkey to a platter, adjust the seasonings in the sauce, and thin if desired with more stock. Add fresh lime juice to taste.

To serve: Sprinkle with the remaining sesame seeds, hot fresh tortillas, some crumbled queso fresco, and cilantro sprigs.

Turkey Pibil

This is based on the classic recipe *conchinita pibil*, which uses pork in the Yucatan in Mexico. *Pibil* is Mayan for "pit," where this dish is traditionally cooked. Annato seeds, which are the basis for the achiote paste below, are used extensively in the Yucatan. They contribute a bright orange-red color. You can buy prepared achiote pastes in Mexican markets that are perfectly fine to use. *El Yucateco* brand is widely available. Below is a recipe to make your own that I think is superior.

MAKES 4 TO 6 SERVINGS

ACHIOTE PASTE

2 tablespoons finely ground annato seeds (sometimes labeled achiote)
1 tablespoon olive oil
1 tablespoon pure chili powder (such as ancho)
2 tablespoons chopped garlic
1 teaspoon whole allspice (about 5), toasted and ground
1/2 teaspoon ground cinnamon
2 teaspoons honey, or to taste
2 teaspoons dried oregano, preferably Mexican
1 teaspoon salt
1/3 cup (80mL) fresh orange or tangerine juice (enough to make a smooth paste)

TURKEY

4 pounds (1.8kg) whole turkey legs, separated into leg and thigh portions
1 pound (450g) fresh or defrosted frozen banana leaves, or aluminum foil

PICKLED ONIONS

2 large red onions, peeled and sliced 1/8 inch (3-mm) thick
1 1/2 cups (360mL) orange juice
1/2 cup (120mL) white wine vinegar
1 teaspoon kosher salt
1 small cinnamon stick

ROASTED JALAPEÑO SALSA

10 red jalapeño or serrano chiles (about 3 ounces, 84g), stemmed and coarsely chopped
3 large garlic cloves, unpeeled
2 tablespoons lime juice
Kosher or sea salt

ACCOMPANIMENTS

Corn tortillas
Finely shredded cabbage
Thinly sliced radishes
Fresh cilantro sprigs
Lime wedges

To make the achiote paste, place all the ingredients in a blender and blend until very smooth. Add the orange juice a bit at a time to facilitate the making of the paste. Store, covered and refrigerated, for up to 2 weeks.

Mix the paste with a 1/2 cup of water in a small bowl. In a large bowl or large plastic food bag, combine the turkey pieces and the achiote marinade, turning to coat the turkey evenly. Marinate the meat, covered and refrigerated, for at least 6 hours or overnight.

Preheat the oven to 325°F. Line a roasting pan with the banana leaves, leaving enough space hanging over the rim to wrap the leaves around the turkey. Place the turkey pieces on the banana leaves in a single layer and pour the marinade over top. Wrap the leaves over the turkey, adding another leaf or two if needed to completely cover the turkey. Cover with aluminum foil and place in the oven for 2 1/2 to 3 hours, or until the turkey is very tender and falling off the bone.

Meanwhile, make the pickled onions. Add the onions to a nonreactive bowl and pour boiling water over them. Immediately strain and return the onions to the bowl along with the orange juice, vinegar, salt, and cinnamon stick. Set aside to cure while the turkey is cooking.

continued on page 214

Make the salsa. In a dry skillet over medium heat, roast the chiles and garlic until they have softened and are darkened in spots, 5 minutes for the chiles and 10 minutes for the garlic. When cool, clip the skins off the garlic. Add the garlic, chiles, lime juice, and a couple of tablespoons of water to a blender and blend until smooth. It should have a spoonable consistency. Taste very carefully and season to taste with salt. The salsa will keep, covered and refrigerated, for at least 3 days.

When the turkey is finished, remove it from the oven and set it aside for 10 minutes. Toast the tortillas in a hot skillet. Serve warm, topped with pieces of turkey, pickled onions, and a little salsa and other accompaniments.

San Marzano Tomatoes

San Marzanos are legendary among lovers of canned tomatoes. They have a distinctive bittersweet flavor, making them ideal for sauces. Tomatoes were part of the new world larder and came to Europe from Central America in the sixteenth century. They were used ornamentally and not considered food until the eighteenth century. San Marzanos evolved into a DOP-designated fruit in Italy, which means there are strict rules regarding where they can be grown and how they are cultivated, and they must be picked by hand. The area of production of San Marzano tomatoes is located in the Campania region and, more specifically, in communes in the provinces of Naples, Salerno, and Avellino. The soils there are richly volcanic, which many believe give Italian San Marzanos their distinctive flavor. San Marzanos are also grown in California and New Jersey. They are more expensive than regular canned tomatoes but definitely worth seeking out.

Chipotle-Rubbed Turkey Breast
Stuffed with Spinach

This recipe comes from Mary Karlin, gifted cook and author of *Wood-Fired Cooking: Techniques and Recipes for the Grill, Backyard Oven, Fireplace, and Campfire* and *Artisan Cheese Making at Home*. She notes: "This roasted turkey breast is rubbed with a mixture of chipotle powder, cumin, and orange zest then stuffed with spinach. The spinach has a slightly tannic profile which I love as a backdrop to the other zesty ingredients. To guarantee a very moist roast, brine the breast for four to six hours before stuffing."

MAKES 6 TO 8 SERVINGS AS A MAIN COURSE

STUFFING

1/4 cup (55g) olive oil

1 pound (450g) leeks, trimmed and sliced lengthwise

1 cup (240mL) orange juice

Zest of 1 orange

1/2 cup (30g) fresh Italian parsley leaves, coarsely chopped

2 teaspoons toasted cumin seeds

Kosher or sea salt and freshly ground white pepper

CHIPOTLE RUB

2 tablespoons chipotle powder

2 tablespoons sweet paprika

2 tablespoons ground toasted cumin seeds

1/4 teaspoon garlic powder

Zest of 1 orange

2 teaspoons kosher salt

1 teaspoon pure maple syrup

3 to 4 tablespoons olive oil

3 pounds (1.4kg) boneless, skinless turkey breast, brined, rinsed, and patted dry

2 cups (60g) packed spinach leaves, long stems removed

For the stuffing, heat the oil in a sauté pan over medium heat and add the leeks. Cook until the leeks are soft, about 5 minutes, and then add the orange juice. Cook until most of the liquid is cooked out, about 5 minutes. Take the pan off the heat and add the orange zest, parsley, cumin seeds, and salt and white pepper to taste. Set aside.

Make the rub by combining the chipotle powder, paprika, cumin, garlic powder, orange zest, and salt in a small bowl. Stir in the maple syrup and the olive oil to make a spreadable paste.

Cut a deep lengthwise slit in the turkey breast up to 1 inch from the end of the breast to form a pocket. Lightly season with salt and pepper. Spread the stuffing mixture inside the pocket. Lay the spinach leaves over the top. Close and secure the slit every 3 inches with kitchen string or with a water-soaked bamboo skewer.

Coat the stuffed turkey with the rub and set aside for 10 minutes.

For grilling: Preheat the grill to 400°F or 425°F. Place the turkey on the hot grill and cook, rotating, until all sides are golden and lightly crispy, about 15 minutes total. Move the roast to the side of the grill, on indirect heat (350°F to 355°F). Put the lid on the grill and continue to cook for another 25 to 30 minutes, turning the meat every 10 minutes or so. Cook until the roast is evenly golden and the internal temperature is 170°F.

When the desired internal temperature is reached, transfer the breast to a cutting board, tent with foil, and let it rest for 15 minutes. Remove any string or skewers.

Slice diagonally across the breast into 1/2-inch pieces. Serve the turkey with a citrusy olive tapenade or fruity salsa.

Dan Dan Noodles

This is a version of perhaps the most famous of Sichuan street foods, and there are many variations, of course. Here I've used ground turkey, but you could use other poultry meats as well as pork, beef, or even mushrooms. I sometimes add a little chopped Sichuan preserved vegetables for garnish.

MAKES 4 SERVINGS

2 tablespoons rice wine or dry sherry
4 tablespoons (60mL) soy sauce, divided
2 teaspoons cornstarch
1/2 pound (230g) ground dark meat turkey
1 package (about 12 ounces, 340g) fresh Chinese egg noodles
2 tablespoons vegetable oil
Kosher or sea salt and freshly ground black pepper
1 teaspoon Sichuan peppercorns, ground (optional)

1 tablespoon peeled and finely chopped ginger
1/4 cup (60g) Chinese sesame seed paste or tahini
1/2 cup (120mL) canned or homemade turkey or chicken stock (see page 70)
2 tablespoons oyster sauce
2 tablespoons rice vinegar
2 teaspoons chili garlic sauce
1/4 cup (33g) chopped roasted unsalted peanuts
4 scallions, thinly sliced

Combine the rice wine, 2 tablespoons of the soy sauce, and cornstarch in a bowl. Add the turkey, mix well, and let sit for 10 minutes.

Add the noodles to a large pot of boiling, salted water. Cook until just tender but still a little firm to the bite. Drain and then place the noodles in a large bowl of ice water to quickly chill and stop the cooking. Drain well and set aside.

In a 12-inch skillet or wok, heat the oil over medium-high heat and swirl the pan to coat the sides. Add the turkey mixture and a little salt and pepper and cook, stirring, for 2 minutes or so. Add the Sichuan peppercorns, if using, and the ginger and cook until the turkey is cooked through and starting to brown, about 5 minutes. Stir in the sesame paste, stock, remaining 2 tablespoons soy sauce, oyster sauce, vinegar, and chili garlic sauce and stir to make a smooth sauce with the meat. Taste for seasoning and adjust to your taste. Add the noodles to the skillet and toss to heat through. Transfer to warm bowls, top with peanuts and scallions, and serve immediately.

Turkey Bolognese Sauce

This is a version of the famous slow-cooked meat sauce of the Emilia-Romagna region in Italy, of which Bologna is the capital. It takes a while to cook, so I'm making a big batch and putting some in the freezer for use later. It's my go-to sauce for all shaped pastas.

MAKES 3-PLUS QUARTS

1 ounce (28g) dry porcini mushrooms

1/3 pound (150g) diced pancetta

1/4 cup (55g) good extra-virgin olive oil

2 medium onions, finely chopped (about 3 cups)

2 medium carrots, peeled and finely chopped (about 2 cups)

2 celery stalks, finely chopped (about 1 cup)

3 pounds (1.4kg) ground dark meat turkey (don't use breast meat)

2 cup (475mL) dry white wine or vermouth

2 cups (475mL) whole milk

1 teaspoon freshly grated nutmeg

2 (28-ounce, 784g) cans crushed tomatoes with puree, preferably San Marzano

2 cups (475mL) canned or homemade chicken stock (see page 70)

Kosher or sea salt and freshly ground black pepper

Put the porcini in a small bowl and cover with 1½ cups of hot water. Let sit for at least 30 minutes for the mushrooms to soften. Drain the porcini over a bowl and reserve the soaking water. Finely chop the mushrooms and set aside.

Add the pancetta to a food processor and pulse until it is very finely chopped. Over moderately high heat, heat the oil in a heavy Dutch oven, add the pancetta and cook, stirring, until the pancetta begins to brown, about 8 mintues. Add the onions, carrots, and celery and continue cooking until the vegetables just begin to brown, 8 to 10 minutes.

Add the turkey and break it up with a wooden spoon until the meat has lost its red color, about 5 minutes. You don't want to brown the meat. Add the wine and cook, stirring, until it has mostly evaporated, 15 to 18 minutes. Add the milk and nutmeg and cook until the milk has mostly evaporated, another 15 minutes or so. Add the tomatoes, chicken stock, and reserved porcini soaking water. Stir well to combine, bring to a boil, and then reduce the heat to a simmer. Cook, uncovered, stirring occasionally to prevent the sauce from sticking to the bottom and burning, 2 hours or so, or until the sauce is thick and rich. Season to taste with salt and pepper. If the sauce is too dry, then add more stock.

Ricotta Herb Gnocchi
with Turkey Bolognese

These gnocchi are easy to make and are a base for all kinds of sauces. They freeze well and can be taken straight from the freezer and cooked in boiling salted water. It's key that you use well-drained whole milk ricotta. My favorite is the sheep and cow's milk ricotta from Bellwether Farms: www.bellwetherfarms.com.

MAKES 4 TO 6 SERVINGS

8 ounces (227g) whole milk ricotta

1 large egg, beaten

1 teaspoon kosher or sea salt

1/2 teaspoon freshly ground black pepper

3 tablespoons chopped fresh herbs, such as basil, parsley, chives

1/3 cup (33.3g) freshly grated Parmesan or other grating cheese of your choice

1 1/4 cups (150g) all-purpose flour, plus more as needed

2 tablespoons olive oil

2 tablespoons unsalted butter

2 cups (475mL) Turkey Bolognese Sauce (see page 216)

Drain the ricotta in a strainer over a bowl for at least 30 minutes. Discard the liquid. Bring a large pot of salted water to a boil.

In a large bowl, combine the drained ricotta, egg, salt, pepper, herbs, and Parmesan. Gradually add the flour, a third of a cup at a time, and with your hands, blend the dough until it just holds together. Try not to over mix. Take a heaping teaspoon of the dough, roll it into a ball on a floured surface, and drop it into boiling water to make sure that it will hold together. If it falls apart, then work in more flour a couple of tablespoons at a time. Try again in the boiling water until it holds together and rises to the surface. Taste for seasoning and adjust if needed.

Divide the dough into 4 equal parts. On a floured board with your hands roll each fourth into a rope about 1 inch in diameter. Cut the ropes into 3/4-inch-long pieces and slightly indent with a fork or gnocchi board. You should have about 30. If you aren't cooking right away, dust the gnocchi with flour and refrigerate, covered, or freeze them and place in an airtight container. Gnocchi will keep for up to 3 days in the refrigerator and 3 months in the freezer.

Drop the gnocchi into boiling water and stir gently to prevent sticking. When they float to the top, cook for another 30 seconds or so. Remove with a slotted spoon to a plate.

Heat the olive oil and butter in a large skillet over moderately high heat until the butter melts. Add the gnocchi and sauté for 2 to 3 minutes or until lightly browned. Serve in bowls with the Bolognese Sauce.

Smoked Turkey on the Grill

One of the best turkeys you'll ever eat is one that is both slowly grilled and smoked. It's simple to do. You'll need a barbecue with a tight cover so that you can control the amount of oxygen and heat. To maximize the flavor and moisture, brine the bird first, then select a good hardwood to use as the smoking medium. You can find them in various sizes from sawdust to small chips to chunks. They all work. Hickory and oak are probably the most commonly available, but also look for fruit woods such as apple, pear, cherry, walnut, or pecan. You will need a good thermometer. I prefer the digital version, which you can leave in the bird the entire time. Use the indirect method described in the recipe and be sure to regulate the heat so that the bird doesn't cook too quickly.

Traditional brines are made from a combination of salt, sugar, and water (see page 53) with some spices and herbs often added for more flavor. I've taken this brine a step further with some additional flavorings. This brine is delicious with a variety of poultry or meats. The following recipe makes a gallon or so of brine, which should be plenty for a 12- to 14-pound turkey.

MAKES 12 SERVINGS

2 cups (400g) packed brown sugar

1 cup (250g) pure maple syrup

¾ cup (170g) coarse salt

3 whole heads garlic, cloves separated and bruised

6 large bay leaves

1 ½ cups (144g) coarsely chopped unpeeled fresh ginger

2 teaspoons dried red chili flakes

1 ½ cups (350mL) soy sauce

3 quarts (2.85L) water

12- to 14-pound (5.4 to 6.3kg) dressed fresh turkey

Combine all the ingredients except the turkey in a large enamel or stainless steel stockpot that is large enough to hold the brine and the turkey. Bring to a simmer and then remove from the heat and allow to cool thoroughly. Rinse the turkey well; remove the neck and giblets, and save them for stock or discard.

Submerge the turkey in the cooled brine. Be sure there is enough brine to cover the bird. If not, add water to cover. Refrigerate for at least 2 days and up to 4. Turn the bird in the brine twice a day.

Remove the bird from the brine and pat dry. Lightly brush the bird with olive oil and set aside. Prepare the barbecue by lighting 24 charcoal briquettes (preferably in a chimney starter). When hot and spotted gray, divide the briquettes in half and push to opposite sides of the grate. Place a metal drip pan that is at least 1 inch deep in the center with the hot coals on either side. The pan should be large enough to catch the drips from anywhere on the turkey.

Place a half cup or so of the wood smoking chips in the center of a double layer of heavy duty foil cut approximately 10 inches square. Form the foil into a ball shape and poke some holes in it. Place on top of one of the mounds of hot coals*.

Put the upper rack of the barbecue in place and then center the turkey on the rack over the drip pan. Cover the barbecue and partially close the air vents to restrict the oxygen (but not so much so that you put out the coals). Within a few minutes, the wood chips should start smoking. Regulate the vents to keep the chips smoking and the coals slowly burning. Check every 25 minutes or so to make sure the coals are still hot and smoke is continuing. Add charcoal and additional chips as needed. The internal temperature of the barbecue should be in the 275ºF to 300ºF range.

Keep the smoke going for 1½ to 2 hours. After that, remove any remaining wood chips and continue cooking without smoke until the bird is done. This ensures that the turkey will not be too smoky in flavor, but you can adjust to taste. The total cooking time for a 12- to 14-pound bird will be approximately 3 to 3½ hours. The internal temperature of the bird should be 165ºF when tested at the thickest part of the thigh or breast. Make sure the thermometer is not touching bone. You can also test by cutting a little incision at the leg-thigh joint and making sure the meat is cooked and juices run clear.

Remove the turkey from the barbecue and allow it to rest at least 30 minutes before carving.

Alternatively, you can use a small 6-inch cast iron skillet to hold the wood chips. Look at garage sales and keep it for this purpose.

The Best
Mashed Potatoes

It would seem that nothing could be simpler than mashed potatoes. They are simple, but there are a few basics that will help make sure yours are the best:

Pick the right potato! Russets from Idaho and Washington are the standard. My favorite are Yukon gold, which have a thin skin but starchy meat, which is what you need for good mashed potatoes. Don't use new potatoes (red or white) or fingerlings. Because of their texture and water content, these are great for steaming, boiling, and frying, but not for mashing.

Peel the potatoes, cut into relatively even 2-inch chunks, and place them in lightly salted boiling water. Cook until a paring knife or fork easily pierces the potatoes. Drain the water when they are done and then return them to the pan and stir over moderate heat to dry them out as much as you can.

My favorite tool for mashing is the food mill, which yields a nice texture. Second choice would be a potato ricer that looks like a giant garlic press, and after that, the good old hand masher. Never, never use a food processor! It's too powerful and will quickly turn the potatoes to glue.

Stir in seasonings and serve mashed potatoes as soon as possible. If you're adding cream, heat it so that the potatoes stay warm. Lots of butter is a nice addition too. Some restaurants actually make mashed potatoes to order because they feel they lose subtle flavors even sitting just a short time. If you need to hold mashers for a while, do it via the double-boiler method, with a stainless steel or glass bowl over barely simmering water. Don't cover with plastic or foil. This creates condensation that drips back into the potatoes, making them soggy and creating off flavors.

Storing Potatoes
How potatoes are stored also makes a big difference in the final product. Make sure you store potatoes in a dark, well-ventilated space. Stored in the light, they will sprout and turn green, which for some can cause a toxic reaction. You can cut out and discard the green, but the flavor will still be affected. Cool, room temperature (around 60°F) is best. Don't refrigerate mashing potatoes, especially russets. Refrigeration softens potatoes and causes them to convert their starch to sugar and lose their potato flavor. Finally, potatoes are sensitive to ethylene gas. Many fruits (like apples, melons, and tomatoes) naturally give off ethylene, which is an odorless, colorless gas that promotes ripening, resulting in sprouting and deterioration of the potato. Keep them separate!

Roast Turkey

Every year it seems there appears another new way of roasting the holiday turkey: high heat, low heat, roasting legs separately from the breast, roasting in a brown paper bag, with stuffing or without. My preference is for not stuffing the bird. It cooks faster, the skin get crispier, and I love the crispy exterior of stuffing when it's baked in a dish, uncovered of course. I'm of the KISS school (Keep It Simple Stupid). It really isn't that difficult, and I've roasted a lot of turkeys and chickens in my life. The important thing for keeping your bird moist is to brine it first, using the wet or dry brine method on pages 53–54.

BRINE
2 cups (400g) packed brown sugar
1 cup (250g) pure maple syrup
3/4 cup (230g) coarse salt
3 whole heads garlic, cloves separated and bruised
6 large bay leaves
1 1/2 cups (144g) coarsely chopped unpeeled fresh ginger
2 teaspoons dried red chili flakes
1 1/2 cups (355mL) soy sauce
3 quarts (2.8L) water

TURKEY
12- to 14-pound (5.4 to 6.3kg) dressed fresh turkey
3 carrots, peeled and roughly chopped
5 celery stalks, roughly chopped

2 potatoes, roughly chopped
2 oranges, quartered
4 lemons, quartered
3 cups (700mL) canned or homemade turkey or chicken stock (see page 70)

GRAVY
3 tablespoons (43g) unsalted butter
3 tablespoons (24g) all-purpose flour
White wine or brandy
2 cups (475mL) canned or homemade turkey or chicken stock (see page 70)
Fresh herbs (such as thyme, rosemary, basil, oregano, sage)
Kosher or sea salt and freshly ground black pepper

Combine all the ingredients except the turkey in a large enamel or stainless steel stockpot that is large enough to hold the brine and the turkey. Bring to a simmer and then remove from the heat and allow to cool thoroughly. Rinse the turkey well; remove the neck and giblets and save for stock or discard.

Submerge the turkey in the cooled brine. Be sure there is enough brine to cover the bird. If not, add water to cover. Refrigerate for at least 2 days and up to 4. Turn the bird in the brine twice a day.

Remove the bird from the brine and pat dry. Lightly brush the bird with olive oil and set aside for at least an hour before roasting. Preheat the oven to 450°F. Set the turkey in a roasting pan fitted with a V-shaped rack. Throw the chopped vegetables and citrus in the cavity. Add the chicken or turkey stock to the pan. Slip a flavored butter up under the skin of the turkey if you want.

Cook the turkey for 20 minutes and then reduce the heat to 350°F (325°F in a convection oven). Roast for 2 1/2 to 3 hours. It's done when juice from the thigh runs clear and an instant-read thermometer reads 165°F in the thickest part of the thigh not touching the bone.

Remove from the oven. Lift the turkey out of the pan and loosely tent with foil to keep warm. Don't wrap tightly or the skin will lose its crispness. Let the turkey rest at least 25 minutes before carving.

To make the gravy: Pour off all fat from the roasting pan, leaving the delicious browned bits in the bottom. Make a roux by whisking the butter in the roasting pan over moderate heat with the flour. Continue to whisk for a couple of minutes. Add a splash of white wine or brandy and scrape up the browned bits. Add the stock and any herbs you like and continue to whisk and simmer for a few more minutes. Season to taste with salt and pepper. Serve the gravy along side the carved meat.

DUCK AND GOOSE

From a culinary standpoint, duck and goose are very similar. They both have lots of fat under their skin that helps keep them buoyant and warm. You will want to remove much of this delicious fat during cooking and save it for other uses. (The fat is not marbled into the meat, so you can also easily remove it if you are deboning the bird.) Duck and goose fat have long been staples in European kitchens. They add delicious flavor to sautéed potatoes, eggs, and vegetables, can be used in place of butter or olive oil for cooking fish, and can be used to make pastry doughs, biscuits, and breads with excellent results.

The simplest way to remove the fat is to prick the skin (not the meat) all over with the point of a small knife or skewer before cooking. This will help the fat render (or melt) during cooking. You can periodically collect fat during cooking. Do this regularly so that it doesn't brown.

You can also render fat from the skin of uncooked ducks and geese that have been trimmed. Cooking the fat will yield a prized byproduct called cracklings.

To Render Fat and Make Cracklings

• Trim all excess skin and fat from the body of the bird and cut it into $\frac{1}{2}$-inch pieces.

• Place in a heavy saucepan with $\frac{1}{3}$ cup of water for each pound of skin and fat to prevent sticking.

• Place the pan over low heat and gently cook, stirring occasionally, for about 2 hours or until the skin has become golden brown and crisp. Don't cook it too fast or the fat will brown or burn; it must stay clear. If the cracklings (pieces of skin) are not browning, then scoop them out with a slotted spoon and cook them with a bit of the fat in a separate small skillet over medium heat.

• Strain the fat through a fine mesh strainer into a jar with a tight-fitting lid. Then cool and refrigerate. It will keep for up to a year.

• The cracklings will become crispier as they cool. Season them lightly with salt. If not using right away, store them in an airtight container and refrigerate them. Reheat them briefly before using them as a garnish in salads or soups. Use anywhere you'd use bacon bits.

DUCK

In America, most of the ducks served trace their origins to China, where duck has always been an important food. Though there are several domesticated breeds of duck, the best selling by far in American markets is the white pekin, not to be confused with Peking Duck, which is a popular Chinese recipe for duck. The pekin originated in northern China thousands of years ago and was domesticated at least two thousand years ago. It comprises roughly 95 percent of US duck production and consumption. They are young when harvested, typically between six and eight weeks old, which ensures that they are very tender and surprisingly nutritious. White pekin has a nutritional makeup that surprises most people, considering the fact that ducks don't have any white meat. According to the US Department of Agriculture, pekin duck breast is lower in fat and calories than skinless chicken breast.

While chickens and turkeys might seem like fast-growing birds, the duck is the most rapidly growing animal of all poultry species. A typical duck will weigh seven pounds in only six or seven weeks.

Supposedly, nine pekin ducklings imported from China started the industry on New York's Long Island. The humid climate, abundance of running water and sandy soil were well suited to raising duck, and those farmed in the area became known as "Long Island duck" or "Long Island duckling."

According to historians, duck farming in the United States began in the Speonk and Eastport area in 1873. By 1885, it had the largest duck farm in the world, setting a record by raising a quarter of a million ducks in a year. The hurricane of 1938 wiped out the industry.

A Quick Primer on Fats

In the 1980s, Americans started to buy into the conventional wisdom that "fat is bad," "fat makes you fat," and "eat less fat and you'll live longer." Animal fats especially were thought to be deadly and cause heart disease. As it turns out, this is not quite true. According to the Harvard School of Public Health, the world's healthiest cultures vary widely in terms of fat consumption—from less than 20 percent of calories from fat to more than 50 percent. Duck and goose fat, as it turns out, are "healthier" than butter with nearly 40 percent less saturated fat and significantly more good mono and polyunsaturated fats. It's still a matter of debate and beyond the scope of this book, but one thing I know for sure is that duck and goose fat are real treasures in the kitchen and, I believe, worth using in moderation.

Apart from swans, geese are the largest waterfowls.

After that, Long Island property became too valuable for duck farming, and now most ducks come from Indiana, Wisconsin, California, and Canada.

Three other primary duck breeds available in the United States are the muscovy, moulard, and mallard.

The muscovy duck (also known as the Barbarie in England) is a gorgeous greenish-black duck with red wattles, found wild in Mexico and northern South America. The muscovy was domesticated in South America before the arrival of Columbus. Muscovy ducks are raised to eleven weeks. They are most often selected for their breast meat and liver, which is used to make foie gras. Muscovy makes up something like 3 to 4 percent of US consumption.

A moulard is a sterile hybrid of the male pekin or mallard and the female muscovy and is bred for breast meat and foie gras. The moulard is larger than the Pekin and has a stronger, gamier taste; it is also considerably fattier. This breed is raised for its liver for foie gras and for its breast, known as "Magret" in French. Moulard ducks comprise 1 to 2 percent of US duck consumption.

There are dozens of wild duck varieties, including

The male mallard duck is known as a drake.

Foie Gras

Foie gras, or "fat liver," is a specially fattened and rich liver. Ancient Egyptians first observed the fattening of the liver in wild ducks who were gorging themselves before beginning their yearly migration. The result was a rich, delicate, buttery liver. They developed a technique to create the foie gras by a process called gavage: overfeeding ducks with corn so that their liver grows to four times its normal size. Historically, this practice was done with geese, but the far more gentle ducks are used today. Geese can be very aggressive and cantankerous. The force feeding of ducks may seem like a brutal procedure, and activists decry the possible health consequences to the duck or goose of an enlarged liver. However, the birds are being raised for slaughter and their long, collagen-lined esophagus can accept a feeding tube without pain or damage (think of a pelican swallowing a fish). In fact, it can be argued that foie gras ducks have a better life than factory-raised birds. They are free range and will patiently wait for their feedings each day. Some cities have banned the production and serving of foie gras. I personally love foie gras, but we all have to make up our own minds about its consumption and our ethical position.

Foie gras, truffles, and saffron are expensive delicacies and what we might call "luxury" foods. Foie gras traditionally is served barely seared or made into a pâté (terrine) or mousse.

teal, pintail, canvasback, shoveler, coot, scoter, and widgeon. The mallard, though, is probably the most familiar breed of duck in the wild. It's the duck with the emerald green head and is the one most often hunted in the United States. It has a white collar and is the ancestor of almost all domestic ducks. The Rouen duck of France is a large domesticated descendent of the mallard. Farm-raised mallards are available on a limited basis.

Farm Raised vs. Wild Ducks

They couldn't be more dramatically different. For this book, I'm focusing on farm-raised varieties, and in most instances I call for the white pekin as the choice of duck. Farm-raised ducks have considerably more fat than their wild counterparts. This is because wild ducks are more physically active than farm-raised ducks, and they eat a diet of fish rather than the corn and grain diet of most farm-raised birds. Full-grown wild birds are older than full-grown farm-raised birds and, therefore, they are "gamier." Because they usually have so little fat, wild birds have a tendency to dry out very quickly when cooking; it is important to baste, bard, or braise wild duck to try to keep it moist.

A Note on Cooking Duck

You can buy duck parts like the breasts and legs separately. Like chicken and other birds, it's much more economical to buy the whole bird and cut it up yourself. This is especially relevant for dark-meat birds such as duck and squab. The breasts of these birds are typically very tender, and it's better to slightly undercook them because they are so lean. The legs and thighs do all the work and generally are cooked much longer in order to make them tender. In buying a whole bird, you have the ability to use each part in the way that works best. With duck, I typically use the breast for one meal and the legs and thighs for another unless I'm cooking it whole, as in roast duck (see page 246).

Roasting Duck

A simple roasted duck is one of life's great pleasures. As with goose, the strategy with roasting a duck is to remove and save the delicious fat. Here is my three-step method. It begins twenty-four hours ahead with pre-salting and ends with a blast in a hot oven to obtain deliciously crispy skin.

Step 1: Salt and season the duck at least 12 hours and up to 24 hours ahead. This salting ahead, as discussed in the dry brining section on page 54, does two things: adds flavor and makes it moister. (It also produces crispy skin that we love.) For the average 5-pound duck, sprinkle 1 tablespoon of kosher salt evenly over the skin and in the cavity of the bird. Place on a V-shaped rack over a rimmed cookie sheet or roasting pan to catch any drips, and refrigerate, uncovered, for 12 and up to 24 hours.

Step 2: Remove the duck from the refrigerator and let it sit at room temperature for at least an hour. Preheat the oven to 350°F. Coarsely chop some aromatic vegetables such as garlic, onions, and carrots and place them in the bottom of a large roasting pan.

Prick the duck all over, piercing just the skin with the point of a sharp knife to help release the fat. Add a splash of white wine if you want. Place the duck breast side down in its rack set inside the roasting pan and roast for 1 hour.

Turn the bird breast side up and continue to roast for another 45 to 60 minutes or until the legs feel loose in their sockets and an instant-read thermometer reads 175°F in the thickest part of the thigh, not touching the bone, and the juices run clear.

Remove the duck from the oven and allow it to sit for at least 10 minutes before slicing. Strain the fat and reserve it in the refrigerator for other uses. (You can use any juices that separate out for making delicious pan sauces.) Discard the vegetables. When the duck has cooled, cut it in half and remove and discard the backbone. At this point, you can wrap and refrigerate it for up to 2 days. Season the duck with salt, pepper, and other spices before serving.

Step 3: If you are serving the duck the next day, remove it from the refrigerator an hour before serving. Preheat the oven to 500°F and roast on a flat rack, skin side up, for 10 to 12 minutes or until the skin is crispy and the duck is warmed through. Carve, season with salt, pepper, and other seasonings, and serve immediately.

GOOSE

Goose is most associated with Christmas, especially in Europe. Perhaps the most famous roasted goose was served by the Cratchit family in Charles Dickens' *A Christmas Carol,* complete with applesauce and mashed potatoes. Goose never really caught on in America because we have such a long history with our native bird, turkey. In recent years, however, restaurants and high-end supermarkets have begun to make it available, especially around the holidays, and people are discovering how delicious it can be.

It definitely can be a little daunting to cook because it's a big bird and there is so much fat (delicious as it is) to deal with. It's not unlike duck but has a richer, fuller flavor, and the texture is a little chewier even when fully cooked, which it must be. In the market, the typical goose will run eight to twelve pounds. You probably won't eat as much goose as you do turkey because it is so rich.

The largest goose producer in America is Schiltz Foods in Sisseton, South Dakota. They sell fresh and prepared goose products of all kinds on their website, www.schiltzfoods.com.

Goose, like duck, can be prepared in a number of ways, but the classic approach is to roast it simply and serve it with a pan sauce or gravy. Perfect roast goose will have crispy skin and not too much fat. Part of the secret is to steam the bird before roasting to get rid of the large amount of fat under the skin.

The
Recipes

Duck Gyoza

You could make these dumplings out of any dark-meat bird, but I think duck is especially tasty. I'm using raw duck meat here, but you could also substitute shredded confit (see page 235).

MAKES 36 SERVINGS

4 cups (280g) finely shredded cabbage
1 cup (230g) ground or finely minced raw duck meat
3 scallions, finely chopped
5 garlic cloves, finely chopped
1 tablespoon grated fresh ginger
1 tablespoon soy sauce
1 tablespoon rice wine

1 tablespoon toasted sesame oil
36 gyoza or wonton wrappers

DIPPING SAUCE

3 tablespoons (45mL) soy sauce
3 tablespoons (45mL) rice or white wine vinegar
Hot chili oil to taste

2 tablespoons vegetable oil for frying

Over gently boiling water, steam the cabbage until it just begins to wilt, about 2 minutes. Drain and, when cool, squeeze out as much water as you can with your hands. In a large bowl, combine the cabbage, duck, scallions, and garlic. Add the ginger, soy sauce, rice wine, and sesame oil and stir to combine to make the filling.

Dust a baking sheet with cornstarch, and pour a cup of water into a small bowl. Place a gyoza wrapper in the palm of your hand and scoop a generous teaspoon of filling into the center of the wrapper. Dip your index finger into the water and moisten the edge of the wrapper. Fold together two corners of the wrapper and pinch to seal. Bring the bottom of the wrapper over the meat filling and press into a pleat. Continue pleating a couple more times, being sure to pinch the edges together. Place on the prepared baking sheet and repeat with the remaining wrappers and filling. (You can freeze them at this point; simply place the sheet of dumplings in the freezer for several hours. When they are frozen, transfer to a zippered freezer bag. You don't have to defrost them to cook, but you'll need to increase the cooking time by a couple of minutes if cooking from frozen.)

To make the dipping sauce, combine the soy sauce, vinegar, and chili oil in a small bowl, and stir to mix.

To fry the dumplings, add the oil to a large skillet with a lid over medium heat. Add the number of gyoza that will fit comfortably in one layer, flat side down. Fry for 2 minutes or so or until the bottoms are lightly browned. Pour ½ cup water into the pan, cover, and cook for 3 minutes to steam the dumplings. Remove the cover and continue cooking until the water has evaporated, about 1 minute. Loosen the dumplings with a spatula and place them on a warm plate. Repeat with rest of the dumplings and serve warm with the dipping sauce.

To boil the dumplings, simply fill a deep saucepan with lightly salted water and bring to a boil. Drop half the dumplings in and cook until they rise to the top. Cook for an additional 2 minutes and then remove the dumplings with a slotted spoon to a warm serving platter. Repeat with rest of dumplings and serve immediately with the dipping sauce.

Duck Sausage or Crépinettes

French in origin, a crépinette is a small, slightly flattened sausage made of minced meat, sometimes including truffle, wrapped in caul fat instead of stuffed into a casing. Caul fat is very delicate lacy fat that surrounds the internal organs of four-footed animals. It's worth seeking out, but chances are you aren't going to find it in stock in supermarkets. So here I'm making the sausage into meatballs. The flavors here are Moorish Spanish. Serve as an appetizer with Romesco Sauce (see page 42) or with pasta and your favorite tomato-based sauce.

MAKES ABOUT 20 MEATBALLS

1 pound (450g) ground duck

¼ cup (37g) blanched slivered almonds, lightly toasted and chopped

¼ cup (37g) golden raisins, chopped

2 teaspoons finely chopped garlic

⅓ cup (35g) freshly grated Parmigiano-Reggiano cheese

¼ cup (20g) bread crumbs, such as panko

1 teaspoon ground cumin

¼ teaspoon ground allspice

1 teaspoon salt

1 teaspoon smoked paprika

2 teaspoons dried crumbled mint

1 large egg, lightly beaten

Olive oil for sautéing

Combine all the ingredients except the olive oil. With wet hands, form the mixture into rounded 2-tablespoon–size balls. Heat about ¼ inch of olive oil in a large, nonstick sauté pan over moderate heat. Fry the meatballs until they are browned on all sides, about 8 minutes. Serve immediately or simmer in sauce for a few minutes.

Duck Rillette

Rillette is a form of French charcuterie, really a kind of pâté. It's commonly made from pork but is also excellent when made from duck, goose, or rabbit. It takes a little time but is very easy to make. Seasoning can change depending on your taste. It does need to be made at least a day ahead of serving, however. In France, you'll see it traditionally packed in small ceramic terrines with lids. I've made it here as a whole loaf, but you can do whatever pleases you.

MAKES 12 SERVINGS FROM A 6-CUP MOLD

2 large ducks, approximately 4 pounds (1800g) each

3 tablespoons sea salt, divided

2 tablespoons plus 1 teaspoon fresh thyme (or 1 tablespoon plus $1/2$ teaspoon dried,) divided

3 teaspoons freshly ground black pepper, divided

1 teaspoon red chili flakes

2 teaspoons fennel seeds

1 teaspoon dried lavender flowers (optional)

3 cups (700mL) dry white wine

1 cup (226g) finely chopped shallots or scallions

3 tablespoons minced garlic

1 teaspoon rubbed sage

1 teaspoon whole oregano

$1/3$ cup (80mL) brandy

2 tablespoons drained and lightly crushed green peppercorns

3 tablespoons minced fresh parsley

$1/3$ pound (150g) good quality ham cut in thick julienne

Accompaniments: whole grain mustard, cornichons, fruit chutney of your choice, crisp croutes or crackers

Preheat the oven to 350°F. Line a 6-cup pâté mold with parchment or plastic wrap. Remove the livers from the ducks and reserve. Rinse the giblets and necks and place them back in the cavities of the ducks. Mix together 2 tablespoons of the salt, 2 tablespoons of the thyme, 2 teaspoons of the pepper, chili flakes, fennel seed, and lavender and sprinkle over and in the cavities of the ducks. Prick the ducks all over with a cooking fork and place in a deep, heavy roasting pan. Add the wine and cover with foil. Roast for $2^{1}/2$ to 3 hours or until the meat falls off the bone easily. Remove the ducks, cool, and reserve the cooking juices and fat, including scrapings from the bottom of the pan. Quickly sauté the duck livers until cooked but still pink inside, about 4 minutes, and set aside.

Place the reserved juices and fat in a deep sauté pan and heat over moderate heat. Add the shallots, garlic, the remaining tablespoon of salt, the remaining teaspoon of thyme, sage, oregano, and the remaining teaspoon of pepper and sauté until soft but not brown.

Add the brandy (avert face) and cook for 5 minutes more. Remove from the heat and add the peppercorns and parsley.

Pull the meat off the ducks and remove any skin, cartilage, or bone. Shred the meat by hand or in short bursts in a food processor. Stir in the shallot mixture. Taste the duck mixture and adjust seasonings.

To assemble the rillette: Fill the prepared mold halfway with the duck meat mixture. Roughly chop the livers and scatter over the duck meat along with the ham. Fill the mold with the remaining duck meat to overflowing. Press the mixture down hard and wrap it in plastic. Place the mold in a larger pan and weight the top so that excess fat is squeezed out. Refrigerate overnight. Rillette will keep refrigerated for up to 2 weeks.

To serve: Unmold by running a knife around the edges. Remove parchment or plastic wrap and wipe off any excess fat. Slice carefully and place on chilled plates with croutes, whole grain mustard, a dab of chutney, and cornichons.

Duck Confit

You can also add the hearts and gizzards to this mixture. The seasoning mix can be changed to your taste. The key here is the very slow cooking to create the meltingly tender meat that almost falls off the bone. If you have trouble regulating the heat on top of the stove place this in a 275°F oven. If you choose to use lard in this recipe, be sure it's "real" (unhydrogenated with no trans fats). You can find it online or in ethnic markets, especially Mexican. You can confit any bird, including the whole bird if you want. (See Turkey Confit on page 196.)

MAKES 6 SERVINGS

1/4 cup coarse salt
2 teaspoons cracked black pepper
4 large garlic cloves, peeled and sliced
  (about 2 tablespoons)
2 whole cloves, crushed
2 dried bay leaves, crumbled
2 teaspoons dried thyme
1/4 teaspoon freshly grated nutmeg
6 duck legs
6 cups (1.kg) rendered duck or goose fat or real lard

In a glass or earthenware bowl, combine the salt, pepper, garlic, cloves, bay leaves, thyme, and nutmeg and mix well. Add the duck legs to the bowl and toss with the salt mixture. Cover and marinate, refrigerated, for 24 hours.

Wipe away the marinade with a damp towel. Melt the fat in a heavy stock pot or roasting pan. Place the duck in the fat and heat it to just under a simmer. You'll need enough fat to completely cover the duck.

Timing will depend on the type and size of the legs.

Pekin can cook in 1 1/2 to 2 hours, while large muscovy can take 2 1/2 to 3 hours. To test, remove a leg from the fat and feel it. During the cooking process, the meat at first is tough and tight but then relaxes. When it's done, it is soft and pulls easily away from the bone. Be careful not to overcook or it will fall apart in the pot.

Gently remove the confit from the fat and place it in a ceramic or glass storage dish. Let the fat cool to room temperature and pour it over the duck. It should completely cover the duck with no meat showing. Cover and refrigerate, and it will keep for at least 3 months.

Crisp Duck Confit
with Braised Red Cabbage

Here's a traditional example using confit. I'm suggesting legs, but you could use whatever part of the bird you like. Crisp confit, on or off the bone, is also a delicious topping for a salad of spicy greens, pasta, and more.

MAKES 4 SERVINGS

2 tablespoons duck fat or vegetable oil

2 cups (300g) sliced onion

4 large garlic cloves, peeled and sliced (about 2 tablespoons)

8 cups (560g) shredded red cabbage

1/2 cup (120mL) orange juice

1 large bay leaf

1/2 cup (120mL) dry white wine

1 cup (240mL) duck or chicken stock

1 teaspoon packed brown sugar, or to taste

2 teaspoons cider vinegar, or to taste

Salt and freshly ground black pepper

4 duck legs confit

Over moderate heat, warm the duck fat in a deep 4-quart saucepan. Add the onion and garlic and cook until softened but not brown, about 5 minutes. Add the cabbage and cook for another 5 minutes or until it just begins to wilt. Add the orange juice, bay leaf, wine, and stock and cook slowly, covered, for 20 minutes or until the cabbage is tender. Season to taste with sugar, vinegar, salt, and pepper.

While the cabbage is cooking, preheat the oven to 400°F. Heat a large, heavy cast-iron skillet over medium-high heat. Carefully remove the duck legs confit from the fat and add it skin side down to the hot skillet. Cook, crisping the legs, for about 6 minutes. Turn the legs skin side up and place the skillet in the oven for 8 to 10 minutes to heat through.

Serve the cabbage in warm bowls topped with the crispy duck confit.

Terrine de Foie Gras

This luxurious dish is a classic of French cuisine. The word terrine traditionally refers to the loaf-shaped earthenware cooking dish with a tightly fitting lid that can be reversed to gently weight and compact the food that is cooked in it.

MAKES 10 TO 12 SERVINGS
1 ½ pounds (680g) fresh duck or goose foie gras

⅔ cup (160mL) good quality sauternes or late harvest Riesling
Salt and freshly ground black pepper

Prepare the foie gras by allowing it to warm up. Cold liver is brittle, and the veins are harder to locate and remove intact. Pull any bits of translucent membrane from the surface, and separate the two lobes, using a knife to sever any connecting veins. Inspect the folds for any patches of bitter green bile and extract them with a knife. Remove the thick, branched main vein that runs through the center of each lobe. Probe for the vein and its branches with your fingers, pulling them out as you follow their length. Season it with salt and pepper and marinate it for 2 hours in the wine.

Preheat the oven to 200°F. Remove the foie gras from the marinade and press it into a 4-cup terrine, leaving a bit of space at the top. Place the terrine on 3 folded-over paper towels in the bottom of a deep roasting pan to keep it from slipping and fill the pan with boiling water to reach halfway up the sides of the terrine. Cook until the internal temperature of the foie gras reaches 115°F on a meat thermometer, about 40 minutes.

Remove the pan from the oven and place the terrine in a pan filled with ice water. Place the terrine cover on, which will force enough fat to the surface to cover the liver. If the terrine doesn't have the "official" cover, cut out a piece of cardboard that will just fit and wrap it in several layers of plastic wrap. Place it on top and weight it down with a couple of small cans of food.

When the foie gras is completely covered by the fat, remove the lid, cover tightly, and refrigerate for at least 2 days before serving. To serve, remove the fat from the surface, dip the terrine in a bowl of warm water for 30 seconds, run a knife along the edges, and invert the terrine onto a plate. Cut into serving slices. The liver will keep for up to 3 weeks if kept under its layer of fat. Save any fat for other uses.

Lentil Soup with Duck Foie Gras

This is a simple soup to make and relies upon having a rich stock to give it full flavor. As noted in the recipe, you need to very quickly sauté the foie gras at the last minute. You could also top the soup with boned crisped duck confit (see page 236).

MAKES 6 SERVINGS

3 tablespoons peeled and finely diced carrots

3 tablespoons finely diced onions

3 tablespoons finely diced celery

3 tablespoons finely diced leeks

Toasted walnut oil for sautéing the vegetables

1 cup (192g) black beluga or green Puy lentils, rinsed thoroughly

Bouquet garni (fresh parsley, thyme sprigs, bay leaves tied together)

6 cups (1.44L) duck or chicken stock

3 tablespoons unsalted butter

2 cups (140g) finely diced wild mushrooms (such as chanterelle, shiitake, morel)

Balsamic or red wine vinegar

Kosher or sea salt and freshly ground black pepper

6 (2-ounce, 57g) uniform slices well chilled fresh foie gras

Deep-fried basil sprigs, if desired

In a deep saucepan or soup pot, sauté the vegetables in the walnut oil over medium heat until just beginning to color, about 5 minutes. Add the lentils, bouquet garni, and enough duck stock to cover by about 1 inch. Bring to a boil over high heat, partially cover, and then reduce the heat to low and simmer until the lentils are tender but not mushy, 15 to 20 minutes.

Drain the lentils, reserving the cooking broth. Discard the bouquet garni. Purée half of the lentils with some of the broth. Add this and the remaining lentils back into the pot along with more broth to make a medium-bodied soup of your preference.

In a skillet, melt the butter over medium heat and sauté the mushrooms until nicely browned. Stir the mushrooms into the soup and season to taste with drops of vinegar, salt, and pepper. Spoon soup into warm bowls.

In a heavy sauté pan over high heat, sear and brown the slices of foie gras, about 30 seconds on each side. Season with salt and pepper to taste and top each bowl with a slice of the foie gras. Serve at once, garnished with fried basil sprigs if using.

Warm Duck Breast Salad

The goal here is to have the salad greens and dressing as cold as possible and ready to go before you put the warm duck on top. It needs to be served immediately. This recipe works equally well with squab breast, which also is best served rare to medium rare.

MAKES 8 SERVINGS

4 pekin duck breast halves

MARINADE

1 tablespoon olive oil
2 teaspoons minced garlic
2 tablespoons minced green onion
2 tablespoons oyster sauce
1 tablespoon soy sauce
2 tablespoons rice wine or dry sherry
2 teaspoons sugar
1/2 teaspoon 5-spice powder (see page 57)

DRESSING

1 tablespoon mashed roasted garlic
1/2 cup (120mL) toasted hazelnut oil
3 tablespoons (45mL) balsamic vinegar
1 tablespoon fresh lemon juice
1 tablespoon minced chives
1 tablespoon soy sauce
1 teaspoon honey, or to taste
Salt and freshly ground black pepper to taste
1/2 cup (113g) toasted and skinned hazelnuts, halved
6 cups (200g) gently packed mixed baby spicy greens (such as cress, arugula, mizuna, tat soi)

Trim the duck breasts of excess fat and score the skin sides in a diamond pattern with the point of a sharp knife through the fat but not into the meat. In a large bowl, combine the marinade ingredients and coat the breasts thoroughly. Allow to marinate for at least 2 hours, covered and refrigerated, turning occasionally.

In a small bowl, mix the dressing ingredients together, except the hazelnuts. Cover and refrigerate at least 1 hour before serving for the flavors to develop.

In a heavy skillet over moderately high heat, cook the duck breasts, skin side down, to brown and render the fat, about 4 minutes. Turn over and cook for another 3 to 4 minutes. Be careful not to overcook. Place the breasts on a cutting board and allow them to rest while you compose the salad. Artfully arrange a mixture of baby greens on 8 plates. Add the hazelnuts to the dressing and spoon over the greens. Thinly slice the breasts on the diagonal and arrange on the greens. Serve immediately while the breasts are still warm.

Sautéed and Roasted Magret "4-4-6-6"

In France, the term "magret," as noted previously, refers specifically to the breast of a fattened moulard duck, usually one that has been grown to produce foie gras. The meat is dark red, very earthy, and rich from the contribution of the expanding liver. Like all duck breast, it is generally cooked rare to medium rare. Anything past medium rare and it becomes chewy and dry. This recipe was adapted from Junny Gonzales, who, with her husband, Guillermo, own Sonoma Artisan Foie Gras in Northern California. Serve with the simple sauce below or any other savory-sweet sauce you like, such as the Cinnamon-Port Sauce (page 281) or Sun-Dried Cherry Sauce (pages 254). If using the smaller pekin duck breast, the roasting time will be around 4 to 5 minutes.

MAKES 4 SERVINGS
DUCK
2 magret duck breast halves
¼ cup (55g) olive oil
2 teaspoons pressed garlic
1 teaspoon dried thyme or herbs de provence
Salt and freshly ground black pepper

SAUCE
¼ cup (40g) peeled chopped shallots
2 cups (475mL) rich chicken or duck stock
3 tablespoons (45mL) Cognac or brandy
1 teaspoon Dijon mustard or to taste
1 cup (240mL) whipping cream
2 tablespoons drained green peppercorns in brine, slightly crushed

Score the duck skin through the fat but not into the meat in a criss-cross pattern. Mix the olive oil, garlic, and thyme together and rub on both sides of the breasts. Season liberally with salt and pepper. Refrigerate for at least 4 hours.

Preheat the oven to 425°F. Wipe the marinade off the magret. In a heavy skillet over high heat, sauté the duck skin side down for 4 minutes, then skin side up for another 4 minutes. Place the pan in the preheated oven and roast for 6 minutes. Remove from the oven, place the breasts on a platter, and cover loosely with foil and allow the magret to rest for 6 minutes before slicing, saving the juices for the sauce. Dump the fat from the skillet, but do not clean the pan.

While the breasts are resting, make the sauce by adding the shallots to the skillet and sautéing for 2 minutes over medium heat. Add the stock, cognac, and mustard and stir to get all the crispy browned bits on the bottom of the skillet. Add the cream and green peppercorns. Boil until the mixture thickens to sauce consistency, about 6 minutes. Stir in any juices from the duck breasts and season the sauce to taste with salt and pepper. Spoon the sauce onto warm plates. Thinly slice the magret on the bias, and fan the slices over the sauce. Serve immediately.

Roast Duck Breasts with Grapefruit

This recipe could also be done with chicken breasts. You could also prepare the meat on the grill rather than roasting. My favorite grapefruits are the Texas pinks or reds that come to the market from October to June.

MAKES 4 SERVINGS
1 tablespoon honey
Juice of 2 grapefruits, divided
$\frac{1}{2}$ teaspoon ground allspice or juniper berry
4 pekin duck breast halves
Salt and freshly ground black pepper

GRAPEFRUIT SAUCE
2 tablespoons balsamic vinegar
2 tablespoons sugar

2 cups (475mL) rich chicken or duck stock
1 cup plus 1 tablespoon (255mL) grapefruit juice
1 cup (240mL) heavy cream
Kosher or sea salt and freshly ground black pepper

2 grapefruits, sectioned
1 large bunch watercress, preferably Upland Cress, with big stems discarded

Preheat the oven to 425°F. Whisk the honey, 3 tablespoons of the grapefruit juice, and the allspice together in a small bowl. Trim the breasts of excess fat and score the skin in a crosshatch pattern, cutting almost but not quite through to the meat. Brush the breasts with the honey mixture, season with salt and pepper, and set aside for at least 15 minutes.

Heat an ovenproof sauté pan over moderately high heat. Add the duck breasts skin side down and sear until golden brown, about 4 minutes. Turn the breasts over and place them in the oven for 5 to 6 minutes more or until the meat is medium rare. Be careful not to overcook. Remove the pan from the oven and then remove the breasts from the pan to a cutting board and allow to rest for at least 3 minutes. Cover loosely with foil to keep warm.

To make the Grapefruit Sauce, combine the balsamic vinegar and sugar in a saucepan and cook over high heat until the sugar is melted and the mixture is reduced to a syrupy consistency, about 2 minutes. Add the stock and 1 cup of the grapefruit juice and reduce over high heat to ¾ cup or so, about 10 minutes. Whisk in the cream and continue to reduce until the sauce is nicely thickened, about 5 minutes. Remove from the heat, stir in the remaining 1 tablespoon of grapefruit juice, season to taste with salt and pepper, and keep warm. This can be made an hour ahead and kept warm.

To serve: Arrange the grapefruit sections and watercress on 4 plates. Thinly slice the duck breasts and arrange them on top, spoon warm Grapefruit Sauce around, and serve immediately.

Crispy Duck Rolls

In the preceding recipes we used the skin and the breast meat. Here is a delicious way to use the meat from the duck legs. This would make a fun appetizer or first course and could be done with any roasted bird meat.

MAKES 16 ROLLS

2 cups (230g) finely chopped cooked duck leg meat
1/2 cup (62g) chopped water chestnuts
1/4 cup (25g) finely chopped scallions, white and green parts
2 tablespoons chopped fresh cilantro

Kosher or sea salt and freshly ground black pepper to taste
1 large head iceberg lettuce
16 (8-inch) round rice papers
Vegetable oil for frying
Hoisin sauce

In a medium bowl, mix together the chopped duck, water chestnuts, scallions, cilantro, and salt and pepper to taste. Separate the lettuce into 16 large leaves and keep refrigerated until ready to use.

Fill a large bowl with warm water and dip a rice paper round into it to soften for a few seconds. Don't allow it to soften all the way or it will be difficult to handle. Drain briefly and place the paper on a clean hard surface, where it will continue to soften.

Place 2 tablespoons of the duck mixture on the bottom third of the rice paper and then roll it tightly to cover the mixture. Fold both ends over and continue to roll to the end. This is very much like rolling a burrito.

The roll should be a compact sausage shape about 3 inches long. Continue in the same way with the rest of the rolls until you've used up all the filling. They can be made up to 4 hours ahead. Store in a single layer, covered with plastic and refrigerated.

Preheat the oven to 200°F and place a baking sheet in it lined with paper towels. Heat about 2 inches of oil in a deep saucepan or wok to 375°F. Deep-fry a couple rolls at a time. They like to stick to one another at the beginning of frying, so don't do too many at a time. Continue with the rest of the rolls, keeping the completed ones warm in the oven.

To serve: Roll up a duck roll in a lettuce leaf with a dab of hoisin sauce and enjoy.

BBQ Duck Legs with Polenta

This is a recipe from my friend and chef Mark Stark. He and his wife, Terri, own four (and by now maybe five) wonderful restaurants in Sonoma County, California, where I live (www.starkrestaurants.com). He is a master of big bold flavors and interesting ingredient combinations.

MAKES 4 SERVINGS

COFFEE BBQ SAUCE
2 cups (300g) sliced yellow onion
5 garlic cloves
3 tablespoons unsalted butter
1 cup (240mL) strong brewed coffee
1 cup (240mL) Worcestershire sauce
2 cups (440g) ketchup
1 cup (240mL) apple cider vinegar
1 tablespoon chili powder
1 tablespoon salt or to taste
8 ounces (150g) brown sugar (about 3/4 cup packed)

DUCK
4 meaty duck legs

Kosher or sea salt and freshly ground black pepper
3 tablespoons olive oil or duck fat
1 medium yellow onion, sliced (about 2 cups, 300g)
6 garlic cloves
2 cups (475mL) chicken stock
1/2 bunch fresh cilantro (reserve the rest for garnish)
1 tablespoon chilled unsalted butter

SMOKED CHEDDAR POLENTA
1 cup (240mL) milk
1 ear corn
1/2 cup (61g) polenta meal
1/4 cup (28g) freshly grated smoked cheddar cheese
1/4 cup (28g) freshly grated white cheddar cheese
1 tablespoon unsalted butter
Salt and white pepper to taste

To make the coffee BBQ sauce, in a medium saucepan, cook the onions and garlic in the butter until they are soft but not browned, about 3 minutes. Add the remaining ingredients and simmer for 45 minutes. Let cool slightly and then purée in a blender until smooth. This recipe will yield more than needed, but will keep for several weeks if refrigerated and tightly sealed.

Preheat the oven to 325°F.

To prepare the duck, season the duck legs with the salt and pepper. In a skillet, cook the duck legs in the olive oil until well browned all over and then transfer them to a casserole dish large enough to fit them snugly in one layer. Add the sliced onions and garlic cloves to the skillet and sauté until golden, about 5 minutes. Add the chicken stock and 2 cups of the BBQ sauce to the skillet. Bring to a boil. Season with a little more salt and pepper. Pour this sauce over the duck legs, enough to just cover them. Tuck in the cilantro and then cover with foil. Place in the oven and braise the legs until tender, 1 to 1½ hours. Let the duck cool in the liquid. When cool enough to handle, remove the duck legs and pick all the meat off the bones. Discard the bones and skin and strain the cooking liquid, pressing down on the solids and discarding the vegetables. Reserve the BBQ sauce and duck meat (this can be done up to 2 days before serving).

To make the Smoked Cheddar Polenta, preheat the oven to 350°F. Combine the milk with 1 cup of water in a deep saucepan. Using a hand grater, grate the corn into the pan. Bring the liquid to a simmer, then slowly whisk in the polenta. Keep stirring until the liquid comes back to a simmer and begins to thicken. Season to your taste with salt and pepper and then cover with foil and cook in the oven for 1 hour. Remove the pan from the oven and whisk in the cheeses and the butter. The polenta should be smooth and the consistency of soft mashed potatoes. You can adjust the consistency with water or chicken stock. Keep warm until needed.

Place the pulled duck meat in a pan along with enough of the BBQ sauce to nicely coat. Gently heat and bring to a simmer. Stir in the chilled butter until incorporated. Place generous portions of polenta into 4 bowls. Top with the duck and garnish with sprigs of cilantro. Pray for leftovers!

A Simpler Peking Duck

Beijing's most famous dish, peking duck is traditionally served with mandarin pancakes, with the crispy skin and meat eaten separately. Here I've tried to simplify the lengthy process used to make it.

MAKES 4 SERVINGS
1 (4-pound, 1.8kg) pekin duck
2 teaspoons salt
2 teaspoons 5-spice powder (see page 57)

**1 TEASPOON FRESHLY GROUND WHITE
  PEPPER BASTING SAUCE**
1/4 cup (60mL) soy sauce
1/3 cup (80mL) orange juice

1/2 cup (120mL) rice wine
3 tablespoons honey

CHINESE PANCAKES
2 cups (240g) all-purpose flour
2 tablespoons minced green onion
2 tablespoons toasted sesame oil

1/3 cup (35g) finely sliced scallions, cut on the bias
1/2 cup (120mL) hoisin sauce

Remove any excess fat from the duck and, with your fingers or a chopstick, gently push under the skin to loosen it from the meat. Be careful not to poke a hole in the skin. Bring a pot of water, large enough to hold the duck, to a boil. Remove the pot from the heat and plunge the duck into the water for 2 minutes. Remove the duck and pat dry. Hang the duck and allow it to dry in a cool, drafty spot for 6 hours or in front of a fan for 4 hours. When it is properly dried, the skin will feel like parchment paper. Season the inside of the duck with salt, 5-spice powder, and white pepper.

Combine the basting ingredients in a small saucepan and bring to the boil. Remove from the heat and brush the duck several times with the liquid. Allow the duck to dry again for 2 hours.

While the duck is drying, make the Chinese Pancakes. Combine the flour and 1 cup boiling water in a bowl and mix, stirring constantly, until all the water is absorbed. Add more water if the mixture seems dry. The dough should just hold together in large lumps.

Add the green onions and gather and knead the dough on a lightly floured board (or in a mixer) until smooth, about 5 minutes. Wrap the dough in plastic and allow to rest at room temperature for 30 minutes.

Unwrap and knead the dough again for 5 minutes. Form into a log about 18 inches long and 1 inch in diameter. Cut the roll into 20 pieces and roll each piece into a ball. Roll out each ball into a circle about 6 inches in diameter. Brush each side with a little of the sesame oil.

Heat a dry nonstick sauté pan over low heat. Cook the pancakes for 45 seconds on each side or until dry. Cover with plastic wrap.

Preheat the oven to 450°F. Place the duck breast side up on a rack in a roasting pan, add a couple of cups of hot water to the bottom of the pan, and roast for 20 minutes. Reduce the heat to 350°F and roast for another 1 1/2 hours or until the temperature in the thickest part of the thigh registers 170°F. The skin should be crisp and mahogany colored. Check occasionally and reduce the temperature more, if necessary, so that the coating does not burn.

To serve: At serving time, steam briefly or wrap the duck in plastic and cook it in the microwave at full power for 30 seconds. Carefully remove the crispy skin and carve the duck. Slice the breast and roll up the meat and skin in Chinese pancakes with scallions and a dab of hoisin sauce.

Duck Enchiladas with Roasted Salsa Verde

Note that this recipe has a couple of components that need to be made ahead or while the duck is roasting, such as the caramelized onions and Roasted Salsa Verde.

MAKES 4 SERVINGS (2 ENCHILADAS PER SERVING)

1 (4- to 5-pound, 1.8 to 2.25kg) duck

2 tablespoons plus 1 teaspoon toasted cumin seeds, divided

1 teaspoon whole coriander seeds

1 teaspoon ground cinnamon

1 teaspoon ground cloves

Kosher or sea salt and freshly ground black pepper

3 cups (700mL) duck or chicken stock

½ ounce dried wild mushrooms, rinsed until soft and finely chopped

1 teaspoon chopped chipotle in adobo, or more to taste

2 tablespoons olive oil

3 large onions, sliced

1 teaspoon packed brown sugar

ROASTED SALSA VERDE

1 pound (450g) fresh husked tomatillos

1 large yellow onion, peeled and quartered

1 medium serrano or jalapeño pepper, seeded

6 whole peeled garlic cloves

2 tablespoons olive oil

½ teaspoon each whole coriander and cumin seeds

Salt and freshly ground black pepper

⅓ cup (16g) chopped fresh cilantro

2 cups (475mL) chicken stock

8 large corn tortillas, softened by steaming briefly

3 cups (340g) shredded pepper jack or cheddar cheese or a combination

¾ cup (180g) seeded and diced fresh tomato

Fresh cilantro sprigs

Preheat the oven to 350°F. Rinse the duck. Remove and discard any excess fat and pat dry. Combine 2 tablespoons of the cumin, coriander, cinnamon, cloves, 2 teaspoons of salt, and 1 teaspoon of black pepper in a spice grinder. Grind the spices and rub the inside and outside of the duck with the mixture. Place the duck on a rack in a roasting pan and roast in the oven for 1½ hours or until the temperature in the thickest part of the thigh registers 170°F.

While the duck is roasting, combine the stock, mushrooms, the remaining teaspoon of cumin, and the chipotle in a saucepan. Bring to a simmer and reduce by half, about 15 minutes. Set aside. Heat a large heavy skillet over moderate heat. Add the oil, onions, and sugar and sauté until the onions are golden brown, about 12 minutes, stirring occasionally. Set aside.

Meanwhile, prepare the salsa verde. When the duck is finished cooking, increase the oven to 375°F. Toss the tomatillos, onion, chile, and garlic with the olive oil in an ovenproof baking dish. Add the coriander and cumin seeds. Season lightly with salt and pepper and roast, uncovered, for 30 minutes or until the tomatillos and onions are lightly brown and soft. Add to a food processor or blender, being sure to include all juices and brown bits. Add the cilantro and stock and process to make a smooth sauce. Strain through a coarse mesh strainer if desired and season to taste with salt and pepper. Keep warm.

When the duck is cool, pick and shred the meat, discarding the bones and saving the skin for cracklings.

Add the meat to the reduced sauce and simmer over low heat for a couple of minutes or until the liquid is absorbed by the meat. Season to taste with salt and pepper.

Divide the duck and caramelized onions among the tortillas. Roll them up and place them in a baking dish, seam side down. Spoon the salsa verde over and top with the cheese. This can be made a day ahead, covered, and refrigerated until ready to use.

Bake the enchiladas for 20 to 25 minutes or until the cheese is melted and the enchiladas are hot. Top with the tomatoes and cilantro sprigs and serve immediately.

Roasting and Peeling
Peppers

Position the broiler rack about 4 inches from the heat source and preheat the broiler. Cut the peppers in half, discarding the stems and seeds. Cover the bottom of a rimmed baking sheet with foil. Lightly oil the peppers with vegetable oil and place them cut-side down on the sheet pan. Broil until the skins are mostly charred, about 10 minutes depending on the broiler. Remove the pan from the broiler, fold the foil up over the peppers, and allow them to steam for a couple of minutes. When they are cool enough to handle, scrape off the charred skin with a paring knife and/or your fingers and discard. Do not rinse the peppers, which would wash away all the toasty, roasty flavors. Strain any juices left on the pan and pour over the peppers.

Duck Jambalaya

There are countless variations on this Cajun-Creole dish. You can find about as many recipes for this dish as there are households that make it. Gonzales, Louisiana, is the self-proclaimed Jambalaya capital of the world and holds a famous annual Jambalaya cooking contest (www.jambalayafestival.org) on Memorial Day weekend each year. Add that to your bucket list! The "broken" rice referred to below is just as it says and is the lower grade of rice. It's available in Louisiana and also used in Vietnamese dishes. You can find it in Southeast Asian markets. Regular medium grain white rice can be substituted.

MAKES 6 SERVINGS

1 (5-pound, 2.25kg) duck, trimmed of excess fat and cut into 8 pieces

Kosher or sea salt

1 teaspoon cayenne pepper

1 cup (120g) all-purpose flour

3 tablespoons vegetable oil

12 ounces andouille or other spicy sausage, cut into large dice

1 medium onion, finely chopped (about 1 cup, 160g)

2 large garlic cloves, finely chopped (about 1 tablespoon)

1 large green bell pepper, diced (about 1½ cups, 115g)

1 large celery stalk, diced (about ¾ cup, 76g)

3 cups (700mL) canned or homemade chicken stock (see page 70), divided

2 cups (480g) ripe fresh or canned diced tomatoes

2 bay leaves

1 tablespoon Worcestershire sauce

1½ cups (281g) white rice, preferably broken

1 cup (96g) sliced green onions, cut thinly on the bias

½ cup (30g) chopped fresh parsley

Hot pepper sauce of your choice

Pat the duck dry with paper towels and score the skin to help remove the fat. Season all sides with salt and cayenne. Dust the pieces with flour and shake off excess. In a heavy Dutch oven or stock pot, heat the oil over moderate heat and brown the duck pieces on all sides. You may have to do this in batches. Transfer the duck to a large plate.

Pour off all but 3 tablespoons of fat from the Dutch oven, add the sausage, and brown lightly, about 7 minutes. Set aside with the duck. Stir in the onions, garlic, bell pepper, and celery and cook until the onions are translucent and softened but not brown, about 5 minutes. Stir in 2 cups of the chicken stock and the tomatoes and bay leaves and bring to a boil over high heat, scraping up any browned bits from the bottom of the pot.

Return the duck and sausage to the pot along with any juices on the plate. Bring to a boil over high heat and then reduce the heat to low and simmer, partially covered, for 1 hour and 15 minutes or until the duck is just tender. Stir in the remaining cup of chicken stock, the Worcestershire, and the rice and bring to a boil. Reduce the heat to low, cover, and simmer for 20 minutes or until the rice is tender and the grains have absorbed most of the liquid. Stir in the green onions and parsley and season to taste with salt and hot sauce.

Duck Braised with Prunes

This simple braise could be done with any culinary bird. Here, it is served with sautéed apples. Pick an apple that doesn't turn mushy, but holds its shape when cooked: Cortland, Jonagold, Northern Spy, Winesap, and Golden Delicious all fit the bill nicely.

MAKES 4 SERVINGS

4 large duck leg-thighs, about 12 ounces each
4 tablespoons (55g) olive oil, divided
1 medium onion, sliced (about 1 1/2 cups, 173g)
4 large garlic cloves, peeled and chopped (about 2 tablespoons)
1 small carrot, peeled and chopped (about 1/2 cup, 64g)
1/2 celery stalk, chopped (about 1/2 cup, 50g)
1 teaspoon whole black peppercorns
2 large bay leaves
4 crushed juniper berries
2 cups (475mL) hearty red wine (such as cabernet)
4 cups (950mL) canned or homemade duck or chicken stock (see page 70)
1 cup (174g) pitted prunes, sliced in half
Salt and freshly ground black pepper
3 tablespoons unsalted butter
2 peeled, cored, and sliced apples

Trim the excess fat from the duck legs. Heat 2 tablespoons of the oil in a saucepan over medium heat. Add the onion, garlic, carrot, and celery and sauté until lightly browned, about 10 minutes. Add the peppercorns, bay leaves, juniper berries, and wine and simmer for 10 minutes, partially covered. Cool completely, about 1 hour, and then add the duck legs and marinate in the refrigerator for at least 4 hours and up to 12.

Remove the legs from the marinade and pat dry, reserving the marinade. Sauté the duck legs in the remaining 2 tablespoons of oil until golden brown on all sides, about 4 minutes per side. Place the duck in a skillet big enough to snugly fit the legs in one layer. Heat the reserved marinade with the vegetables and the prunes to a simmer. Pour over the duck, add the stock, and simmer gently, covered, for 1 1/2 hours or until the duck is tender. Remove the duck and keep warm.

Strain the cooking liquid, pressing down on the solids. Discard the solids. Remove as much fat as you can from the liquid. Pour the liquid into a saucepan and reduce over high heat to a nice sauce consistency, about 30 minutes. Season to taste with salt and pepper.

Heat the butter in a sauté pan over medium heat and sauté the apple slices in the butter until lightly browned, about 2 minutes. Divide the apples among four warm plates, top with the duck, and ladle the prune sauce over the top.

Duck à l'Orange

This is one of those warhorse recipes that introduced America to the glories of French food. It still is delicious and of course can be done with any culinary bird. Note that the sauce can be made ahead.

MAKES 4 SERVINGS

¼ cup (30g) sugar
2 tablespoons sherry wine vinegar
1½ cups (350mL) fresh orange juice
2 tablespoons finely minced shallots
1½ cups (350mL) low-sodium chicken broth
4 large naval oranges

2 large pekin or muscovy duck breast halves
Kosher or sea salt and freshly ground black pepper
2 tablespoons canola oil
½ stick (55g) unsalted butter
1 tablespoon finely grated orange zest

Stir the sugar and 2 tablespoons of water in a heavy medium saucepan over medium-high heat until the sugar dissolves, about 2 minutes. Bring to a boil, occasionally brushing down the sides of the pan with a wet pastry brush to prevent the sugar from recrystalizing. Swirl the pan until the syrup turns a golden amber, about 8 minutes. Remove from the heat and stir in the vinegar. Be very careful because the mixture will bubble energetically. Add the orange juice and shallots and boil, stirring continuously, until reduced to about ½ cup, about 10 minutes. Add the chicken broth and continue to boil until reduced to ¾ cup, about 15 minutes. Set aside.

Using a microplane grate 1 tablespoon zest from the orange, reserving for later, and then cut off the peel and white pith from the oranges, reserving 1 tablespoon of peel. Working over a bowl, cut between the membranes to release the segments. The sauce and oranges can be prepared up to 4 hours ahead.

Using a small knife, score the duck skin but not the meat in a crosshatch pattern. Season liberally with salt and pepper. Heat the oil in a large heavy skillet over medium-high heat. Place the duck breasts skin side down in the skillet. Cook until brown and crisp, about 4 minutes. Turn the duck and cook to desired doneness, about 6 minutes longer for medium rare. Transfer to a plate and let stand for 5 minutes to let the juices redistribute.

Meanwhile, bring the sauce to a simmer. Whisk in the butter and orange zest just until the butter melts. Also whisk in any juice from the plate with the duck breasts. Drain the orange segments and mix into the sauce. Slice the duck breasts crosswise on the diagonal and arrange the slices on 4 warm plates. Spoon the sauce with orange segments around.

Duck Breast with Sun-Dried Cherry Sauce

A riff on the classic from the days of "Long Island Duckling." The cherry sauce can be made ahead and reheated. It could be used with any bird throughout the book.

MAKES 4 SERVINGS
4 pekin duck breast halves
3 tablespoons olive oil
2 teaspoons finely minced shallots
2 tablespoons balsamic vinegar, preferably white or golden
Salt and freshly ground black pepper

SUN-DRIED CHERRY SAUCE
2 tablespoons olive oil
2 large shallots or 3 green onions, peeled and chopped (about 1/4 cup, 28g)

1 cup (100g) chopped shiitake or cremini mushrooms
6 cups (1.4L) canned or homemade chicken stock (see page 70)
1 cup (240mL) hearty red wine (such as Zinfandel)
1 cup (138g) sun-dried cherries, divided
1 tablespoon finely grated orange zest
1/2 cup (120mL) fresh orange juice
2 teaspoons chopped fresh thyme (1 teaspoon dried)
1/2 cup (120mL) vintage style or Ruby port, or to taste
Salt and freshly ground black pepper

Trim the breasts of excess fat and score the skin in a crosshatch pattern, cutting almost but not quite through to the meat. Whisk the olive oil, shallots, and vinegar together in a small bowl and brush the breasts with the mixture. Season the breasts well with salt and pepper and set aside for at least 30 minutes.

Meanwhile, make the Sun-Dried Cherry Sauce. Heat the oil in a saucepan over medium heat and sauté the shallots and shiitakes until very lightly browned, about 6 minutes. Add the stock and wine and reduce by half, about 20 minutes. Add half of the cherries and the orange zest, orange juice, thyme, and port and reduce to a light sauce consistency, about 5 minutes. Strain, skim off any fat, and add the remaining cherries to plump in the warm sauce. Adjust the seasoning with salt and pepper to taste. This can be made up to a week ahead and stored in the refrigerator.

Preheat the oven to 425°F. Heat an ovenproof sauté pan over medium-high heat. Add the duck breasts skin side down and sear until golden brown, about 4 minutes. Turn the breasts over and place them in the oven for 5 to 6 minutes or until the meat is medium rare. Be careful not to overcook. Transfer the breasts to a cutting board and allow them to rest for at least 3 minutes. Cover the breasts loosely with foil to keep warm.

To serve: Spoon some of the cherry sauce on warms plates. Thinly slice the duck breasts, arrange the slices on top of the sauce, and serve immediately.

Classic Roast Goose

We want to follow the same method as for roast duck on page 228, except we are going to steam the goose after it has gone through its dry salt brine to remove the copious amounts of fat under the skin.

MAKES 6 TO 8 SERVINGS

Step 1: Remove the wing tips with kitchen shears and store them in the refrigerator along with the giblets for making gravy. Salt the goose inside and out at least 12 hours and up to 24 hours before roasting. For an 8- to 10-pound goose, use 2 tablespoons or so of kosher salt. Place on a rack in a deep roasting pan (preferably with a lid) and refrigerate uncovered for 12 to 24 hours. With a sharp skewer or the point of a paring knife, gently prick the skin, trying to avoid going all the way into the meat, around the legs and lower part of the breast. This will allow the fat to escape during steaming and roasting.

Step 2: Remove the goose from the refrigerator and let it sit at room temperature for at least 1 hour. Add an inch or so of water to the pan and place it over a large burner. Cover the pan tightly with the lid or heavy duty foil and seal well around the edges. Bring the water to a boil and then reduce the heat so that it is gently simmering (you'll have to take a peek). Steam the covered goose for 45 minutes. Turn off the heat, carefully remove the cover, and allow it to cool for 20 minutes or so. Lift the goose with its rack and transfer it to a rimmed baking sheet to catch any drips. Strain the steaming liquid into a tall, clear container or fat separator, and reserve the fat for other uses. Discard the steaming water.

Step 3: Preheat the oven to 350°F. Return the goose breast side down in its roasting rack to the roasting pan and roast, uncovered, for 1½ hours. Turn the bird breast side up and continue to roast for another 1½ hours or until the legs feel loose in their sockets, an instant-read thermometer reads 175°F in the thickest part of the thigh (not touching the bone), and the juices run clear. Be sure to monitor the goose the whole time, removing excess fat with a bulb baster. Turn the oven up to 500°F and cook the goose until its skin is beautifully browned and crispy, 10 to 15 minutes. Keep your eye on it so that you don't burn the bird. Set the bird aside for at least 20 minutes on a rimmed baking sheet to catch any drippings.

Step 4: Make a pan sauce such as one of the ones on page 42, incorporating any of the drippings. Carve the bird and serve with the pan sauce.

Corned Goose

This is a very old technique, not unlike corned beef, which was done to help preserve the bird when refrigeration was at a premium. You can use this for all culinary birds. Once cooked, the meat can be used in main courses, in soups, on sandwiches, in salads, or for corned goose hash! "Corned" has nothing to do with actual corn but is an old English word for "kernel." It referred to any kind of small, hard object, like, say, a large grain or "corn of salt."

MAKES ABOUT 3 POUNDS OF MEAT

1 cup (224g) kosher or sea salt
½ cup (100g) brown sugar, firmly packed
6 garlic cloves, peeled and bruised with the side
  of a knife

12 whole cloves
1 teaspoon freshly grated nutmeg
1½ tablespoons juniper berries, crushed
1 (6- to 8-pound, 2.7 to 3.6kg) goose, steamed to
  reduce the fat

Combine the salt, sugar, and 3 quarts of water in a stock pot and simmer until the salt dissolves, about 2 minutes. Remove from the heat and stir in the garlic, cloves, nutmeg, and juniper berries. Let the mixture cool to room temperature. Put the goose in the cooled mixture, adding additional water if necessary to just cover the goose. Cover and store refrigerated for 4 days, turning the goose twice each day.

Drain the goose, rinse well, and cover with cold water in a large bowl or pot. Place a heavy plate or large can on the bird if necessary to keep it submerged, and let it stand in the refrigerator for 8 hours. During this time, change the water at least 4 times.

Preheat the oven to 350°F. Drain the goose, pat dry, truss and roast it on a rack in a roasting pan for 2½ hours or until the temperature in the thickest part of the thigh registers 170°F. Be sure regularly to "drain off" the fat with a bulb baster.

Fricassee of Goose

Fricassee is a French term and is basically a braise of almost any bird cooked slowly in a seasoned broth and, in this case, finished with crème fraîche. It's important here to remove as much fat from the goose as you can before cooking. Render it and make cracklings per the instructions on page 226.

MAKES 8 TO 10 SERVINGS
1 (6- to 8-pound, 2.7 to 3.6kg) goose
6 tablespoons (90mL) goose fat or olive oil, divided
Salt and freshly ground black pepper
2 medium onions, sliced (about 3 cups, 450g)
2 celery stalks, chopped (about 1 cup, 150g)
1 medium carrot, peeled and chopped (about 1 cup, 150g)
2 bay leaves
2 teaspoons fennel seeds
2 teaspoons dried thyme

3 cups (700mL) canned or homemade chicken stock (see page 70)
1½ cups (350mL) dry white wine
5 tablespoons (71g) unsalted butter
⅔ cup (80g) all-purpose flour
1½ cups (350mL) crème fraîche or heavy cream
3 cups (216g) quartered cremini mushrooms
2 tablespoons lemon juice, or to taste
¼ cup (20g) chopped fresh parsley
Cooked rice or noodles (optional)

Cut all of the goose meat off the bones, removing the skin and reserving the fat. Cut the meat into 2-inch cubes. A little hint here: Make sure the goose is very cold when cutting it up. As the bird warms, so does the fat, which makes it slippery.

Heat 3 tablespoons of the reserved fat in a large Dutch oven over medium-high heat and brown the meat on all sides, seasoning generously with salt and pepper. You may have to do this in batches. Set the meat aside and pour out all but 3 tablespoons of fat. Add the onions, celery, and carrots and brown lightly over medium heat. Add the bay leaves, fennel seeds, and thyme. Return the goose meat to the pan and give it a stir. Add the chicken stock and wine and enough water to cover the meat by a ½ inch. Bring to a simmer and cook, covered, for 40 to 45 minutes or until the goose is very tender.

Transfer the goose to a platter and strain the broth, discarding the vegetables and removing any surface fat. Wipe out the Dutch oven, return the strained stock, and bring to a boil over high heat. Cook until the liquid is reduced to 3 cups, about 15 minutes.

Meanwhile, add the butter to a saucepan over moderate heat. Whisk in the flour and continue whisking for 3 minutes to cook out any raw taste in the flour and prevent lumps. Slowly whisk in the reduced broth and crème fraîche and simmer for 4 or 5 minutes until thickened and smooth. Add additional chicken stock if desired for a thinner sauce.

Add 3 tablespoons of goose fat to a large sauté pan over moderately high heat. Add the mushrooms and cook until nicely browned, about 4 minutes. Add the reserved goose meat, lemon juice, and parsley. Season to taste with salt and pepper. Serve with rice or noodles, if desired.

SMALL
BIRDS

(Quail, Squab, Partridge, and Dove)

There is a whole range of small game birds that can share similar preparations. These include quail, squab, dove, grouse (prairie chicken), chukar, ptarmigan, and partridge. They are all part of a large group of non-waterfowl birds described as having "upland-ground-like shape." All are lean, usually darker-meat birds, and I think they are superb grilled. They are all lean birds. Be careful not to overcook them or they become dry.

Quail

Scientifically named *Coturnix coturnix*, the common quail originated from the migratory quail birds of the Asian, African, and European continents. They eventually reached America, and these species interbred naturally and were crossbred artificially, giving rise to the many subspecies and mutations we have today.

Most quail have a crest or plume, called a topknot, on their head.

Bobwhite quail is the most common species of quail in America and is often referred to as the number one game bird of the eastern and southern United States. It is also farm raised for the table along with Japanese quail (*Coturnix coturnix japonica*) and is still an important source for meat and eggs in Japan and other parts of Asia.

Though you don't typically see them offered every day in American markets, farm-raised quail can be ordered easily with a few days' notice (see pages 310–11 for sources for quail and other specialty birds). Note that wild game birds and animals cannot be served in restaurants or sold in retail markets unless they have been slaughtered and dressed under US Department of Agriculture or equivalent foreign inspection.

Quail are harvested at five weeks or so depending on the species and are usually shipped frozen (which is fine) and range in size from four to eight ounces. Chefs love quail, and I've asked some of my chef friends to share their favorite recipes here. We typically serve two quail per serving for a main course and one for a first or salad course. They can be purchased whole or partially boned with the breast and back bones removed, leaving only the bones in the wings and leg-thigh sections.

I personally love to cook them whole so that I can nibble the juicy meat right off the bone. The birds are so small that trying to use a knife and fork makes no sense.

Other small birds such as partridge and dove can be substituted in any of the following quail recipes.

Squab

"Squab," or young pigeon, has been bred for food for centuries, dating back to early Asian and Arabic cultures. Parent birds, or "breeders," mate for life and share the responsibilities of raising their young. True squabs have never flown. Dressed for market four weeks after hatching, they range in weight from sixteen to twenty ounces, depending on the breed or breed mix. There is a large number of breeds of pigeons, many of which are suitable for the production of squabs. The most popular is the king, which is often bred with a French breed called carneau, since they produce large breasts.

The meat of a squab is unlike domestic poultry or wild game birds. All dark, moist, and distinctly flavorful, each bird is prepared for market before it is old enough to fly. Since the fat on squab is "baby fat" (just under the skin), the meat is actually quite lean. Like quail, you can buy squabs whole or semi boneless.

When cooking squab, make sure it isn't cooked past medium rare. You want to make sure the meat is rosy and moist. If you cook it too long, the bird develops a distinctly "livery" taste.

In *How to Cook a Wolf*, M.F.K. Fisher claims that "a roasted pigeon is and long has been the most heartening dish to set before a man." Her favorite way of cooking squab was a covered-pot version that included lemon and parsley in the cavity, followed by a quick brown in bacon fat and a slow braise in red wine, cider, beer, orange juice, or tomato juice. The bird was then served on toast with bacon and Belgian endive with a fruity, young Beaujolais. Comfort food at its best!

Squab are considered one of the most intelligent birds on the planet.

The Recipes

Grilled Quail Salad
with Lavender Pepper Rub

This rub is one that I use on any bird, and it's also good with lamb.

MAKES 4 SERVINGS

4 semi-boneless quail

Lavender Pepper Rub (recipe follows)

1/2 cup (60g) walnut halves

1 1/2 cups (52.5g) 1/2–inch cubes rustic bread, crusts removed

4 tablespoons (55g) toasted walnut oil, divided

1 teaspoon orange zest

1/3 cup (80mL) orange juice

1/2 teaspoon ground ginger

1/8 teaspoon ground nutmeg

Pinch ground cloves

Kosher or sea salt and freshly ground black pepper

4 cups (120g) gently packed baby salad greens

2 cups (60g) gently packed frisée leaves (preferably white leaves only)

1 honeycrisp apple (or other tart-sweet apple), cored and thinly sliced

Rinse the quail and pat dry. Rub the exterior with some of the Lavender Pepper Rub and set aside.

Preheat the oven to 350°F. Place the walnuts in a pie plate. Toss the bread with 1 tablespoon of the walnut oil and arrange on another pie plate. Place both pie plates in the oven and cook until the walnuts are lightly toasted, about 6 minutes. Remove the walnuts and continue cooking the croutons until crisp, about 6 more minutes.

In a large bowl, whisk the remaining 3 tablespoons of the walnut oil with the orange zest, orange juice, ginger, nutmeg, cloves, and salt and pepper to taste.

Heat a grill to moderately high heat or heat a ridged grill pan over medium heat. Grill the quail until the juices run clear, about 4 minutes on each side.

Toss the greens, frisée, apple, walnuts, and croutons with the orange dressing and arrange on 4 plates. Top with the quail and serve immediately.

Lavender Pepper Rub

2 teaspoons kosher or sea salt

2 teaspoons whole black peppercorns

2 teaspoons whole fennel seeds

1 teaspoon white peppercorns

2 teaspoons dried lavender flowers (available at health food stores)

Place all the ingredients in a spice or coffee grinder and pulse to a fairly fine powder. Rub on the meat at least 30 minutes before cooking.

Pan-Roasted Quail and Pear Salad

This salad uses something the French call *gastrique*. It's a syrup made by reducing vinegar or wine, sugar, and often fruit. It is served with meats and fishes, vegetables such as fresh tomatoes, and also as an addition to sauces to add depth and flavor. It also adds complexity to fruit-based cocktails. Any bird could be used here.

MAKES 4 SERVINGS

Canola oil

2 firm ripe pears, peeled, cored, and halved

Kosher or sea salt and freshly ground black pepper

½ cup (115g) sugar

1 cup (240mL) red wine (such as cabernet)

2 tablespoon balsamic vinegar

2 teaspoons finely chopped fresh rosemary

2 teaspoons finely chopped shallots

4 semi-boneless quail

6 cups (180g) gently packed mixed baby greens (such as frisée, mache, arugula)

1 large navel orange, peeled and segmented

4 ounces (113g) creamy blue cheese such as Point Reyes Farmstead, cut up

⅓ cup (39g) lightly toasted walnut halves

Preheat the oven to 375°F. Lightly oil a baking sheet and place the pears on it, cut side down. Brush the top of each pear with a little oil and sprinkle with salt and pepper. Roast until the pears are lightly browned and easily pierced with the point of a knife, 15 to 20 minutes depending on ripeness and variety. Remove from the oven and set aside. When cool, using a small knife, cut the pears lengthwise 3 or 4 times up to but not through the stem end and gently press to form a fan.

While the pears are roasting, make the *gastrique*. In a deep saucepan, dissolve the sugar with 2 tablespoons of water over medium heat. When the sugar is dissolved, increase the heat to medium high and swirl the pan occasionally until the sugar is golden brown, about 4 minutes. Carefully (the mixture will bubble up dramatically) add the wine and vinegar and reduce to a light syrup, about 4 minutes. Stir in the rosemary and shallots and set aside.

Season the quail inside and out with salt and pepper. Tuck the wings behind the body and tie the legs together with kitchen twine, if desired. Heat a heavy-bottomed ovenproof sauté pan over moderately high heat, add 2 tablespoons of canola oil, and brown the quail on both sides, about 5 minutes per side. Place the pan with the quail breast side up in the oven and roast for 4 to 5 minutes or until the juices run clear. Be careful not to overcook. Remove the twine, if any, from the legs.

To serve: Arrange greens, pears, orange segments, blue cheese, and walnuts on 4 plates. Drizzle with *gastrique*, top each with a quail, and serve immediately.

Warm Quail Salad
with Yogurt-Grapefruit Vinaigrette

I've also made this salad with grilled or roasted duck or squab breasts fanned over the greens. There is something seductive about cold and warm ingredients in the same dish.

MAKES 4 SERVINGS
MARINADE
2 tablespoons olive oil
1 small onion, finely sliced (about ⅔ cup, 106g)
¼ cup (60mL) sherry wine vinegar
3 tablespoons finely chopped fresh mint leaves
1 teaspoon crushed white peppercorns
½ teaspoon salt
¼ teaspoon ground allspice

8 boned quail

VINAIGRETTE
2 tablespoons olive oil
1¼ cups (300g) plain whole-milk yogurt
3 tablespoons finely chopped fresh mint leaves
1 tablespoon minced shallots
3 tablespoons (45mL) sherry wine vinegar
3 tablespoons toasted walnut oil
4 tablespoons (60mL) red ruby grapefruit juice
2 tablespoons honey, or to taste
Salt and freshly ground white pepper to taste

4 large ruby red grapefruit, sectioned
6 cups (180g) gently packed mixed baby savory
    greens (such as frisée, mache, arugula)

To make the marinade: Heat the olive oil in a sauté pan over medium heat, and cook the onions until they just begin to color, about 4 minutes. Remove the pan from the heat. Add the sherry vinegar to the pan, stir to deglaze the pan, and cool. Add the mint, peppercorns, salt, and allspice and set aside.

Tuck the quail wings behind the body and pin or tie the legs into an attractive shape if desired. Add the quail to the marinade and gently toss to coat the quail. Cover and marinate in the refrigerator for at least 4 hours.

To make the vinaigrette: Combine all the ingredients in a small bowl and allow to sit for at least 1 hour, refrigerated, for the flavors to develop.

At serving time, arrange grapefruit sections and greens on plates and spoon the vinaigrette around. Grill or broil the quail until just done, 8 to 10 minutes, turning once (flesh should be just barely pink). Place the quail on top of the salad and serve immediately.

Roasted Quail
with Wild Mushroom Stuffing

The sauce can be made ahead of time, so this dish can be put together very quickly. We're roasting the birds here, but they are also delicious finished over a wood-fired grill.

MAKES 6 MAIN COURSE OR 12 APPETIZER SERVINGS

12 partially boned quail

6 tablespoons (80g) olive oil, divided

Kosher or sea salt and freshly ground black pepper

20 thin slices pancetta, divided

3 large shallots, thinly sliced (about $1/2$ cup, 56g)

2 cups (172g) diced wild mushrooms (such as shiitake, oyster, chanterelle)

$1/3$ cup (80mL) dry white wine

1 tablespoon chopped fresh herbs (such as chives, basil, oregano)

$1/4$ cup (60mL) good balsamic vinegar

2 cups (475mL) quail or canned or homemade chicken stock (see page 70)

3 tablespoons unsalted butter

8 cups (320g) lightly packed young spinach, stems removed

$1/2$ cup (120g) seeded and finely diced ripe tomato

Rub the skin of the quail with 2 tablespoons of the olive oil. Tuck the wings behind and lightly season inside and out with salt and pepper. Chop 8 slices of the pancetta and add to a sauté pan with 2 tablespoons of the olive oil. Add the shallots and mushrooms and sauté over medium-high heat until the shallots are very lightly browned, about 5 minutes. Add the wine and cook until the liquid evaporates, about 2 minutes. Stir in the herbs and season to taste with salt and pepper. Cool.

Preheat the oven to 425°F. Stuff the cavities of the quail with the mushroom mixture, tuck in the legs, and skewer shut if necessary. Season with salt and pepper. Add the remaining oil to a sauté pan over medium heat and lightly brown the quail, about 5 minutes. Wrap a slice of the remaining pancetta around each quail and roast for 8 to 10 minutes or until just done. Be careful not to overcook. While the quail are cooking, add the vinegar and stock to a small saucepan and reduce over high heat until thickened to a light sauce consistency, about 5 minutes. Whisk in any pan juices from the cooked quail and keep warm.

Add the butter to a hot sauté pan and allow it to just begin to brown. Add the spinach, stir-fry quickly just to wilt, and mound in the center of warm plates. Top with the quail, stir the tomato into the sauce, and spoon the sauce over and around the quail just before serving.

Grilled Quail and Asparagus
with Asian Flavors

This would work nicely as a first course. For a main course I'd suggest doubling the quantities. Grilling is my preferred way of cooking asparagus. It brings out a sweetness that blanching or steaming doesn't.

MAKES 4 SERVINGS

2 tablespoons soy sauce
$^1/_4$ cup (60mL) rice wine or sake
1 tablespoon finely minced ginger
$^1/_4$ teaspoon 5-spice powder (see page 57)
4 semi-boneless quail, halved
1$^1/_2$ pounds (680g) asparagus
Olive oil

Kosher or sea salt and freshly ground black pepper
$^1/_3$ cup (75g) mayonnaise
2 teaspoons seasoned rice vinegar
1$^1/_2$ teaspoons soy sauce
$^1/_2$ teaspoon toasted sesame oil
Drops of hot sauce to taste
1 tablespoon toasted sesame seeds

Prepare a moderately hot grill. Whisk the soy sauce, rice wine, ginger, and 5-spice powder together in a bowl. Add the quail and turn to coat inside and out. Marinate for 30 minutes.

Meanwhile, cut off the tough bottoms of the asparagus and discard. Lightly coat the asparagus with olive oil and season generously with salt and pepper. Place the asparagus on the grill and cook until they are nicely marked but still crisp-tender, about 3 minutes. Cut diagonally in half and arrange on four plates.

Whisk the mayonnaise, rice vinegar, soy sauce, sesame oil, and drops of hot sauce together in a small bowl and adjust the seasonings to your taste. Set the sauce aside.

Remove the quail from the marinade and pat dry. Brush with a little olive oil and grill on both sides until they are nicely marked and their juices run clear, about 6 minutes total.

To serve, spoon the sauce over the asparagus and top with quail halves and a sprinkling of sesame seeds, and serve immediately.

Deep-Fried Quail
with Dried Fruit Chutney

The accompanying chutney in this recipe needs to be made ahead and makes much more than you'll need, which is a good thing. It's delicious with all manner of grilled and roasted meats and a lovely accompaniment for cheese, plus it lasts almost indefinitely refrigerated.

MAKES 4 SERVINGS

2 tablespoons olive oil
3 tablespoons (45mL) dry sherry
2 tablespoons orange juice
2 tablespoons finely chopped ginger
3 tablespoons (30g) chopped scallion, white part only
Salt and freshly ground black pepper
4 semi-boneless quail
$\frac{1}{3}$ cup (43g) cornstarch
Dried Fruit Chutney (recipe follows)

Combine the olive oil, sherry, orange juice, ginger, green onions, and a little salt and pepper in a blender and blend until relatively smooth. Rub all over the quail, including the inside, and marinate for at least 4 hours or overnight, covered and refrigerated. Remove the quail from the marinade and pat dry.

Combine the cornstarch with $\frac{1}{2}$ cup of water in a bowl and mix until smooth. Dip the quail in the cornstarch mixture until evenly coated. Set the quail aside on a rack.

Pour oil to a depth of at least 1 inch in a deep saucepan or wok. Heat the oil to 375°F and cook the quail, breast side down, for 3 minutes. Turn and cook for another 3 minutes on the other side or until the quail is cooked through. Check for doneness at the leg joint. The juices should run clear when the thickest part of the thigh is pierced, and the leg will move easily in the socket. Remove the quail from the pan and drain on paper towels. Serve hot with a $\frac{1}{4}$ cup or so of room temperature chutney on the side.

Dried Fruit Chutney

This chutney is a delicious accompaniment to smoked and roasted meat and poultry dishes and a great addition to any cheese plate.

MAKES ABOUT 1 QUART

1 (750ml) bottle dry white wine, such as sauvignon blanc

¾ cup (170g) sugar

2 whole star anise

2 bay leaves

1 tablespoon coriander seeds, crushed

1 tablespoon black peppercorns, crushed

1 cup (165g) raisins (preferably golden, unbleached)

¾ pound (340g) assorted dried fruits such as apricots, cherries, mangos, figs, coarsely chopped

3 tablespoons minced candied ginger

2 large tart-sweet apples or pears, peeled, cored and cut into 1-inch (2.5cm) chunks

3 tablespoons (45mL) fresh lime or lemon juice

Combine the wine, sugar, and spices in a nonreactive saucepan and simmer, uncovered, over medium heat for 10 minutes. Remove the pan from the heat and let cool. Strain the liquid, discarding the spices. You should have about 2½ cups of strained liquid. Return the liquid to the pan, add the raisins, dried fruits, and candied ginger, and simmer, covered, for 5 minutes. Add the apples and simmer gently until they are just tender, about 3 minutes. Remove the pan from the heat and let cool. Stir in the lime juice.

Store the chutney, covered, in the refrigerator for several weeks. Serve at room temperature for maximum flavor.

Coffee-Spice Roasted Quail
with a Vanilla Sauce

This rub is an intriguing one and could be used on any bird. I like to serve this with sautéed spinach or chard. Some thinly sliced and crispy fried parsnips would also add a nice crunchy touch.

MAKES 6 SERVINGS

COFFEE-SPICE RUB

1 tablespoon white sesame seeds

12 black peppercorns

20 coriander seeds

3 whole cloves

2 juniper berries

½-inch (13-mm) piece cinnamon stick

1 small bay leaf

3 tablespoons freshly and very finely ground espresso

1 teaspoon salt

2 teaspoons sugar

12 bone-in quail

5 tablespoons (75mL) olive oil, divided

VANILLA SAUCE

3 tablespoons chopped shallots

½ cup (43g) sliced mushrooms

3 tablespoons unsalted butter, divided

3 cups (700mL) quail or chicken stock

1 cup (240mL) dry white wine

⅔ cup (160mL) heavy cream

1 (3-inch) vanilla bean, split

1 tablespoon lemon juice

Kosher or sea salt and freshly ground white pepper

To make the rub, preheat the oven to 350°F. On a baking sheet, arrange in separate piles the sesame, peppercorns, coriander, cloves, juniper berries, and cinnamon and toast until the sesame seeds are golden, about 10 minutes. Remove the spices from the oven, and with a spice grinder, finely grind the toasted spices along with the bay leaf. Add the coffee, salt, and sugar and continue grinding until the mixture is finely ground. Turn the oven up to 450°F.

Lightly rub the quail with 2 tablespoons of the olive oil and then rub with the spice mixture. Refrigerate, covered, for 2 to 3 hours.

Meanwhile, prepare the vanilla sauce. Sauté the shallots and mushrooms in 1 tablespoon of the butter until the vegetables are soft but not brown. Add the stock and wine and reduce by half over high heat, about 8 minutes. Add the cream and vanilla bean and reduce again to a light sauce consistency, about 8 minutes. Strain through a fine-mesh strainer, pressing down on the solids. Scrape the soft center of the vanilla bean into the strained sauce and discard the bean. Adjust the seasonings with drops of lemon juice and salt and pepper. Whisk in the remaining butter in bits. Hold the sauce in a warm water bath or thermos until serving time (up to 3 hours).

Remove the quail from the refrigerator. In a large, heavy, ovenproof sauté pan, heat the remaining oil and brown the quail on all sides over moderate heat. Turn the quail breast side up and place the pan in the oven for 5 to 7 minutes to finish cooking. Test by inserting the point of a knife at the thigh joint. Juices should run clear and the leg should move easily. Serve 2 quail per person with sauce spooned around.

Grilled Quail
with Pickled Figs and Prosciutto

If you make the figs ahead, refrigerate them in their poaching liquid and return them to room temperature before serving. You get a bonus with this recipe: The leftover fig-poaching syrup is delicious on grilled meats or even ice cream. Be sure to strain it before using. The figs are served at room temperature, but the quail should be hot, right off the grill.

MAKES 4 SERVINGS

PICKLED FIGS

1 cup (225g) sugar
1 1/2 cups (350mL) red wine vinegar
1/2 cup (120mL) balsamic vinegar
1 (3-inch, 7.6-cm) cinnamon stick
6 cardamom pods, slightly crushed
2 star anise pods
6 quarter-size coins fresh ginger
4 lemon slices, seeds removed

6 whole black peppercorns
12 fresh, firm, ripe figs such as black mission

QUAIL

8 semi-boneless quail
2 tablespoons olive oil
Kosher or sea salt and freshly ground black pepper

12 thin slices prosciutto

In a medium nonreactive pot, place the sugar, vinegars, cinnamon, cardamom, star anise, ginger, lemon, and peppercorns. Simmer, uncovered, for 10 minutes. Add the figs, cover, and continue simmering for 3 minutes. Remove from the heat and let the figs cool in the syrup. Figs can be prepared to this point and stored in their syrup in the refrigerator for up to 2 weeks. Using a slotted spoon, carefully remove the figs, reserving the poaching syrup for another use.

To make the quail, prepare a charcoal fire or preheat the broiler. Brush the quail with the oil and season with salt and pepper. Grill the quail, breast side down for 3 to 4 minutes. Turn the quail and continue cooking until nicely browned, 4 minutes or so. Alternately, place the quail skin side up on a baking sheet and cook under the hot broiler until crisp on the outside, 4 minutes or so. Turn the quail and continue broiling for another 3 minutes or until done. The quail should be slightly pink and juicy inside. Be careful not to overcook.

Meanwhile, wrap each pickled fig with a slice of prosciutto. Grill or broil the figs for 3 minutes or until the prosciutto is lightly browned. Serve alongside the quail with a little drizzle of strained fig poaching liquid.

Grilled Quail
with Arugula, Radishes, and Crushed Peas

This recipe is from Hugh Acheson, author of *A New Turn in the South* and chef/partner of the Athens, Georgia, restaurants Five and Ten, The National, and Empire State South. He's a wonderfully inventive chef and a very busy guy. He is a six-time James Beard nominee for Best Chef South and currently stars as a judge on Bravo TV's *Top Chef*.

MAKES 4 SERVINGS

1 shallot, minced
1 cup (240mL) cider vinegar
1/2 teaspoon Dijon mustard
1 cup (220g) extra-virgin olive oil
1 tablespoon sorghum molasses or pure maple syrup
1/2 teaspoon coriander seeds, toasted and finely ground

2 teaspoons freshly grated orange zest
Salt and freshly ground black pepper to taste
4 semi-boneless quail
2 cups crushed peas (recipe follows)
2 cups (56g) gently packed arugula
1/2 cup (58g) shaved radishes

In a small saucepan, combine the shallot and the vinegar. Reduce by half over medium heat and then cool. Place the mustard in a small mixing bowl and slowly drizzle in the olive oil, whisking constantly. It doesn't have to emulsify, just combine. Add the sorghum, coriander, and orange zest, and then add the reduced vinegar. Season to taste with salt and pepper.

Take half of the vinaigrette and marinate the quail, covered and refrigerated, for 1 hour. Save the other half for plating the salad.

Prepare a hot grill and remove the quail from the marinade. Grill for 3 to 4 minutes per side and then let rest for 5 minutes. Cut each quail in half and set aside in a warm place.

Place 1/2 cup of crushed peas on each of four plates. In a mixing bowl, lightly dress the arugula and radishes with the reserved vinaigrette. Arrange the salad on the plates and then finish with two halves of quail per plate. Circle a little more vinaigrette around each plate.

Crushed Peas

1 tablespoon unsalted butter
1 shallot, minced
3/4 cup (180mL) chicken stock
2 cups freshly shelled English peas

2 tablespoons crème fraîche
2 tablespoons chopped fresh mint
Pinch of Aleppo pepper flakes
Salt to taste

Warm a small saucepan over medium heat and add the butter. When it shimmers, add the shallot and cook for 2 minutes. Add the stock and bring to a boil. Add the peas, cover, and cook for 3 minutes. Remove from the heat, place the peas and stock in a food processor, and pulse to work the peas into a crushed consistency. Add the crème fraîche and pulse again. With a spatula scrape the peas back into the pot and finish by stirring in the mint and the Aleppo. Season with salt to taste and serve.

Quail in Grape Leaves Roasted in Coals

The idea of grilling or roasting small birds is an ancient one. Here, instead of roasting over the fire, I'm placing the grape-leaf-wrapped bundles of quail right down in the hot coals, which means that you'll need to do this with a charcoal grill. Wait to place the birds in the coals until the coals are no longer flaming but are completely covered with gray ash. You'll note that I'm wrapping the birds with foil for the first part of their cooking. You can omit this step if you want, but it adds a little safety net and helps ensure that the quail don't end up getting charred before they're done. Alternately, you can cook the grape-leaf-wrapped quail on the grill without the foil instead of placing them down in the coals. Try it both ways and see which works for you.

MAKES 4 SERVINGS

50 to 60 large grape leaves packed in brine
1 teaspoon whole coriander seeds
1 teaspoon ground cumin
1 teaspoon freshly ground black peppercorns
1 teaspoon salt

2 teaspoons ground sumac or 1 tablespoon
  lemon juice
3 large garlic cloves, finely chopped
1/2 teaspoon ground allspice
1/4 teaspoon ground cinnamon
3 tablespoons or so extra-virgin olive oil
8 fresh bone-in quail

Rinse the grape leaves well and then soak them in cold water for at least 1 hour, changing the water 3 or 4 times.

Make a spice mixture by combining the coriander, cumin, peppercorns, salt, sumac, garlic, allspice, cinnamon, and oil in a small bowl. Rinse the quail and pat dry with paper towels and then rub the spice mixture on the inside and outside of the quail. Drain the grape leaves, pat dry, and wrap each quail with 6 or so leaves and tie with kitchen twine. Make sure the quail are completely covered with at least 2 layers of leaves. Wrap the quail completely in heavy-duty foil.

Place the quail bundles in the hot coals and cook for 10 minutes, turning a couple of times. Remove the foil from the quail and place them in their grape-leaf wrappings right in the coals and cook for another 10 minutes or so, turning 3 or 4 times until the outer layers of the grape leaves are lightly charred. To test for doneness, insert an instant-read thermometer into the thickest part of the thigh. When it registers at least 165°F, it is done.

Serve, discarding the leaves, and eat with your fingers!

Quail a la Plancha
With Roasted Grapes

This is another bold recipe from Chef Mark Stark of Stark Reality Restaurants (see head note on page 245). Saba is fresh grape juice cooked down to a syrupy consistency called a "must." It is the precursor to balsamic vinegar.

MAKES 4 SERVINGS
QUAIL
4 sprigs fresh lavender or rosemary, minced
1 garlic clove, minced
2 tablespoons olive oil
¼ teaspoon freshly ground black pepper
4 semi-boneless quail

ROASTED GRAPES
1 pound (350g) red seedless grapes
2 tablespoons extra-virgin olive oil
2 tablespoons (30mL) cognac or brandy
Kosher or sea salt and freshly ground black pepper
2 tablespoons (28g) unsalted butter
½ cup (57g) toasted hazelnuts, halved
2 tablespoons (30mL) saba or good aged balsamic vinegar

Combine the lavender, garlic olive oil, and black pepper in a small bowl. Rub the marinade over the quail, inside and out. Let the quail marinate for 4 hours or up to 12 hours, refrigerated.

To make the roasted grapes, preheat the oven to 400°F with a baking sheet inside. Remove all the grapes from the stem. Toss the grapes with the oil, cognac, and salt and pepper to taste. When the baking sheet is hot, remove it from the oven, add the grapes, and return it to the oven. Roast until the grapes just start to pop, about 4 minutes. Transfer the grapes, with their juices, to a plate to cool.

Heat a cast-iron pan over medium heat. Season the quail with salt and then place them in the hot pan with only the oil coating. Cook for about 2 minutes until they are browned and crispy and then flip over and repeat on the other side. The quail should be well browned but still slightly pink on the inside. Set on a plate and keep warm.

Reduce the heat on the skillet. Discard any residual fat from the pan. Add the butter and the hazelnuts and cook for 30 seconds, until the nuts are aromatic. Add 1 cup of the grapes and any accumulated juices from the grapes and quail. Cook until the grapes are just warmed through. Spoon the mixture onto 4 warm plates, top each with a quail, and drizzle the saba over the quail to finish.

Pan-Roasted Quail
with Foie Gras and Apple-Pepper Sauce

This is a recipe from my friend Michele Anna Jordan. A prolific writer of cookbooks and newspaper and magazine articles and a James Beard award winner, she is one of the most colorful people in Northern California wine country. She is a fantastic teacher. She notes that "you can easily omit the foie gras from this dish, as it is pure gilding of the lily, delightfully delicious but superfluous. Wilted spinach would be a great accompaniment for this dish."

MAKES 4 SERVINGS

FOIE GRAS

1/2 pound (230g) duck foie gras, chilled
Kosher or sea salt and freshly ground black pepper

SAUCE

3 cups (700mL) filtered apple juice, divided
3/4 cup (180mL) apple cider vinegar

QUAIL

4 bone-in quail, about 4 ounces (113g) each
Kosher or sea salt and freshly ground black pepper
4 tablespoons (55g) unsalted butter, divided
2 apples, peeled, cored, and cut lenthwise into
1/4-inch-thick (6-mm) slices
4 small sprigs of fresh tarragon, chervil, or Italian parsley

---

Cut the foie gras into four equal slices, season it all over with salt and pepper to taste, set on a plate in a single layer, cover, and refrigerate.

For the sauce, pour 1 cup of the apple juice into a small saucepan, set the pan over medium heat, and simmer until reduced to about 2 tablespoons, about 10 minutes. Add the remaining apple juice, the vinegar, and several generous grinds of black pepper and simmer until the sauce is reduced to about 1 to 1¼ cups, about 10 minutes. Set aside.

Preheat the oven to 375°F.

For the quail, season them inside and out with salt and pepper. Melt 1 tablespoon of the butter in a large heavy skillet over medium heat. When the butter is foamy, add the quail, cook for about 4 minutes, turn, and cook for 4 minutes more, until evenly browned on both sides. Transfer the quail to a plate, add 2 tablespoons of the butter to the pan, and add the apples and sauté, turning once, until golden brown.

Return the quail to the pan, set the pan on the middle rack of the oven, and cook for about 10 minutes, or until the quail are cooked through.

Remove the pan from the oven, cover, and let rest for 5 minutes.

Uncover the pan and use a spatula to transfer the apple slices to warmed plates, mounding them slightly off center. Lean a quail against the apples, leaving room on top of the apples for the foie gras.

Working quickly, set a heavy skillet over high heat and set the pan used for the quail over medium heat. Pour the sauce into the second pan, swirl to pick up pan juices, and when the sauce just begins to simmer, remove it from the heat, season with a couple generous pinches of salt, add the remaining tablespoon of butter, and swirl.

When the first pan is very hot, add the foie gras in a single layer. Cook for 30 seconds, turn, and cook for 30 seconds more. Quickly transfer the foie gras to the plates, setting it on top of the apples. Spoon the sauce over and around the quail, apples, and foie gras. Season lightly with salt and generously with black pepper, garnish with herb sprigs, and serve immediately.

Pan-Seared Squab
with Figs and Cinnamon-Port Sauce

Remember that squab needs to be cooked "pink" or medium rare.

MAKES 2 SERVINGS
CINNAMON-PORT SAUCE
1 tablespoon olive oil
1/3 cup (53g) minced white onion
1 cup (240mL) port wine
2 1/2 cups (595mL) rich chicken stock
1/2 cup (75g) chopped dried figs
1 (4-inch, 10-cm) cinnamon stick,
   broken into 3 or 4 parts
2 star anise pods

2 teaspoons minced fresh thyme
Salt and freshly ground black pepper

SQUAB
2 whole squab
Salt and freshly ground black pepper to taste
2 tablespoons vegetable oil, such as canola
Fresh thyme sprigs for garnish

To make the cinnamon-port sauce, heat the oil in a saucepan over medium heat. Sauté the onion in the oil until lightly browned, about 8 minutes. Add the port, stock, figs, cinnamon, and star anise and bring to a boil. Cook until the sauce is reduced to a light sauce consistency, about 15 minutes. Strain through a fine strainer and stir in the thyme. Season to taste with salt and pepper. Keep warm.

To make the squab, cut each one in half and season liberally with salt and pepper. Cut off the wing tips and discard or save them for stock. In a heavy sauté pan over medium-high heat, add the oil. Sauté the squab, skin side down, for 4 to 5 minutes, until the skin is richly browned. Turn the squab and continue cooking for 2 to 3 minutes. Be careful not to overcook the squab; it should be juicy and pink inside. To serve, spoon the sauce on warm plates and place a squab half on top of each. Garnish with the thyme sprigs.

Minced Squab in Lettuce Cups

This is a classic recipe served widely in Chinese restaurants. Any other dark bird meat could be used, such as chicken thighs. Make sure you have everything ready before cooking and assembling.

MAKES 4 SERVINGS

6 dried Chinese black dried shiitake or mushrooms
1 (16- to 20-ounce) squab
2 tablespoons (30mL) dry sherry or rice wine
1 tablespoon soy sauce
1 tablespoon oyster sauce
2 teaspoons toasted sesame oil
1/2 teaspoon sugar
1/2 teaspoon chili garlic sauce

2 teaspoons cornstarch
Vegetable oil, such as peanut
2 ounces thin rice sticks (often labeled vermicelli)
2 teaspoons finely minced ginger
3 tablespoons finely chopped green onions
1/4 cup (31g) chopped fresh or canned drained water chestnuts or bamboo shoots
1/3 cup (45g) toasted pine nuts
12 small Bibb or iceberg lettuce leaves
Hoisin sauce

Soak the mushrooms in hot water to cover until soft, about 20 minutes. Discard the stems, finely dice the caps, and set aside. Bone the squab, discard the skin, chop the meat finely, and set aside. You should have at least 1 1/2 cups of meat. Combine the sherry, soy sauce, oyster sauce, sesame oil, sugar, and chili garlic sauce in a bowl and set aside. In another bowl, combine the cornstarch with 2 tablespoons of water and set aside. Heat 1/2 an inch of oil in a saucepan to 375°F and drop a handful of the rice stick into the oil. They will immediately puff up. Remove to paper towels. Repeat as necessary until all the vermicelli is fried.

Heat a wok or large heavy skillet over high heat and add 2 tablespoons of oil. When the oil is hot, add the ginger and green onions and sauté for 20 seconds. Add the squab and mushrooms and cook until the meat is just cooked through, about 2 minutes.

Add the sherry mixture, water chestnuts, and pine nuts and bring to a simmer. Stir in just enough of the cornstarch mixture to lightly thicken and glaze the squab mixture. Serve at once by spooning into lettuce cups with little dabs of hoisin. Break the rice sticks into small pieces and sprinkle on top of the squab. Roll and eat with gusto!

Broiled Squab
with Pomegranate, Orange, Marsala, and Honey

This is a recipe from my friend Joyce Goldstein. Joyce is the author of important cookbooks and an authority on the cuisines of the Mediterranean. Her ground-breaking restaurant, Square One, in San Francisco changed us all, and this recipe appeared in her award winning cookbook *Square One*. She is one of the most gifted teachers I know. She notes that "this is a recipe from the Veneto. The sauce would work well on quail or duck. Serve with saffron risotto and sautéed spinach with pine nuts and you have a most elegant and dramatic plate that tastes as wonderful as it looks."

MAKES 4 SERVINGS

½ cup (170g) pomegranate molasses
1 cup (240mL) orange juice
1 cup (240mL) marsala wine
½ cup (170g) honey or to taste
4 butterflied squab

4 cups (950mL) canned or homemade chicken stock (see page 70)
2 tablespoons orange zest
Salt and freshly ground black pepper
32 orange segments
½ cup (88g) pomegranate seeds

In a medium bowl, combine the pomegranate molasses, orange juice, marsala, and honey. Set aside ¾ cup of this mixture in a separate bowl. Place the birds side by side in a noncorrosive container. Pour the marinade over the birds and marinate, covered, in the refrigerator for 6 to 8 hours or overnight.

Preheat the broiler to high or make a charcoal fire. Bring the birds to room temperature and remove from the marinade. Reserve the marinade for basting. Grill or broil the birds for 4 minutes on each side, or until medium rare. Baste a few times with the reserved marinade.

For the sauce: Bring the chicken stock to a boil in a saucepan over high heat and reduce by half, about 10 minutes. Add the reserved pomegranate mixture (*not* the marinade) and the orange zest to the reduced chicken stock in the small saucepan. Season to taste with salt and pepper. Turn off the heat and add the orange segments. Place the birds on serving plates. Pour the sauce and orange segments over the birds and sprinkle with pomegranate seeds.

Note: You may prepare two five-pound ducks in a similar manner. Roast them in a 500°F oven for an hour, basting often with the pomegranate-orange mixture. Make the sauce with reduced duck stock. Serve with the same accompaniments.

Roasted Squab Breast
with Corn Cakes and Exotic Mushrooms

This recipe is from Tom Schmidt, executive chef of John Ash & Co. in Sonoma County, California. Tom has cooked all over Europe and is a master with game birds of all kinds. The mushrooms he is using here are from one of our favorite producers, Gourmet Mushroom (www.mycopia.com), which ships unusual mushrooms all over the country.

MAKES 4 FIRST-COURSE SERVINGS
CORN CAKES
1 1/2 cups (246g) fresh corn kernels
1/3 cup (53g) cornmeal
1/3 cup (40g) all-purpose flour
Kosher or sea salt and freshly ground pepper
1/2 teaspoon baking powder
2/3 cup (160mL) heavy cream
2 egg yolks
3 tablespoons (43g) melted unsalted butter, divided

SQUAB
2 large whole bone-in squab breasts
Salt and freshly ground black pepper
1 pound (450g) mixed exotic mushrooms (such as velvet, piopinni, clamshell)
1/4 cup (55g) rendered duck fat or unsalted butter, divided
2 large shallots, peeled and finely chopped
2 garlic cloves, peeled and finely chopped
1 tablespoon fresh thyme leaves
2 tablespoons (30mL) saba or reduced balsamic vinegar
4 sprigs thyme for garnish

For the corn cakes, boil the corn for 2 minutes in salted water. Drain and run cold water over to stop the cooking. Sift together the cornmeal, flour, salt and pepper to taste, and baking powder in a large bowl. Mix the egg yolks and cream together and add to the flour mixture. Stir in the corn and 2 tablespoons of the melted butter.

Preheat the oven to 425°F.

Bring the squab to room temperature and season with salt and pepper.

Place the breasts on a small baking tray, skin side up. Roast the squab in the oven for 12 minutes for rare. Let rest for 5 minutes.

While the squab are roasting, trim the ends of the mushrooms but leave them whole. In a nonstick pan over moderately high heat, add 2 tablespoons of the duck fat and sauté the mushrooms and shallots, stirring often, for 5 minutes. Add the garlic and thyme, adding more duck fat if necessary. Sauté for 5 minutes more or until the mushrooms are lightly browned but still holding their shape. Season to taste with salt and pepper.

Make the corn cakes. In a large nonstick pan over medium heat, add the remaining melted butter. Pour one-quarter of the batter into the pan and cook until bubbles form on top, about 3 minutes. Flip the pancake and cook for 2 to 3 more minutes. Repeat until you use all the batter, and then divide the pancakes among four warmed plates. Mound the mushrooms on the pancakes. With a sharp knife, cut the breasts off the bone and slice each once diagonally in half. Place the breasts on top of the mushrooms. Drizzle a little saba on top and garnish with thyme sprigs.

Pan-Seared Squab Breast
with Pinot and Pomegranate–Braised Red Cabbage

Chefs Justin Wangler and Tracey Shepos Cenami head up the amazing food and wine program at Kendall Jackson Winery in Sonoma County, California. If you are in the area, it's definitely worth a stop. The "airline breasts" referred to in this recipe have part of the wing bone attached, which makes for a nice presentation.

MAKES 4 SERVINGS

4 airline squab breasts
1 teaspoon kosher salt
2 tablespoons neutral flavored oil, such as canola
1 tablespoon unsalted butter
2 sprigs fresh thyme
Pinot and Pomegranate–Braised Red Cabbage (recipe follows)
2 ounces fresh goat cheese such as Cypress Grove
1/2 cup (55g) chopped toasted pecans
1/8 cup (42g) pomegranate molasses
1/8 cup (5g) watercress

Rinse and pat the squab breasts dry using a paper towel. Sprinkle with salt on both sides.

Heat a skillet over medium-high heat and add the oil. Place the squab in the pan, skin side down. Using a spatula, lightly press down on the breasts to help them cook evenly. Cook until golden brown, approximately 2 to 3 minutes. Flip the breasts and add the butter and thyme to the pan. Using a spoon, baste the breasts with the pan juices. Cook for 2 minutes more for medium rare. Remove the squab from the pan and place them on a paper-towel-lined plate. Allow to rest for 3 minutes.

Combine 2 cups of the braised cabbage, the goat cheese, and the pecans in a large bowl and toss gently to combine.

To serve, place a spoonful of the cabbage mixture on each serving plate. Top with a squab breast and drizzle lightly with pomegranate molasses. Sprinkle with watercress.

Pinot and Pomegranate–Braised Red Cabbage

1 tablespoon bacon fat or olive oil
1/2 red onion, julienned
2 teaspoons kosher salt
1 bay leaf
4 juniper berries
3 black peppercorns

1 pound (450g) red cabbage, thinly sliced
1 sprig fresh rosemary
1/3 cup (80mL) red wine vinegar
1 cup (240mL) red wine, such as pinot noir
1/8 cup (42g) pomegranate molasses
1/8 cup (30g) sugar

In a large pot over medium heat, combine the bacon fat, onion, and salt. Sauté until soft, without browning, approximately 4 minutes.

Meanwhile, make a sachet using cheesecloth. Add the bay leaf, juniper berries, and black peppercorns; tie with kitchen twine and set aside.

Add the cabbage, rosemary, and sachet to the pot, stir, and wilt the cabbage slightly, about 4 minutes. Add the red wine vinegar, red wine, pomegranate molasses, and sugar. Stir and bring to a boil. Reduce the heat to low and simmer for approximately 30 minutes, or until the liquid reduces almost completely. Remove the sachet and rosemary sprig. Keep warm. Any leftover cabbage can be refrigerated for up to 1 week.

Partridge Escabeche

All around the Mediterranean, there are recipes for pickling fowl or fish in a mixture of olive oil, vinegar, and aromatics. Known in Spain as escabeche, the technique was probably introduced by the Arabs and was an ingenious way of preserving food before refrigeration. In Spain it's still a beloved preparation, and the pickled little birds are often split, partially deboned, and served as a tapa, or appetizer.

MAKES 6 SERVINGS

6 cleaned partridge, quail, or dove
Salt and freshly ground black pepper
1/2 cup (110g) extra-virgin olive oil
1 small onion, peeled and cut into thin wedges
6 large garlic cloves, peeled and slivered lengthwise
1 small carrot, peeled and sliced thinly at an angle

1 teaspoon whole black peppercorns
2 whole cloves
2 bay leaves
1 (4-inch, 10-cm) rosemary sprig
1 cup (240mL) white wine
3/4 cup (180mL) sherry vinegar
2 tablespoons (42g) honey
Chicken stock or water as needed

Preheat the oven to 325°F. Season the birds well inside and out with salt and pepper. Heat the oil in a heavy skillet over medium heat and brown the birds on all sides, about 6 minutes. Remove the birds from the pan and place them in an ovenproof casserole in one layer, breast side up.

In the oil remaining in the skillet, sauté the onion, garlic, and carrot until they begin to brown, about 5 minutes. Add the peppercorns, cloves, bay leaves, rosemary, wine, vinegar, and honey and bring to a sim-mer. Pour the contents of the skillet over the birds in the casserole. If there isn't enough liquid to completely cover the birds, then add chicken stock or water to cover. Place the casserole in the oven and bake, uncovered, for 1 hour until very tender (legs should wiggle easily in the joints).

Remove the casserole from the oven and allow the birds to cool. Remove and discard the bay leaves, cover tightly, and refrigerate for at least 24 hours and up to a week. Serve the birds at room temperature or reheated in their marinade.

Small Birds Sardinian Style

This is a variation on escabeche and a very old and traditional recipe from Sardinia. You can use partridge, quail, squab, dove, or any other small bird.

MAKES 6 SERVINGS

3 large quail, partridge, doves, or other meaty little bird

1 small onion, sliced

2 medium carrots, peeled and chopped

1 large celery stalk, sliced (about ¾ cup, 76g)

6 anchovy fillets, finely chopped

2 large bay leaves

2 cups (475mL) dry white wine

Chicken stock (see page 70)

1 cup (220g) extra-virgin olive oil

¼ cup (60mL) white wine vinegar

3 tablespoons (11g) finely chopped fresh parsley

2 tablespoons (17g) drained chopped capers

Salt and freshly ground black pepper

Rinse the birds and pat them dry. Strew the onions, carrots, celery, anchovies, and bay leaves in the bottom of a saucepan just large enough to hold the birds in a single layer, arrange the birds on top, and add the wine and enough stock to cover. Bring to a simmer and then cover the pan and cook gently for 45 minutes or until the birds are very tender.

Make the sauce by whisking the olive oil, vinegar, parsley, and capers together and seasoning to taste with salt and pepper. Remove the birds from the pan, cut them in half lengthwise and arrange them in a serving dish. Pour the sauce over them and allow to cool before serving.

Strain and save the stewing liquid for other uses.

DOVE

Charlie's Wild Dove

My brother Charlie is an architect in Santa Fe, New Mexico. He has a wonderful but droll sense of humor. He cuts right to the chase with recipes and everything else in life. This is his classic hunting camp recipe. He notes that there isn't much to a dove other than the breasts. When cooking wild dove the first thing you have to do is to check for bird shot pellets.

MAKES 4 SERVINGS

4 thick strips of smoked bacon, chopped
1 small onion, chopped (about 1 cup, 160g)
1 small carrot, peeled and chopped (about 1 cup, 128g)
$\frac{1}{2}$ large celery stalk, chopped (about 1 cup, 150g)
Kosher or sea salt and freshly ground black pepper
2 cups (475mL) white wine

$1\frac{1}{2}$ cups (350mL) canned or homemade chicken stock (see page 70)
2 tablespoons chopped fresh sage
2 tablespoons chopped fresh rosemary
4 wild doves, cleaned and feathers and pin feathers removed
4 thick slices toasted sourdough bread

Heat a heavy Dutch oven and add the bacon. Cook until the bacon is crisp, about 8 minutes. Remove the bacon and set aside.

Add the vegetables to the pot. Season and sauté in the bacon fat until they start to caramelize, about 6 minutes. Add the wine and chicken stock and deglaze the pot. Add the fresh herbs. Bring to a simmer and add the dove breasts. Cover and poach about 10 minutes if using breasts only or 14 minutes if using the whole bird. Remove the birds, strain the chicken stock, and season to taste. Place a thick slice of sourdough bread in each bowl, place the doves on top, ladle the poaching liquid over, and sprinkle with the bacon.

GAME HENS

(Pheasant and Guinea Fowl)

Game Hens

Game hens could have been included in the chicken chapter because they really are just little chickens. We tend to see them as something different, however, so I've given them their own section. Anything you do with chicken you could do with game hens and vice versa. So here are a few more ideas for both.

Rock Cornish game hens are the result of cross breeding white rock hens and Cornish hens. Many sources credit Alphonsine and Jacques Makowsky of Connecticut for developing this small bird in the 1950s. Their intent was to breed a small chicken with mostly white meat suitable for a single serving. They are harvested at twenty-eight to thirty days old as opposed to forty-two or more for regular chickens. That they are all white meat, very tender because of their young age, and cook faster than regular chicken have made them very popular in the United States. Additionally, their delicate flavor lends them to all kinds of seasoning and marinating opportunities.

Pheasant

There are more than forty species of pheasant, but the beautiful ring-necked is the pheasant of choice in North America. Imported from China in 1881, no other game bird species introduced to this continent has been as successful at flourishing as the pheasant. Pheasants are related to the partridge, quail, grouse, and guinea fowl, which make up the order *galliformes*, or chicken-like birds. Females are two to three pounds, and older males can reach five pounds in weight.

There are many pheasant farms in America, most of which raise pheasant for hunting. Like other game birds, truly wild pheasant has a stronger flavor than the farm-raised version. Because it's hard to tell how old wild pheasants are, it's best to use moist cooking methods such as braising to cook them. Farm-raised birds, however, are much more tender and can successfully be roasted, grilled, or sautéed like chicken. See pages 310–11 for pheasant sources.

Although chicken always has to be cooked through, the breasts of farm-raised birds such as pheasant, guinea fowl, duck, and small birds such as squab are different. Because the meat itself is very lean, you should cook it until just pink to make sure it stays moist. As I said in the duck chapter, it's like having two different meats to cook: breasts and leg-thighs. The Braised Pheasant recipe (see page 304) illustrates how to deal with this dilemma.

Guinea Fowl

Guinea fowl or guinea hens originated from one of several wild species from what used to be called the Guinea Coast (hence the name) of West Africa. The ancestors of the domesticated guinea fowl we know today were introduced to Europe during the late fifteenth century, and from there the breed was taken by colonists to many other parts of the world, including North America. Like its cousin the pheasant, the guinea fowl is a beautiful bird with rich coloring. Farmers traditionally loved having a flock of guinea hens around because they are voracious eaters of all kinds of insects, especially ticks, and they are noisy "guard birds," squawking loudly when predators are near.

Farmed guinea fowl are harvested at sixteen to eighteen weeks and run from 1½ to 3 pounds, depending on their age. They have just a hint of gaminess, somewhere between a chicken and a pheasant, and like pheasant, they are very lean. Older birds take well to slow braising, while younger birds can be deliciously grilled or sautéed.

The
Recipes

Tea-Smoked Game Hens

This same technique can be used for all culinary birds, adjusting the time for the size of the bird, of course.

MAKES 4 SERVINGS

1 tablespoon salt

1 ½ teaspoons 5-spice powder (see page 57)

2 game hens

1 small orange or lemon, cut into 4 wedges

1 (2-inch, 5-cm) piece ginger, cut into thick coins

¼ cup (47g) white rice

½ cup (120mL) Lapsang souchong or other black tea

4 large pieces dried orange peel (available at Chinese markets) or fresh peel

1 cinnamon stick, broken into pieces

Toasted sesame oil

Combine the salt and the 5-spice powder and rub the birds inside and out with the mixture. Place a wedge of citrus and a couple of coins of ginger in the cavity of each bird.

Transfer the hens, breast side up, to a steamer and steam over boiling water, covered, for 30 minutes or until just cooked through. Pierce the leg joint with a carving fork. If the juices run clear, it's done. While the hens are steaming, combine the rice, tea, sugar, orange peel, and cinnamon in the bottom of the wok.

Arrange a metal rack about 2 inches above the tea mixture and transfer the hens, breast side up, to the rack. Tightly cover the wok and heat over medium-high heat until wisps of smoke begin to appear, 3 to 5 minutes. Smoke the hens, covered, for 8 minutes. Remove the wok from the heat and let the hens sit, covered, for another 8 minutes or so.

Transfer the hens to a cutting board and brush lightly with the oil. Carve or chop them with a cleaver and serve warm or at room temperature.

Grilled Green Curry Game Hens

This is a simple recipe using prepared Thai green curry paste, which is available in Asian markets and some supermarkets. The prepared pastes are fine, but once you make your own, you might not go back. I've included a recipe for homemade green curry paste below. You can use this recipe with any bird, adjusting the cooking time, of course.

MAKES 2 TO 4 SERVINGS

2 game hens

⅓ cup (80mL) unsweetened coconut milk

3 tablespoons (28g) Thai green curry paste
  (preferably homemade or Mae Ploy brand)

2 tablespoons dark brown sugar

¼ cup (60mL) fresh lime or lemon juice

3 tablespoons (45mL) fish sauce

1 tablespoon vegetable oil

Butterfly each hen by removing the back bone and flattening (see page 51). Using a sharp knife, cut shallow slits ½ inch apart along the legs and thighs and place the hens in a bowl.

In a small bowl, whisk the remaining ingredients until smooth. Rub the curry mixture all over the birds, into the slits, and under the skin. Marinate for at least 4 and up to 12 hours, covered and refrigerated.

Prepare a grill to medium hot. Wipe off any excess marinade from the hens with your hands. Grill the flattened birds, skin side down, until the skin is browned and crisp, about 10 minutes. Turn the birds skin side up, cover, and grill until cooked through, another 15 minutes. The legs should move easily and the juices should run clear when you nick the thickest part of the thigh. Transfer the birds to a cutting board and let them rest for 5 minutes. Carve and serve.

Thai Green Curry Paste

MAKES ABOUT 1 CUP

2 teaspoons Thai shrimp paste

2 tablespoons hot green chiles (such as serrano),
  seeded and chopped

4 medium mild green chiles (such as Anaheim),
  seeded and chopped

½ cup (80g) chopped white onion

6 garlic cloves, peeled and chopped

3 lemongrass stalks, trimmed and chopped

2 tablespoons chopped fresh ginger or galangal

2 tablespoons chopped cilantro stems and/or roots

2 teaspoons freshly ground white peppercorns

2 teaspoons ground coriander seeds

½ teaspoon ground cloves

Grated zest and juice of two large limes,
  preferably Kaffir

1 to 1½ tablespoons peanut oil

Wrap the shrimp paste in a double layer of aluminum foil and dry toast it in a heavy skillet over medium-high heat for 2 minutes on each side. Unwrap and combine the paste with all the other ingredients in a blender and process to a smooth paste, adding more oil, if needed. Store, covered, in the refrigerator for up to 3 weeks or in the freezer for up to 3 months.

Cider-Brined and Smoked Game Hens

This brine works equally well with chicken or turkey. As I've talked about earlier, brining is a magical process that adds both flavor and moistness to the meat. In this recipe I'm using a covered barbecue to both cook and smoke the birds. You want to make sure to use the indirect heat method (described below) in the barbecue and monitor both the temperature of the barbecue and the birds with a thermometer. The objective is to cook the birds slowly enough so that they can pick up a rich smoky flavor, and you also want to be sure that they are cooked through.

MAKES 6 GENEROUS SERVINGS

BRINE

1 quart (32 ounces, 950mL) apple cider
1/2 cup (120mL) soy sauce
1 cup (200g) brown sugar
3/4 cup (168g) kosher salt
6 cups (1.4L) water
2 medium oranges, sliced
1/2 cup (48g) coarsely chopped ginger
1 or 2 whole star anise
2 tablespoons chopped garlic
3 whole bay leaves

HENS

6 whole game hens, split with backbones removed
Olive oil

Combine the apple cider, soy sauce, sugar, salt, and water in a saucepan over medium-high heat and bring to a simmer, stirring all the time to dissolve the sugar and salt. Reduce the heat to medium and add the oranges, ginger, star anise, garlic, and bay leaves. Simmer for 1 to 2 minutes and then remove from the heat and cool.

Divide the cooled brine among a couple of large heavy duty zip-top bags. Divide the game hens among the bags and squeeze out as much air as you can before zipping closed. Refrigerate for at least 4 and up to 12 hours, turning occasionally.

Prepare the grill using the indirect heat method (see sidebar). Add the smoking wood of your choice to the hot coals. Remove the hens from the brine and pat dry. Brush them liberally with olive oil, place them on the grill, and cook/smoke until done. The birds should reach an internal temperature of 160°F in the thickest part of the meat. Depending on the heat of the barbecue, it should take approximately 40 minutes. Let the birds rest, loosely covered in foil, for at least 5 minutes before carving.

The Indirect **Heat Method**

With this method, you cook the food with the heat source off to the side. It's essential that you have a grill with a good, tight-fitting lid so that the heat circulates around the grill to slowly cook the food evenly on all sides. It's the preferred method for cooking large cuts of meat and whole birds. The method is simple. First, put a drip pan in the center of the charcoal bed and then arrange hot coals on either side. The cooking grate goes over the coals and then you arrange the food (in this case, the birds) over the drip pan. This method prevents flare-ups, and the drip pan allows you to capture juices to make a sauce or gravy.

Glazed Game Hens Grilled on a Cedar Plank

Birds that are glazed with sweet glazes are a problem on the grill because the sugar can burn easily. Using a plank helps alleviate that problem. The glaze gets caramelized a bit, but the plank helps protect it from burning and adds its own subtle woody flavor. You can use this method with some of the glazes on pages 106–107.

MAKES 2 TO 4 SERVINGS

GLAZE

½ cup (160g) peach or apricot preserves
½ cup (120mL) orange juice
¼ cup (40g) minced onion
2 garlic cloves, minced
1 tablespoon soy sauce

1 tablespoon chili garlic sauce, or to taste
1 tablespoon rice wine vinegar
1 tablespoon olive oil
½ teaspoon black pepper

2 game hens, split in half with backbones removed

Soak a large cedar plank in water for at least 1 hour before using. Combine the glaze ingredients in a small saucepan over low heat and cook for 5 minutes or until syrupy. Set aside.

Preheat a grill to about 400°F. Place the plank on the grill until it begins to smolder a bit, about 5 minutes. Flip the plank and place the hens on the slightly charred side and generously spoon or brush the glaze over the hens. Close the lid and cook for 15 minutes. Reduce the heat to medium (or if you have a charcoal grill, move the coals to one side) and cook for another 15 to 18 minutes, or until the juices run clear and the legs move easily.

Plank Roasting

Plank roasting is easy. It just requires a little preparation. Planks made from cedar, alder, oak, and fruit woods are all possibilities. Always choose thick planks (at least 1 inch thick) so that they can be used several times. Make sure the wood is untreated. Wash between uses in warm water with a mild detergent and rinse well.

Soak the plank for at least an hour in water. Place a weight on it if necessary to submerge it. Remove from the water and allow excess water to drip away.

Place the plank on the grill over high heat for 3 to 5 minutes or until the underside of the plank starts to smolder and smoke.

Flip the plank over and put the prepared food on the slightly charred side of the plank. This gives the food a "sear," which improves flavor and texture and reduces steaming. Top with whatever sauce you are using and cook until the food is done.

Keep the grill hood closed during cooking to distribute the heat evenly and to reduce the oxygen that might cause the plank to ignite. Serve the food directly off the plank at the table. Put some foil down first to keep from marring the tabletop or cloth.

Braised Pheasant

This rustic preparation is wonderful with egg noodles, polenta, or risotto.

MAKES 2 TO 4 SERVINGS

¼ cup (55g) extra-virgin olive oil

1 (2½-pound, 1.1kg) pheasant, cut into 6 serving pieces

Salt and freshly ground black pepper

1 large white onion, chopped (about 3 cups, 400g)

4 large garlic cloves, peeled and slivered (about 2 tablespoons)

2 ounces pancetta, finely diced

1 teaspoon dried oregano

3 whole cloves

2 bay leaves

2 tablespoons (38g) tomato paste

1¼ cups (300mL) dry white wine

3 cups (700mL) chicken stock

2 tablespoons freshly grated Parmesan cheese

2 tablespoons finely chopped parsley

Heat the oil in a large skillet over moderate heat. Add the pheasant pieces, season with salt and pepper to taste, and brown lightly on all sides, about 5 minutes total. Remove the meat and set aside. To the same skillet, add the onion, garlic, pancetta, oregano, cloves, and bay leaves and cook until the onion just begins to brown, about 5 minutes. Remove excess fat, if desired, and discard.

Return the pheasant to the skillet, stir in the tomato paste, wine, and chicken stock, and bring to a boil. Reduce the heat and simmer, partially covered, until the pheasant breasts are tender, 12 to 14 minutes. Remove the breasts and set aside. Continue cooking the leg and thigh pieces for an additional 20 minutes or until tender. Remove the whole legs (thigh and drumstick) and set aside.

Increase the heat to high and boil until the liquid in the skillet has reduced to 1 cup, about 8 minutes. Strain the sauce through a medium-mesh strainer and return to the pan. Season to taste with salt and pepper. Return the cooked pheasant pieces to the sauce to heat through. Mix the Parmesan and parsley in a small bowl. Serve topped with cheese and parsley mixture.

Roast Pheasant Stuffed with Wild Rice

This is a traditional recipe in which you may use your favorite stuffing.

MAKES 2 TO 4 SERVINGS

2 tablespoons (28g) unsalted butter

1 medium onion, finely chopped (about 1 1/2 cups, 220g)

1 celery stalk, finely chopped (about 1/2 cup, 50g)

2 medium garlic cloves, finely chopped (about 1 tablespoon)

Kosher or sea salt and freshly ground black pepper

1 ounce dried porcini mushrooms, softened in warm water for 30 minutes and chopped

3/4 cup (54g) sliced mushrooms

1/4 cup (60mL) dry white wine

1/3 cup 80mL)canned or homemade chicken broth (see page 70)

1/2 cup (83g) golden raisins

1 1/2 cups (246g) cooked wild rice

1/4 cup (15g) chopped fresh flat-leaf parsley

1 tablespoon chopped fresh thyme (1 teaspoon dried)

1 (2 1/2 pound or so, 1.1kg) whole pheasant

Preheat the oven to 425°F. Heat the butter in a heavy skillet over medium heat. Add the onion, celery, and garlic, season lightly with salt and pepper, and cook, stirring frequently, until the onion just begins to brown, about 5 minutes. Add the mushrooms and cook until their liquid has evaporated, about 5 minutes. Add the wine and chicken stock and stir to scrape up any browned bits from the bottom of the pan. Cook until most of the wine and broth have evaporated, about 8 minutes. Transfer to a bowl and stir in the raisins, wild rice, parsley, and thyme and season to taste with salt and pepper; set aside.

Season the pheasant inside and out with salt and pepper. Loosely stuff the pheasant with the rice mixture, then arrange on a rack in a roasting pan. Roast for 10 minutes; reduce heat to 350°F and roast for 40 minutes or until the juices in the thigh run clear when it is pierced with a knife. Let the pheasant rest for 5 minutes before carving.

How to cook **wild rice**

Wild rice is not rice at all but a grass, an annual aquatic grass seed *Zizania aquatica* found mostly in the upper freshwater lakes of Canada, Michigan, Wisconsin, and Minnesota in North America. Almost all of it are not even wild, but rather cultivated varieties that do not occur naturally. Its easy to cook. Bring three cups of water or stock to a boil, season lightly with salt and pepper, stir in one cup of uncooked wild rice, and then reduce the heat and simmer, covered, for 40 to 45 minutes or just until the kernels puff open. Uncover, fluff with a fork, and simmer an additional 5 minutes. Drain off any excess liquid.

Roasted Guinea Hen with Chili Butter

Adding a compound or flavored butter (see pages 39–40) under the skin helps flavor and keep the bird moist—a useful technique with any bird. Flavored or compound butters can be made ahead, wrapped in plastic and then foil, and frozen. Allow to soften before using. They also make a simple topper for grilled or roasted birds and meats.

MAKES 2 TO 4 SERVINGS

1 tablespoon olive oil

4 large garlic cloves, peeled and minced (about 2 tablespoons, 17g)

1/2 pound, 230g (2 sticks) unsalted butter, softened

1 teaspoon ground cumin

1/8 teaspoon ground cinnamon

1 tablespoon pure chili powder, such as ancho, or 1 teaspoon chipotle powder

1 tablespoon minced fresh cilantro

2 teaspoons fresh lime or lemon juice

Salt and freshly ground black pepper

2 (2- to 3-pound, .9 to1.3kg) guinea hens

In a small sauté pan, heat the olive oil and sauté the garlic over moderate heat until soft but not brown, about 2 minutes. Set aside and cool.

Preheat the oven to 450°F.

In a mixing bowl, blend together the butter, cumin, cinnamon, chili powder, cooled garlic, cilantro, lime juice, and salt and pepper to taste. Loosen the skin around the breast and legs of the guinea hens and, with your fingers, spread a layer of chili butter under the skin. Be careful not to tear the skin. Rub any remaining chili butter on the hens and place them, breast side down, on a roasting rack in a pan and roast for 15 minutes.

Turn the hens breast side up, reduce the temperature to 350°F, and continue to roast the hens, basting with pan juices frequently (add a little white wine if desired). Roast for an additional 30 to 35 minutes or until a meat thermometer inserted into a fleshy part of the thigh registers 165°F. Transfer to a cutting board and let stand, covered loosely with foil, for 10 minutes before carving.

Grilled Guinea Fowl Piri Piri

Piri piri is the Portuguese name for a very spicy type of birds-eye chile and an all-purpose sauce/rub/dip from the southern part of Portugal and the Portuguese colonies of Mozambique and Angola. While hot chiles are from the New World, they somehow made their way from the Americas to Portugal and then to Africa, where they call them piri piri, the Swahili word that means "pepper pepper." This is a great go-to sauce that can be used for almost any bird.

MAKES 2 TO 4 SERVINGS

1 (2- to 3-pound, .9 to1.3kg) butterflied guinea fowl (see page 51 for method)
1 cup lemon juice
3/4 cup (240mL) olive oil
6 large garlic cloves, minced (about 3 tablespoons, 26g)
1/4 cup (40g) chopped onion
3 tablespoons (9g) chopped fresh cilantro
2 tablespoons orange zest
2 tablespoons hot red pepper flakes
2 teaspoons dried oregano
1 teaspoon ground cumin
1 1/2 teaspoons salt
2 tablespoons (28g) unsalted butter
Lemon wedges for garnish

Rinse the guinea fowl and pat dry. Combine the rest of the ingredients, except the butter and lemon wedges, in a blender and pulse to make a smooth marinade. Put the bird in a bowl, pour the marinade over it, and turn to coat. Cover and refrigerate for at least 4 hours or overnight, turning occasionally.

Prepare a medium-hot grill and lift the bird from the marinade, draining well and reserving the marinade. Place the bird on the well-oiled grill, skin side up to start. Close the lid and cook for 15 minutes. Turn the bird skin side down and continue to cook and turn until the skin is nicely brown and the meat at the bone is no longer pink (cut if necessary to test), another 20 minutes or so.

Meanwhile, pour the reserved marinade into a saucepan and, over medium-high heat, bring it to a boil. Reduce the heat to medium and simmer for at least 5 minutes. It's important to bring the marinade to a boil when making the sauce to make sure you have killed any bacteria from the raw bird. Add the butter and stir until melted. Turn the heat to low and stir occasionally until ready to serve.

When the bird is done, transfer it to a cutting board and let it sit, covered loosely with foil, for at least 5 minutes before carving. Carve and serve with the sauce and lemon wedges.

RESOURCES

COMPANY NAME	ADDRESS
CHICKEN	
Coleman Natural	1667 Cole Blvd Building 19, Suite 300, Golden, CO 80401
Petaluma Poultry	P.O. Box 7368, Petaluma, CA 94955
Pepper Ranch Poultry	1545 Pepper Road, Petaluma, CA 94952
D'Artagnan	280 Wilson Avenue, Newark, NJ 07105
Greenling	Austin, TX (online store)
Family Friendly Farm	834 State Highway V, Cape Girardeau, MO 63701
Open A Bar 2 Ranch LLC	100133 County Road 4, Lyman, NE 69352
EGGS	
Born Free, LLC	313 Pleasant Street, Watertown, MA 02472
C C Family Farm	6030 Butler Road, Penryn, CA 95663-9657
Hodge Rance, LLC	3267 Tyus Carrollton Road, Carrollton, GA 30117
TURKEY and/or GOOSE	
Rocky Ridge Ranch	PO Box 175, Reardan, WA 99029
Peaceful Pastures	69 Cowan Valley Lane, Hickman, TN 38567
Kingbird Farm	9398 W. Creek Road, Berkshire, NY 13736
Ayrshire Farm	21846 Trappe Road, Upperville, VA 20184
Good Earth Farms	10431 Mayflower Road, Milladore, WI 54454
DUCK	
Eastern Plains Natural Food Co-op	P.O. Box 224, Bennett, CO 80102
Liberty Ducks	520 Fair Ave, Petaluma, CA 94952
Veritas Farms	32 Rousner Lane, New Paltz, NY 12561
PHESANT, OSTRICH & OTHER LARGE GAME BIRDS	
MacFarlane Pheasants, Inc.	2821 South U.S. Hwy, 51, Janesville, WI 53546
Blue Heaven Ostrich, Inc.	3140 C Road, Loxahatchee, FL 33470
Songline Emu Farm	66 French King Hwy, Gill, MA 01354
QUAIL, SQUAB & OTHER SMALL GAME BIRDS	
Nicky USA	223 SE 3rd Avenue, Portland, OR 97214
Texas Quail Farms	265 Brushy Branch Road, Lockhart, TX 78644
Quail Hill Farm	Old Stone Hwy, Amagansett, NY 11930
D'Artagnan (Squab; Partridge)	280 Wilson Avenue, Newark, NJ 07105
Angel Acres Farm (Cornish Game Hens)	60500 Maple Ridge Road, Mason, WI 54856

PHONE	WEBSITE
(800) 442-8666	www.colemannatural.com
(800) 556-6789	www.petalumapoultry.com
(707) 321-9638	www.localharvest.org/pepper-ranch-poultry-M49446
(800) 327-8246	www.dartagnan.com
(888) 789-2352; (512) 440-8449	www.greenling.com
(573) 335-1622	www.familyfriendlyfarm.com
(308) 787-1111	www.openabar2ranch.com
(800) 370-1439	www.bornfreeeggs.com & www.radlo.com
(916) 663-1630	www.penrynfarm.com
(770) 605-6385	www.hodgeranch.com
(509) 953-0905	www.rockyridgeranchspokane.com
(615) 683-4291	www.peacefulpastures.com
(607) 657-2860	www.kingbirdfarm.com
(540) 592-7018	www.ayrshirefarm.com
(715) 652-3520	www.goodearthfarms.com
(303) 644-4079	www.easternplains.com
(707) 795-3797	www.libertyducks.com
(845) 384-6888	www.veritasfarms.com
(800) 345-8348; (608) 757-7881	www.pheasant.com
(561) 655-0441	www.gourmetostrich.com
(413) 863-2700	www.allaboutemu.com/songline-emu-farm
(800) 469-4162; (503) 234-4263	www.nickyusa.com
(512) 376-2072	www.texquail.com
(631) 267-8492	www.peconiclandtrust.org/quail_hill_farm.html
(800) 327-8246	www.dartagnan.com
(888) 207-6903	www.angelacresfarm.net

INDEX

Numbers in bold indicate pages with illustrations